American Book Company's

PASSING THE NEW ALABAMA HIGH SCHOOL GRADUATION EXAMINATION

IN

READING

(Revised October 2000)

DR. FRANK PINTOZZI
DEVIN PINTOZZI

AMERICAN BOOK COMPANY
P O BOX 2638
WOODSTOCK, GEORGIA 30188-1383
TOLL FREE: 1 (888) 264-5877 PHONE: 770-928-2834 FAX: 770-928-7483

ACKNOWLEDGEMENTS

We are grateful to Kelly Berg for her assistance in creating the graphics for this book. We would also like to thank the editors of *National Geographic* for the use of selections from their periodical.

P.O. Box 2638
Woodstock, GA 30188-1383

Printed in the United States of America

06/03 10/04 01/05 09/05 05/06 06/07

TABLE OF CONTENTS

ALABAMA READING

Preface

PASSING THE NEW ALABAMA GRADUATION EXAM IN READING will help students preparing for the reading test during their junior year in high school. This book will also assist students who have failed the reading test and who want to review skills and strategies before taking the test again. **The materials in this book are based on the objectives and content descriptions of the New Alabama Graduation Examinations published by the Alabama State Department of Education.**

This book contains several sections. These sections are: 1) General information about the test; 2) A Diagnostic Test; 3) Chapters that teach the concepts and skills emphasized on the test; 4) Two Practice Tests. Answers to the tests and exercises are in a separate manual.

We welcome comments and suggestions about the book. Please contact the authors at:

American Book Company
PO Box 2638
Woodstock, GA 30188-1383

Toll Free: 1 (888) 264-5877
Phone: (770) 928-2834
Fax: (770) 928-7483

ABOUT THE AUTHORS

Dr. Frank Pintozzi is Professor of Reading / ESOL Programs at Kennesaw State University, Marietta, Georgia. For over 27 years, he has taught English and reading at the high school and college levels. He holds a doctorate in education from North Carolina State University in Raleigh, North Carolina. He is the author of ten textbooks on reading, writing, and study strategies.

Devin Pintozzi is a recent graduate of Oglethorpe University in Atlanta where he majored in psychology and minored in history. He is a full-time writer who strives for accuracy and clarity in all of his publications.

The Pintozzis have written best-selling books on passing graduation exams in Florida, Georgia, South Carolina, Tennessee, and Alabama.

PREPARING FOR THE NEW ALABAMA GRADUATION EXAMINATION IN READING

INTRODUCTION

If you are a student in an Alabama high school, you must pass the **New Alabama Graduation Exam in Reading** to receive a secondary school diploma. This test is one of four tests now required for graduation from Alabama high schools.

In this book, you'll prepare for the **New Alabama Graduation Examination** in **Reading**. The questions and answers that follow will provide you with general information about this exam.

In this book you'll take a **Diagnostic Exam** to determine your strengths and areas for improvement. In the chapters, you'll learn and practice the skills and strategies that are important in preparing for this exam. The last sections contain two practice tests that will provide further preparation for the actual **Alabama Reading Exam**.

What Is On The New Alabama Graduation Exam in Reading?

For the **Alabama Reading Exam,** you will answer a large number of multiple-choice questions based on concepts and skills in reading. This new exam is more challenging than the previous one.

Why Must I Pass the Alabama Graduation Exam in Reading?

You are required to pass this exam for several reasons. First, the state of Alabama, your future employers, and your community need an educated workforce. Secondly, today's high school graduates will need to adapt to rapidly changing technology throughout their lives. Employees without basic language skills and comprehension will be unable to communicate effectively in the workplace. Without these skills, there's a great chance they will not only be unemployed but unemployable. Thirdly, by demonstrating your language ability, you can show what you have learned in school and apply this knowledge to new situations and experiences.

When Do I Take the Alabama Graduation Exam in Reading?

During your junior year in high school, you must take the **New Alabama Graduation Exam in Reading**.

How Much Time Do I Have To Take the Exam?

Timing for the **New Alabama Graduation Exam in Reading** will vary. Check with your teacher or counselor about how much time you will have for the exam.

What Happens If I Don't Pass the Exam?

You may take the **New Alabama Graduation Examination in Reading** several times before the end of the twelfth grade. The first time that you take this exam is in the eleventh grade. You will then have several more chances to pass the exam in high school.

If I Fail the Reading Exam, Where Can I Get Help To Pass It the Next Time?

In some school districts, you can sign up for special classes. The instructors in these classes will teach you how to study and prepare for the **Alabama Graduation Examination in Reading.** You can also seek extra help in Reading / English classes during your years in high school. Finally, you can work with tutors or counselors who can help you pass the **Reading Exam.**

How Is My Test Scored?

Check with your teacher or counselor about the passing score on the **New Alabama Graduation Exam in Reading.** Scoring for your exam is based on several areas of reading. These areas covered are listed below:

Word Meaning
Analogies
Finding the Main Idea
Reading for Details, Sequence, and Cause-Effect Relationships
Inferences
Conclusions
Generalizations
Predictions
Summary
Fact and Opinion
Reference Sources
Rhetorical Devices
Propaganda
Fallacies
Point of View
Figurative Language
Author's Purpose
Word Meaning
Graphic Aids

READING DIAGNOSTIC EXAM

Read the following passage, and answer the questions below.

1) The Aurora Borealis spreads across the night sky, and now you can see clearly in a 180° arc with no obstructions. 2) About 3,000 feet up the mountain, animals such as the arctic fox can be seen hunting for their next meal. 3) When climbing one of the mountains in Alaska's interior, you always get a surprising view of the natural world. 4) At 6,000 feet, the air gets thinner, and each small movement forward and up requires extra amounts of effort. 5) At the base of the mountain, the jagged rock starts to join with the forest cover, making the mountain seem like a majestic island in a sea of forest. 6) At the top of the mountain, it seems like all of the natural world is yours.

1. What is the correct order if you are ordering the sentences from the base of the mountain to the top of the mountain?

   A. 6-5-2-3-4-1
   B. 3-5-2-4-6-1
   C. 1-6-4-2-5-3
   D. 1-4-2-3-5-6
   E. 5-2-3-4-6-1

2. What is the correct arrangement of the sentences if you are ordering the sentences from the top of the mountain to the base of the mountain?

   A. 3-6-1-4-2-5
   B. 5-2-4-1-6-3
   C. 1-6-4-2-5-3
   D. 3-5-2-4-6-1
   E. 1-6-4-3-5-2

Read the following passage, and answer the questions below.

1) Fourth, I want to be active in local civic organizations in my community. 2) Second, I want to meet that special someone, fall in love, and marry. 3) Most importantly, I want to be licensed as a world-renowned oral surgeon in my own practice. 4) Finally, I would like to spend two years in a third-world country helping people in the Peace Corps. 5) As far as my goals in life go for the next twelve years, I have a list of priorities. 6) Third, I would like to have three children and own my own home and a dog. 7) Fifth, I want to travel to Europe while in college for free on some special scholarship.

3. Ordering the sentences from most important to least important, what is the correct order of the sentences?

   A. 5-3-2-6-1-7-4
   B. 3-2-6-1-7-4-5
   C. 5-4-7-1-6-2-3
   D. 4-7-1-6-2-3-5

4. Based on the passage on the preceding page, what is the sixth most important thing that the narrator wants to accomplish?

   A. The narrator wants to be active in the local civic organizations.
   B. The narrator is going to travel to Europe while in college.
   C. The narrator wants to spend two years in the Peace Corps.
   D. The narrator wants to be a world renowned oral surgeon.

Select the word that means the <u>same</u> as the underlined word.

5. Kimanji is <u>proposing</u> that we build a new football stadium.

   A. suggesting
   B. questioning
   C. demanding
   D. ignoring

Select the word that means the <u>opposite</u> of the underlined word.

6. The United States <u>exports</u> many products to Mexico and Canada.

   A. imports
   B. sends
   C. sells
   D. ships

Read the two excerpts below and answer questions 7 and 8.

Document A

. . . the rights of the Cherokees are . . . plain . . . and the duty of the government to secure those rights is as binding as ever. . . . If the white man must oppress us – if he must . . . throw us penniless upon the wild world, and if our cries [mean] nothing at the door of those who have promised to be our guardians and protectors, let it be so.

Document B

During the 1830s, settlers seeking more land began to pressure the United States government to remove the Cherokee nation from Georgia. As Cherokees began to know of their opposition, they split into two camps. One, led by Elias Boudinot, advocated leaving the Cherokee lands in Georgia peaceably before they either went to war with the United States or were forced to leave. The other camp, composed of the majority of the Cherokee, chose to stay on their native lands. Boudinot's group peaceably left three years prior to the United States' forced march of the remaining Cherokee to Oklahoma.

7. Which is the best explanation for why the two writings differ in their presentation of Cherokee views of forced migration?

   A. Document A presents the opinion of Elias Boudinot. Document B does not.
   B. Document B was written to white settlers. Document A was written to Cherokees.
   C. Document A presents the opinion of Elias Boudinot. Document B presents both Boudinot's and the other Cherokees' decisions.
   D. In Document A, Boudinot likes the idea of moving off the Cherokee land. In Document B, the Cherokee people are against leaving their land.

8. Where would these documents most likely first appear?

A. encyclopedias
B. textbooks
C. newspapers
D. catalogues

Read the passages. Select the best answer.

What could possibly be more important to the future of this great nation than the health of the people? That is why we are offering Quitnow – a program designed to enable anyone to quit smoking instantly! Never again will the smoker feel the urge to smoke.

9. The propaganda in this advertisement is used to convince the reader that

A. the nation is in a health crisis.
B. the future of the nation is in the hands of the healthcare industry.
C. buying Quitnow improves the future health of the nation.
D. smoking is undesirable and addictive.

Population Density

And what of the assertion that as the world population grows, poverty is the inevitable result?

Actually, the amount of poverty in a country has little to do with its population density or even its supply of resources. It does have a lot to do with each country's economic system and how free it is.

Japan, for instance, is one of the most prosperous countries on earth, but it has more people per square mile than, say India, one of the world's poorest. Likewise, booming Singapore has a population density of more than 13,000 people per square mile. Yet Singapore's per capita income is over fifteen times that of communist-run Cuba, which has 254 people per square mile.

It is no accident that the world's most prosperous countries are those with the freest and least-regulated, least-taxed economies. Thriving Asian economies like those of Japan, Singapore, Hong Kong, Taiwan, and South Korea are classic examples of these.

10. Based on the information above, one could infer that:

A. Democratic countries tend to have the highest population densities.
B. Communist countries are the most prosperous.
C. Democratic countries are the most prosperous.
D. Communist countries tend to have the highest population densities.

11. Which of the following is the main idea of the passage above?

A. The world’s poorest nations are also the freest.
B. Nations with a free economy are the most prosperous.
C. Communist countries are the most prosperous.
D. The world’s largest economies are also the most populous countries.

12. The author's purpose in writing this passage is

A. to criticize.
B. to motivate.
C. to entertain.
D. to inform.

13. Which of the following statements from the passage above is a **fact**?

A. It is no accident that the world's most prosperous economies are those with the freest and least-regulated, least-taxed economies.
B. Thriving Asian economies like those of Japan, Singapore, Hong Kong, and South Korea are classic examples of these.
C. Booming Singapore has a population density of more than 13,000 per square mile.
D. Singapore's per capita income is over fifteen times that of communist-run Cuba, which has 254 people per square mile.

Read the following passage, and answer questions 14-17.

He was quick and alert in the things in life, but only in the things, and not in the significant things. Fifty degrees below zero meant eighty degrees of frost. Such fact impressed him as being cold and uncomfortable, and that was all. It did not lead him to meditate upon his frailty as a creature of temperature, and upon man's frailty in general, able only to live within certain narrow limits of heat and cold; and from there on it did not lead him to the conjectural field of immortality and man's place in the universe. Fifty degrees below zero was to him just precisely fifty degrees below. That there should be anything more to it than that was a thought that never entered his head.

As he turned to go on, he spat speculatively. There was a sharp explosive crackle that startled him. He spat again. And again, in the air, before it could fall to the snow, the spittle crackled. He knew that at fifty below spittle crackled on the snow, but this spittle had crackled in the air. Undoubtedly it was colder than fifty below – how much colder he did not know. But the temperature did not matter. He was bound for the old claim on the left fork of Henderson Creek, where the boys were already. They had come over across the divide from the Indian Creek country, while he had come the roundabout way to take a look at the possibilities of getting out logs in the spring from the islands in the Yukon. He would be in to camp by six o'clock; a bit after dark, it was true, but the boys would be there, a fire would be going, and a hot supper would be ready. As for lunch, he pressed his hand against the protruding bundle under his jacket. It was also under his shirt, wrapped up in a handkerchief and lying against the naked skin. It was the only way to keep the biscuits from freezing. He smiled agreeably to himself as he thought of those biscuits, each cut open and sopped in bacon grease, and each enclosing a generous slice of fried bacon.

He plunged in among the big spruce trees. The trail was faint. A foot of snow had fallen since the last sled had passed over, and he was glad he was without a sled, traveling light. In fact, he carried nothing but the lunch wrapped in the handkerchief. He was surprised, however, at the cold. It certainly was cold, he concluded, as he rubbed his numb nose and cheekbones with his mittened hand. He was a warm-whiskered man, but the hair on his face did not protect the high cheek-bones and the eager nose that thrust itself aggressively into the frosty air.

– Jack London

14. What is the conflict in this story?

A. the campers against the loners
B. man against nature
C. fire against ice
D. man against mountain

15. Where does this story take place?

A. the tundra
B. the desert
C. the rain forest
D. the mountains

16. What is the tone of this passage?

A. hopeful
B. critical
C. satirical
D. humorous

17. What is the pattern of events in this passage?

A. A man is lost in the snow and is unsure where he is going.
B. A man is on his way to a campsite and is traveling through the bitter cold.
C. A man is trying to find a way to move logs through the Yukon.
D. A man is on his way to the warmth of the southern United States.

Our Metabolism

Metabolism refers to how the body burns energy. People with high metabolisms burn more calories than people with low metabolisms. Consequently, they have an easier time losing weight. One-half of the women and one-fourth of the men in the United States are trying to lose weight and become fit. The sad truth is that most of us will regain our original weight in a year or less.

What's the real secret for losing weight and keeping it off? The answer is developing and maintaining a healthy metabolism. Here are some tips for improving your metabolism and melting away that extra fat:

1) Drink plenty of cold water. Filling up on water decreases the appetite. Three quarts of water each day are ideal.
2) Don't skip meals, especially breakfast. Eat small meals every two to three hours. In this way, carbohydrates and protein will not be converted into fat.
3) Eat fat-burning foods. Raw vegetables, whole grains, fruits, and legumes are your best choices. Consume fruits between meals for extra energy, so they won't be converted to fat.
4) Exercise regularly. Aerobic exercises like running and walking are best. Also try lifting weights – a good muscle builder and fat burner. Exercise before you eat. It will decrease your appetite and increase your metabolism.

18. What is the main idea of the passage above?

A. Extra fat is unhealthy for our weight and our health.
B. Improving our metabolism helps us lose weight.
C. The right foods and regular exercise are crucial for good health.
D. People with high metabolisms have an easier time losing weight than those with a low metabolism.

19. Which of the following is an **opinion**?

A. Metabolism refers to how the body burns energy.
B. Filling up on water decreases the appetite.
C. The sad truth is that most of us will regain our weight in a year or less.
D. Exercise before you eat.

For questions 20-21, select the word or phrase that matches the meaning of the underlined word.

20. More <u>options</u> are possible with a high school diploma.

A. promises
B. choices
C. complications
D. jobs

21. We are covered by a full manufacturer's <u>warranty</u>.

A. product
B. price
C. guarantee
D. tax

An Unwelcome Surprise

Sharice closed her locker and ran to her next class. "I hope I make it in time!" she thought as she ran into the classroom and took her seat. Her mind was already agitated as Cory took a seat behind her. As usual, Cory began telling gross stories to his friends before class started. Sharice had had enough. She turned around and said, "Cory, I am already motion sick from the bus ride to school. Your conversation is making me sicker. Please stop!" She gave Cory a very mean look. Cory didn't care. He just laughed at Sharice and continued on with his gross story. Sharice began looking paler and shouted, "I need to go to the bathroom!" As she began walking, Cory thought it would be fun to trip Sharice. When Sharice tripped, she tried to balance herself by grabbing Cory's desk, but instead, she fell on Cory. Unfortunately for Cory, that surprise was the last straw for Sharice's stomach. When Sharice got up, Cory was wearing her sausage and egg breakfast. Cory ran to the bathroom in disgust and embarrassment while Sharice calmly asked the teacher if she could call her mother.

22. What is the main idea of this story?

A. Bad deeds rarely go unpunished.
B. Cory made Sharice's stomach upset.
C. Sharice got sick on the way to school.
D. Cory ran to the bathroom to wash his shirt.

23. The author's main purpose in writing this passage is to

A. create suspense.
B. persuade students to stay home when they're sick.
C. criticize.
D. tell a story.

24. What is the climax of this story?

A. Cory begins telling gross stories in the back of the classroom.
B. Sharice vomits on Cory.
C. Sharice tells Cory to stop telling gross stories.
D. Cory runs to the bathroom.

Complete the analogies for questions 25-26.

25. Danger is to security as peace is to _______.

A. mischief
B. love
C. war
D. finances

26. Bee is to hive as bird is to _______.

A. worm
B. tree
C. honey
D. nest

Answer the following questions on reference sources.

27. In what section of the newspaper would you find an opinion on a current news event?

A. Editorial section
B. Front page
C. Entertainment section
D. Sports section

28. On the front page of a newspaper, you would find information about

A. advertisements.
B. deaths in the community.
C. the latest sports events.
D. important news items.

29. Which part of the book would you use to find a list of page references of the names, places, and subjects in a book?

A. index
B. title page
C. preface
D. glossary

30. The appendix is the part of the book that gives information on

A. supplementary material not essential to the text itself.
B. the author, title, and publication.
C. page references for names, places, and subjects in a book.
D. chapter titles and page numbers.

31. Where would you look for a book on speed reading?

A. a card catalog
B. a telephone book
C. Reader's Guide to Periodical Literature
D. glossary

32. If you wanted to find the meaning of the word "dividend," where would you look?

A. telephone directory
B. magazine
C. dictionary
D. card catalog

33. If the guide words <u>lance - late</u> were at the top of a page in the dictionary, which word could be included on that page?

A. laundry
B. laser
C. lamp
D. lake

Marketing and Sales Division Building

	Office No.
Mr. Arnold Bass	218
Ms. Susan Chapel	128
Mr. Dale Fletcher	222
Mr. Ken Greene	207
Mrs. Cheryl Love	105
Ms. Gail Spears	109
Mr. Ben Tinley	215
Mrs. Jessie Ulrich	112
Mr. Sam Walton	111

34. Ms. Stone, a new accounts manager in the Marketing and Sales Division Building, will have her name added to the above alphabetized building directory between

A. Mrs. Cheryl Love and Ms. Gail Spears.
B. Mr. Ben Tinley and Mrs. Jessie Ulrich.
C. Ms. Gail Spears and Mr. Ben Tinley.
D. Ms. Susan Chapel and Mr. Dale Fletcher.

Read the following poem and answer the question that follows.

from A Red, Red Rose

And I will love you still, my dear,
Till all the seas go dry.

Till all the seas go dry, my dear,
And the rocks melt with the sun:
O I will love you still, my dear,
While the sands of life shall run.

And fare you well, my only love,
And fare you well awhile!
And I will come again, my love
Although it were ten thousand miles.

– Robert Burns

35. The phrase "Till all the seas go dry" means

A. until there is a drought.
B. forever.
C. about seven years.
D. until sea water can evaporate.

Tomorrow's Jobs

In recent years, the level of educational attainment of the labor force has risen dramatically. Between 1975 and 1990, the proportion of the labor force aged 25 to 64 with at least 1 year of college increased from 33 to 47 percent while the proportion with 4 years of college or more increased from 18 to 26 percent. Projected rates of employment growth are faster for occupations requiring higher levels of education or training than for those requiring less.

The emphasis on education will continue. Three out of the four fastest growing occupational groups will be the executive, administrative, and managerial group; the professional specialty group; and the technical and related support occupations group. These occupations generally require the highest levels of education and skill and will make up an increasing proportion of new jobs. Office and factory automation, changes in consumer demand, and substitution of imports for domestic products are expected to cause employment to stagnate or decline in many occupations that require little formal education – apparel workers and textile machinery operators, for example. Opportunities for high school dropouts will be increasingly limited, and workers who cannot read and follow directions may not even be considered for most jobs.

Employed high school dropouts are more likely to have low paying jobs with little advancement potential, while workers in occupations requiring higher levels of education have higher incomes. In addition, many of the occupations projected to grow most rapidly between 1990 and 2005 are among those with the highest earnings.

36. Based on this passage, what is one effect of the increasing emphasis on education?

A. The janitorial profession will increase dramatically in openings.
B. Textile workers will be in high demand.
C. Miners will see more demand for their services.
D. Sales managers will be in high demand.

37. What is the main idea of this passage?

A. Job openings in many manufacturing fields will increase dramatically in the next century.
B. Jobs requiring higher levels of education will be in greater demand in the next century.
C. The United States population as a whole has attained a higher level of education.
D. Occupations projected to grow the most are technicians and administrators.

38. According to the graph, how many feet does it take to stop a car moving 55 miles per hour?

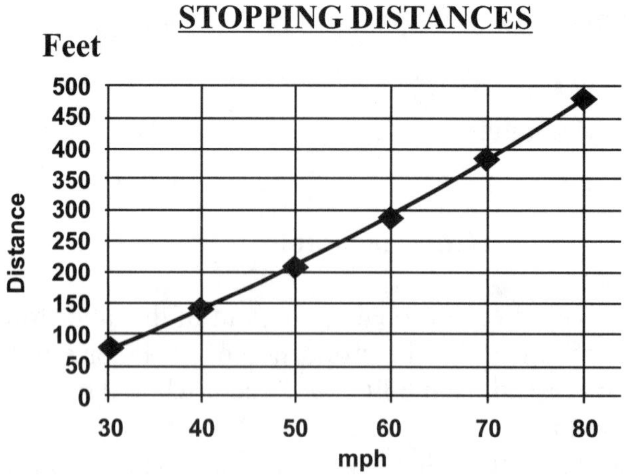

A. 200 feet
B. 225 feet
C. 250 feet
D. 300 feet

Buffalo Soldiers

After the Civil War, many blacks moved to the West to find a better life for themselves. Some became cowhands, ranchers, or shopkeepers. Some farmed the land in a harsh environment with few resources. Several African-American Army regiments served on the frontier and became skilled fighters.

These special soldiers lived among the Indians, but others worked to control and contain the Native American population. In their role as soldiers in the military, African-American men were instrumental in patrolling the Great Plains, the Rio Grande, and areas of New Mexico, Arizona, Colorado, and the Dakotas. Under acts of Congress, four segregated regiments were established in 1866 to use the services of African-American soldiers. Two were cavalry regiments and two were infantry units. Black cavalry regiments consisted of the 9th and 10th Cavalry, and the infantry units included the 24th and 25th Infantry divisions.

The exploits and experiences of the Buffalo Soldiers, a term used by the Native Americans to describe the black troops, are described in a comprehensive account by William H. Lick, *The Buffalo Soldiers: A Narrative of the Negro Cavalry in the West.* (Norman: University of Oklahoma Press, 1963)

39. What is the main idea of the passage above?

A. African American regiments served on the Frontier with distinction.
B. The Buffalo Soldiers lived among the Native Americans.
C. The United States selected four regiments to patrol the West.
D. African American soldiers became fighters in the American West.

40. Which of the following events is in the right order?

A. Buffalo Soldiers was a name Indians gave African-American soldiers before the Civil War.
B. African-American soldiers were patrolling the Great Plains before 1866.
C. The 9th and 10th Infantry units were working to contain American Indian populations before the Civil War.
D. The 24th and 25th Infantry divisions were established after the Civil War.

41. From the passage, one can infer that the writer

A. admired the African-American soldiers.
B. thought that African-Americans should not live with Native Americans.
C. thought that African-Americans should not move to the West.
D. was neutral toward the African-American soldiers.

42. Which passage contains propaganda?

A. The political race for president in the nation of Erewon has been very tight. Emilio Adonaldo, the incumbent president, leads the political party that has remained in power for fifty years. His opponent, Enrique Hernandez, leads the opposition party at a time when a growing number of citizens have been voicing criticism of current presidential policies. Both sides seem equally ready for the coming campaign season.

B. Through all the recent charges of government mismanagement, only Gene Buxton has kept himself above reproach. He is flawlessly dedicated to the needs of his constituents. He remains popular with the vast majority of voters. Vote for Gene Buxton. Integrity is his middle name.

C. Protesters on both sides of this emotional Supreme Court decision were on the verge of violence today as the verdict was read. Those wanting tougher restrictions on prisoner's rights were appalled, while those supporting prisoner's rights were pleased by today's verdict.

D. Kelly Sharp and Vicky Hutchinson are the opposing candidates for the new congressional district carved out of a portion of two other districts. Both candidates have been successful entrepreneurs. Their campaign spending has come out of their own pockets. Because two successful businesswomen are candidates, representing a growing trend in the nation, this race will be closely watched around the country.

Job Interview Tips:

- Respond promptly.
- Use good manners. Learn the name of your interviewer and shake hands when you meet.
- Use proper English and avoid slang.
- Be cooperative and enthusiastic.
- Ask questions about the position and the organization.

43. What should you do when you are called for an interview?

A. Allow a few days to pass.
B. Return the call immediately.
C. Mention that you want an interview right away.
D. Say that you want a high salary.

The Experiment

"Before you drink, my respectable old friends," said he, "it would be well that, with the experience of a lifetime to direct you, you should draw up a few general rules for your guidance, in passing a second time through the perils of youth. Think what a sin and shame it would be if, with your peculiar advantages, you should not become patterns of virtue and wisdom to all the young people of the age!"

The doctor's four venerable friends made him no answer, except by a feeble and tremulous laugh; so very ridiculous was the idea that, knowing how closely repentance treads behind the steps of error, they should ever go astray again.

"Drink, then," said the doctor, bowing. "I rejoice that I have so well selected the subjects of my experiment."

With palsied hands, they raised the glasses to their lips. The liquor, if it really possessed such virtues as Dr. Heidegger imputed to it, could not have been bestowed on four human beings who needed it more woefully. They looked as if they had never known what youth or pleasure was, but had been the offspring of nature's old age and always the gray decrepit, sapless, miserable creatures, who now sat stooping around the doctor's table, without life enough in their souls or bodies to be animated even by the prospect of growing young again. They drank off the water and replaced their glasses on the table.

– Nathaniel Hawthorne
"Dr. Heidegger's Experiment"

44. Based on the passage, we can infer that the doctor believes the drinking of the liquor will probably

A. make the four persons old and gray.
B. make the four persons drunk.
C. restore the youth of the four persons.
D. make the four persons sick.

45. What is the setting of the passage?

A. in the middle of Dr. Heidegger's hospital
B. at the dinner table of one of the four elderly people
C. at a restaurant
D. in Dr. Heidegger's home at the dinner table

How to Clean a Steam Iron

1. Pick out the starch, lint, and dirt buildup from the steam holes on the bottom of the iron with a paper clip or other wire.
2. Fill iron with equal parts water and white vinegar.
3. Set on a clean oven rack on top of a broiling pan while heating the iron to a high setting.
4. Set the iron down flat on the rack and operate the iron on a high setting until all the steam runs out. Then keep the iron on for another half hour.

46. When should you fill the iron?

A. before you pick out the steam holes on the bottom with a wire
B. after you pick out the steam holes on the bottom with a wire
C. after the iron gets hot
D. after all the steam runs out

Dr. Dunk

When Dominique Wilkins moved to Washington, North Carolina with his mother and seven brothers and sisters, his favorite game was marbles. "I was the Larry Bird of marbles," he said, but he soon discovered basketball. By the time he was fifteen, he was challenging older players in the schoolyard for a dollar per game.

While he played basketball at Washington High School, sportswriters started calling him "Dr. Dunk" because of his crowd-pleasing dunks on the court. By then, Dominique was six feet seven inches and led his basketball team to two Triple-A state championships. At the University of Georgia, Wilkins continued his astonishing success. The Georgia Bulldogs were able to appear twice in the National Invitation Tournament (NIT). The National Basketball Association's (NBA) coaches selected Wilkins for the All-American squad. After 78 games for Georgia, Wilkins averaged 21.6 points and 7.5 rebounds.

The rest of Wilkins' story is history. He went to play for the Atlanta Hawks for twelve seasons. During this time, he developed into one of the most prolific scorers in NBA history. His flying above the rim style challenged Michael Jordan's status as the NBA's greatest scorer and performer. In fact, in the 1983-84 season, Wilkins won the Gatorade Slam Dunk Contest at the all-star festivities, even beating out rookie Michael Jordan of the Chicago Bulls. Dr. Dunk would continue to be a box-office draw for many years to come.

47. Based on this passage, we can conclude that Wilkins' success in basketball primarily resulted from

A. luck.
B. size and height.
C. crowd-pleasing dunks.
D. size, hard work, and playing ability.

48. What did Dominique Wilkins do immediately after he led his high school team to two Triple-A state championships?

A. Wilkins went on to play for the University of Georgia.
B. Wilkins played twelve seasons with the Atlanta Hawks.
C. Wilkins beat out Michael Jordan at the Gatorade Slam Dunk Contest.
D. Wilkins began challenging older players for a dollar per game.

49. Why was the passage above written?

A. to urge an action
B. to teach a lesson
C. to motivate
D. to inform

50. According to the table below, which region of the world has the best access to physicians?

	Sub-Saharan Africa	East Asia	South Asia	Latin America
Population growth rate	3.2	1.5	2.3	2.2
Infant mortality (per 1,000 live births)	51	68	57	66
Population per physician	23,760	2,400	3,570	1,230
Daily calories per person	2,101	2,594	2,228	2,701

A. Latin America
B. South Asia
C. East Asia
D. Sub-Saharan Africa

Use the graph below to answer questions 51-52.

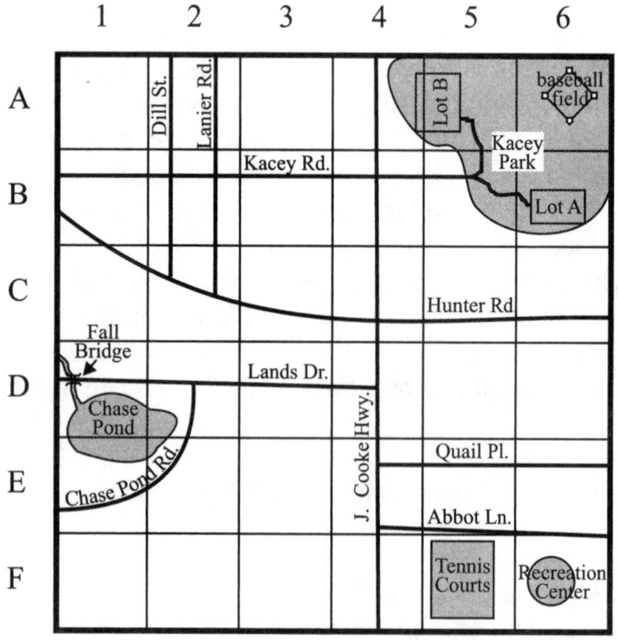

51. Which of the following landmarks would be found in A6?

A. Chase Pond
B. baseball field
C. tennis courts
D. recreation center

52. In which row and column do you find the intersection of Chase Pond Road and Lands Drive?

A. D2
B. E1
C. D4
D. E2

EVALUATION CHART
READING DIAGNOSTIC EXAM

Directions: On the following chart, circle the question numbers that you answered incorrectly, and evaluate the results. Then turn to the appropriate topics (listed by chapters and parts), read the explanations, and complete the exercises. Review the other chapters as needed. Finally, complete the Practice Reading Exams to further prepare yourself for the **New Alabama High School Graduation Examination in Reading**.

		Questions	**Pages**
Chapter 1:	Finding the Main Idea	11, 18, 22, 37, 39	17-31
Chapter 2:	Reading for Details, Patterns of Ideas, and Word Meaning	1-6,17, 20-21, 25-26, 36, 40, 43, 46, 48	32-55
Chapter 3:	Inferences, Conclusions, Generalizations, Predictions, and Summary	7, 10, 41, 44, 47, 49	56-75
Chapter 4:	Fact and Opinion	13, 19	76-80
Chapter 5:	Reading Graphic Aids	38, 50-52	81-99
Chapter 6:	Using and Choosing Reference Sources	8, 27-34	100-122
Chapter 7:	Analysis of Literature	9, 12, 14-16, 23-24, 35, 42, 45	123-158

Chapter 1

FINDING THE MAIN IDEA

The **main idea** is the central point or controlling idea of a passage. Many times it is stated directly in the title, the beginning, or at the end of a passage. Sometimes, however, the main idea may only be implied rather than stated directly. You need to identify two kinds of main idea statements about a reading selection. They are as follows:

1) **A Statement or Paraphrase of a Directly Stated Main Idea**

2) **A Summary Statement of an Implied Main Idea**

A DIRECTLY STATED MAIN IDEA IN A PARAGRAPH

When you read a paragraph where the **main idea is directly stated,** you will usually find some or all of the main idea in the title, beginning, or ending sentences. Consequently, the main idea will be a statement or restatement (paraphrase) of those sentences. Look at the following examples.

The Comeback of Rabies

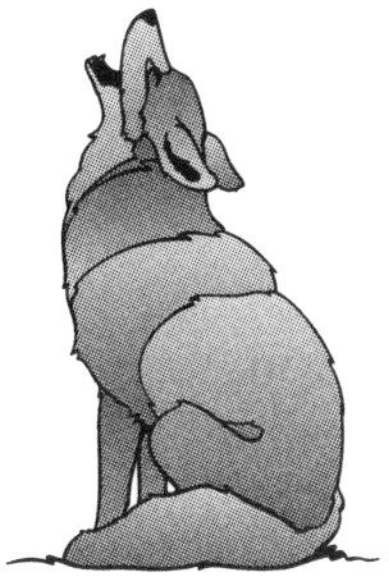

Rabies, a deadly disease to both animals and humans, is on the increase in many areas of Florida. In fact, the number of reported human exposures to rabies has not been as high since the 1940s. This particular strain of rabies was brought to Florida by Texas coyotes. Truckloads of these coyotes are imported into the state by hunting clubs and are used in fox hunts. The disease has always been found among wild animals, but the real problem is that fewer than half of all dogs, cats, and farm animals have been vaccinated against it. In 1994, twenty cats, ten dogs, and three horses contracted rabies: an increase of 500% in the last five years. Domestic animals must be vaccinated, for they are the ones most likely to have contact with humans.

Based on this passage, what is the main idea of the paragraph?

A. Rabies is a very contagious and dangerous disease.
B. Brought to Florida by coyotes, rabies is quickly spreading among domestic animals.
C. Few domestic animals have been vaccinated against rabies.
D. Domestic animals have more contact with humans than do wild animals.

Because the title, first sentence, and last sentence contain the main points of the paragraph, the best choice is B. **Florida, rabies, quickly spreading,** and **domestic animals** are the key words in the answer that state or paraphrase the main idea in the first and last sentences.

Choices A, C, and D contain only parts of the main idea. While they each refer to key topics like rabies, disease, and domestic animals, they do not mention that rabies is **spreading** or **on the increase in Florida.**

A DIRECTLY STATED MAIN IDEA IN A PASSAGE OF SEVERAL PARAGRAPHS

At times you need to locate the **directly stated main idea in a passage of several paragraphs.** In this situation, you need to skim the title, the first sentences, and last sentences of all the paragraphs before choosing the best statement or restatement of the main idea in the passage below.

East Meets West

It is amazing how the Japanese have retained their cultural heritage while simultaneously integrating many parts of Western culture. One of the most popular adaptations is the style of dress. Many Japanese today wear "Western" style clothing such as business suits, active wear, jeans and T-shirts. Traditional clothing is often reserved for special occasions.

Many Japanese also have adopted Western furnishings into their homes. It is not unusual to have a completely westernized home with only one traditional Japanese room. Western influences can be seen throughout Japanese popular culture, such as fast-food restaurants, music, and the movies.

The Japanese also have more time to devote to leisure. Surveys show that spending time with family, friends, home improvement, shopping, and gardening form the mainstream of leisure, together with sports and travel. The number of Japanese making overseas trips has increased notably in recent years. Domestic travel, picnics, hiking and cultural events rank high among favorite activities.

Japan is a land with a vibrant and fascinating history, varied culture, traditions, and customs that are hundreds of years old, yet segments of its society and economy are as new as the microchips in a personal computer.

The best statement of the main idea is:

A. In Japan, you will find evidence of both traditional customs and culture as well as examples of Western-style adaptations.
B. In Japan, jeans, fast-food, picnics, and personal computers are very popular.
C. In Japan, people always enjoy traveling overseas and shopping.
D. Japanese and American culture are so similar that you really cannot tell the difference between them.

As you review this paragraph again, you will use the same strategies for this multiple-paragraph passage as you did for a single paragraph. Once again, the title, the first sentences of each paragraph, and the last sentence of the passage contain the key words **Japan, culture, customs, traditions, Western-style,** and **adaptation.** Since choice A contains all of these key ideas, it would be the best restatement of the main idea of the passage.

Choices B and C focus only on a few details in the passage. Choice D is incorrect because the facts in the passage indicate that the Japanese still maintain some of their traditions. Therefore, Japanese and American cultures are not identical.

Tips for Finding a Stated Main Idea

1. **Read the title.** The main topic for the paragraph or passage is often mentioned in the title.

2. **Read the entire paragraph or passage.** You'll get an overview of who or what the selection is about.

3. **Read the first and last sentence of each paragraph.** Most of the key words and ideas will be stated in these places.

4. **Choose the answer that is the best statement or restatement of the paragraph or passage.** Your choice should contain the key words mentioned in the title, the first sentences, or the last sentences of each paragraph or passage.

AN IMPLIED MAIN IDEA IN A PARAGRAPH

First, let's look at the meaning of the word" implied." Consider the following sentence.

> Outside, the wind was bitterly cold, and the snow was falling fast.

What season of the year is it? It is winter, of course. Does the sentence state that it is winter? The answer is no, but you can tell it is winter because of the description. If the word "winter" were in the sentence, the season would be **directly stated.** Because the season is described without using the word "winter," the season of the year is **implied or inferred.**

You may read a paragraph where the **main idea is implied** rather than directly stated. Then you must develop a different set of strategies to identify the main idea. You are still looking for the central point of the paragraph, but the author includes only details and facts in the selection. No one sentence summarizes the entire paragraph, but together these sentences revolve around a main idea that is not directly stated. The reader must infer what that idea is.

A good approach for determining an implied main idea could be learned by reviewing the paragraph below. Read this paragraph, and answer the question that follows.

Putting Energy Back Into Your Life

Are you getting enough water? Think of your houseplants. When they are short on water, they droop. The same thing happens to you! Our bodies are made up of millions of cells; the principal part of these cells is water. If the cells are low on water, you will function at less than full efficiency. Strive for six to eight glasses of water each day.

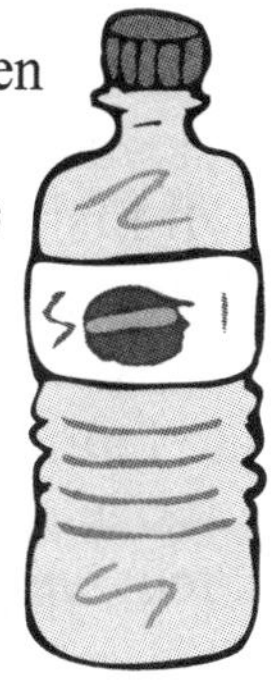

What is the main idea of this paragraph?

A. Houseplants need water to live.
B. The body's cells are composed of a high percentage of water.
C. Our bodies are made up of millions of cells.
D. Drink water because your body needs it to be efficient.

As you reread this paragraph and its question about the main idea, you would learn from the title that the topic is **regaining energy.** However, this paragraph does not deal specifically with regaining energy. Only by examining the whole passage is this topic fully discussed. So the main idea of this paragraph is about the importance of water but not about regaining lost energy.

In a paragraph with a directly stated main idea, you would usually find the main idea by reading the first or last sentence of the paragraph. The first sentence asks the question, "Are you getting enough water?" Though the middle sentences make other assertions about the importance of drinking water, they do not really discuss how to replace the body's energy. The last sentence commands the reader to drink six to eight glasses of water per day but, again, ignores discussion on replacing lost energy in the body.

Since the title, first sentence, and last sentence do not provide a complete main idea statement, the only other choices are the middle sentences. However, they mainly relate facts about how all living cells are mostly composed water and need water to be efficient.

On the other hand, **if you combine all of these factual sentences together,** you can arrive at a main idea about the paragraph. That statement, of course, is D in your choice of answers. Even though D is not directly stated, it is a broad enough summary of all the other sentences in the paragraph. Therefore, it is the **main idea**. The other choices (A, B, or C) are specific facts mentioned in the paragraph, but they are not broad enough to be the main point.

AN IMPLIED MAIN IDEA IN A PASSAGE OF SEVERAL PARAGRAPHS

At times, you may need to determine the implied main idea in a passage of several paragraphs. The main idea will summarize all of the facts and ideas in the passage. The title would help you decide on the topic, but you would need to combine the various ideas in the paragraphs to come up with a main idea statement for the passage.

Read the entire passage about the **Scourge of the South**, and determine the main idea.

Scourge of the South is Heading North

Look out Yankees. The plant that ate Dixie may be coming your way. Kudzu, a vine with lush green leaves and beautiful purple flowers, originated in Japan. It first appeared in the U. S. at the 1876 Centennial Exposition in Philadelphia and became popular in the 1930s when soil conservationists urged farmers to plant it to halt erosion. They succeeded–too well. Kudzu is now a common weed from East Texas to Florida and as far north as Pennsylvania. It can grow a foot a day and covers roadsides, telephone poles, trees, stop signs, and anything else in its way. Kudzu is tough, too: Only repeated doses of strong and expensive herbicide can eradicate it.

Researchers at Duke University have studied the plant and have decided its northward spread is limited by low temperatures. They concluded, however, that just a 3° increase in average temperature could allow kudzu to spread as far as Michigan.

But goat ranchers can rejoice. Research at the University of Georgia has shown that four grazing goats can destroy one acre of kudzu in two years.

The best statement of the main idea is that

A. only powerful herbicides can kill kudzu.
B. kudzu originated in Japan and prevents soil erosion in the United States.
C. some people love kudzu. Others despise it.
D. at one time beneficial, kudzu is now a nuisance which is hard to eliminate.

How did you decide that D was the best choice? You found that D best combines the facts and ideas in each paragraph, even though there is no sentence like D in the passage. It is simply the **broadest statement** of this passage's main idea. Thus, by joining the facts together, you arrive at an implied main idea.

Choice A has only one detail mentioned in paragraph 3. Choice B summarizes only paragraph 2 of the passage, and choice C is not clearly discussed in the passage.

Tips for Determining an Implied Main Idea

1. **Read the title.** The title will help you identify the topic of the selection.

2. **Read the entire paragraph or passage.** You'll get a general understanding of the selection.

3. **Reread the facts and details in each paragraph.** Think of overall ideas that they share in common.

4. **Choose the answer that summarizes all of the facts and ideas in the passage.** Confirm your choice by going back to the passage to check your evidence one more time.

PRACTICE 1: MAIN IDEA IN A PARAGRAPH

Directions: Read each of the following paragraphs. Decide whether the main idea is stated or implied. If the main idea is stated, underline it. If the main idea is implied, write it in your own words in the space provided. Discuss your answers with the class or instructor.

1. A back to the basics movement is shaking up the business of farming agribusiness by getting impressive yields with fewer chemicals. An example of the cycles of a healthy dairy farm includes a farm aerated by earthworms and brimming with fungi and bacteria. Legume roots such as peas, beans, and clover fix nitrogen in the soil. Five year crop rotations on this dairy farm begin with an alfalfa harvest; roots are left for soil enhancement. After corn is harvested, rye is planted for winter cover: a pattern repeated the second year. Oats and alfalfa replace corn and rye in the third year. In years four and five, alfalfa is cut monthly, late in spring to fall. Alfalfa and grasses provide feed for cattle which produce fertilizer as does plant residue. Ladybugs and other insects are introduced to the fields to control pests. With fewer insecticides used and entering the atmosphere to return to earth in rain, the purity of rivers and drinking water improves.

____

____

2. 

Scientists don't know much about the hagfish swimming the waters of the Gulf of Maine except that it has become a nuisance to New England fishermen. The Shoals Marine Laboratory sent out an underwater laboratory to study the fish, but, at first, they could find hardly any. Then they set out some smelly, rotten fish and soon the sub was surrounded by hundreds of hagfish. It was picnic time for the fish, but not the scientists. The hagfish produces large amounts of slime as a defense mechanism; hence the nickname "slime hag." The fishermen have no compliments for these creatures that raid their lobster cages and fishing nets leaving only skin and bones behind. They look similar to an eel. Some fishermen are getting even by selling the skins of the hagfish to Korean tanners who make them into wallets and checkbook covers.

____

____

3. For ship owners, barnacles are a multimillion dollar headache. Workers remove around 15 tons of marine growth– mostly barnacles– from one ship each year. The drag caused by a six month accumulation can force a vessel to burn 40 percent more fuel just to maintain a normal cruising speed. The cost for idle hours in port plus cleanup charges for U.S. shipping interests– military and civilian– comes to several hundred million dollars per year.

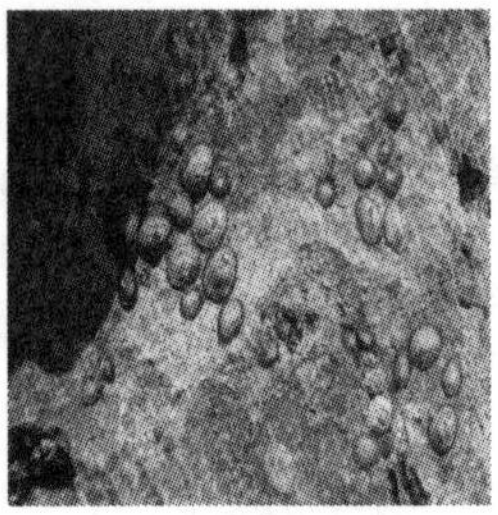

____

____

4. Named for Atropos, a Greek goddess who determined the length of one's life, deadly nightshade (*Atropa belladonna*) is a poisonous plant from Europe, Asia, and North Africa. Now Czech researchers have found a new role for nightshade: In their lab, it absorbs and detoxifies PCBs, major pollutants. Martina Mackova and her colleagues at the Institute of Chemical Technology in Prague are beginning tests in contaminated soil, planting nightshade infected with a bacterial parasite that whets the plants' appetite.

– *National Geographic*, May 1998

____

____

5. Were dogs already "man's best friend" by 6500 B.C.? Did their human masters mourn the loss of human helpers?

The people who lived in the Illinois River Valley 8,500 years ago certainly cared about their domesticated dogs. A team of scientists has uncovered almost complete skeletons of four dogs, carefully laid on their sides, in specially dug, shallow graves. They are the oldest known dog burials in North America and among the oldest domestic dog remains found anywhere, says Darcy F. Morey of the University of Tennessee.

– *National Geographic*, November 1992

____

____

PRACTICE 2: MAIN IDEAS IN PASSAGES

Directions: Read the following passages. Decide whether the main idea is stated or implied. If the main idea is stated, underline it. If the main idea is implied, write it in your own words in the space provided. Discuss your answers with the class or instructor.

1.

Volunteering

Nothing can be more satisfying in life than taking the opportunity to volunteer. Taking time out of your play and work schedule to spend with others can be very rewarding. For instance, spending time with cancer patients in the children's wing of the hospital is really special. Playing games and reading books to the children just make you feel tingly inside knowing you brought a smile to a little child.

One volunteer, Dalilah, made a special impression on the children by teaching them to finger paint with their hands and with their feet. She also taught them magic tricks with coins and handkerchiefs! Everyone who volunteers, whether they teach the children something or just listen to them, makes a difference in their lives. That is what volunteering is all about–making a difference!

____

____

2. **The House is Burning!**

I was so mad when my mom came home from work and announced that we all had to plan and practice a fire escape plan. We had to go outside as quick as possible from whatever room we were in when Mom rang the bell. My job was to grab my little brother Josh. We had to meet under the maple tree outside our house. Since there were eleven of us, Mom assigned us numbers in case she would forget our names. I hated practicing these fire drills because we had to do these drills in school, too.

One day after two years of these monthly drills, my sister, Carolyn, was playing with logs in the fireplace. Sparks jumped out of the fire and started burning up the living room carpet. Eagerly, the flames licked the furniture and the wallpaper. Smoke filled all of the rooms, setting off our twelve smoke detectors. It was our familiarity with the escape plan that saved our lives, valuables, and even our pets, Fluffy and Foofoo. Unlike our neighbors who lost all of their valuables in a fire, we were able to save many important pictures and jewelry that had been in our family for decades.

____

____

3. **The Little Girl That Could**

Little Zack went outside and walked around the outdoor pool. There was something shiny in the bottom of the waters, and when he looked closer, he fell in the water. His sister, Penny, was making her little brother a peanut butter and jelly sandwich when she heard the splash. Seeing that her brother was nowhere in sight, Penny ran outside toward the pool.

When Penny arrived at the pool, she saw that her brother was motionless at the bottom of the pool. Quickly, Penny jumped in and brought Zack to the surface. At nine years old, Penny had just taken a CPR course at her school in her gym class. She immediately started doing what she had learned. Zack was not breathing and did not have a pulse. She turned Zack's head upwards and began doing chest compressions and mouth-to-mouth resuscitation. At this moment, Penny's mom came outside looking for her children. "Mom, call 911. Zack fell into the pool," Penny yelled. Penny's mom ran back inside and did what she was told. Penny's CPR had worked. Zack spit out the water quickly. Soon, Zack's pulse returned, and he was breathing on his own.

By the time the ambulance arrived, Zack's color had returned to his face, and he could talk. The paramedics were amazed that this little girl had saved her brother's life. Instantly, the girl became a celebrity at school, and the school threw a party for her and the firemen that had taught her class CPR.

____

____

4. **All the World's a Stage**

Stella and her new friend, Max, were in line for lunch in the cafeteria. Everyone was eating their food without making too much noise. Max had just finished telling Stella about the self-defense class he was taking after school. Stella asked Max, "Why don't you show me one of the special self-defense moves you learned?"

"Sure," Max said. "Just watch this!" Max, full of concentration, tilted his head back and slammed it into his cafeteria tray. Stella and the rest of the lunch room looked up in shock to see that Max had broken the cafeteria tray, and the skin on his forehead was wide open.

"Are you OK?" Stella asked as Max recovered from his display of power.

"Of course I am," Max said as he lost balance and crashed to the floor.

"What does breaking a cafeteria tray have to do with self-defense?" Stella asked. Max could not respond. He could only see stars spinning quickly around his head.

When Max returned from the hospital, he was just fine except for the thin scar he had on his forehead. One day several weeks later, Max was once again in line next to Stella at lunch. He turned to her and said, "That self-defense move turned out badly. Let me show you a new move I learned in gymnastics class!"

"Please," Stella said, "No more special tricks. Just be yourself, and stick to what you do best."

____

____

5. **The Dish Monster**

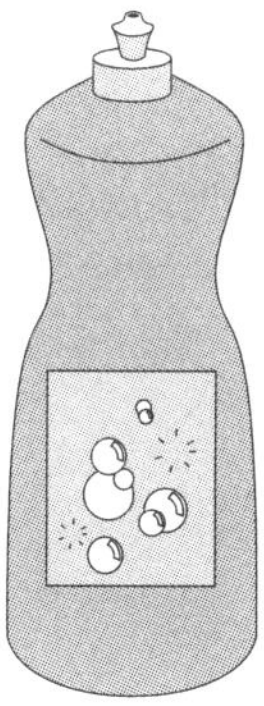

Kenny came home one day and checked the list to see what his daily chore was. Today, Kenny had to do the dishes. He went to the kitchen and rinsed the excess food off the dishes and silverware. He then loaded the dishwasher and made sure the plates did not touch each other. "Oh no!" Kenny said. "There is no dishwasher soap!" He kept looking on top of the sink and found a bottle of soap for washing dishes by hand. "Oh great!" Kenny said. "I'll just load this soap into the dishwasher and use it instead." Kenny put the soap in the dishwasher, turned it on, and went into the living room to watch TV.

About thirty minutes later, Kenny's dad walked into the kitchen with two bags full of groceries. He slipped all over the kitchen floor, and two heads of lettuce dropped into the foamy water. "Kenny!" his dad yelled when he regained his balance. "Come in here now!" Kenny ran into the kitchen and straight into a surprise. Suds covered the entire kitchen floor, and the dishwasher kept making more.

"Whoa!" Kenny said as he fell down and slid into the kitchen table. "Ouch!" Kenny said, "What's happened here? I loaded the dishwasher and turned it on like the note said." "Did you use hand dishwashing soap, Kenny?" his dad asked.

"Yes, Dad." Kenny answered. "So that's what happened!" Kenny's dad chuckled. Soon, they began the biggest foam fight that kitchen had ever seen. Then they cleaned up the mess.

____

____

PRACTICE 3: MAIN IDEAS FROM PASSAGES

On your own or in a group, reread other paragraphs from this book starting with Chapter 2. Are the main ideas stated or implied? If they are stated, underline them. If they are implied, write them in your own words. Then share your findings with the class or the instructor. Have them rate the main ideas in four columns labeled **Too Narrow, Too Broad, Unrelated,** and **Appropriate.**

PRACTICE 4: MEDIA SEARCH FOR MAIN IDEAS

A. **IDEA EXCHANGE:** On your own or in a group, find paragraphs and passages on different topics in newspapers, magazines, or books. Write out the stated or implied main ideas you find on a separate sheet of paper. Bring the articles to class.

Exchange only the articles with another student or group members. See if they identify the same main ideas that you did. Then share the results of your efforts with your instructor. Again, rating the main ideas as **Too Narrow, Too Broad, Unrelated,** and **Appropriate** would be helpful.

B. **PHOTO TITLES:** Share photos or pictures with a partner. Then think of titles (main ideas) to go with them.

C. **NEWS STORY TITLES:** Bring news stories to class. Cut out the titles, and keep them separate. Exchange only the articles, and come up with your own titles. Then see how closely they match the original titles.

CHAPTER 1 REVIEW

Directions: Read the following passages, and answer the question(s) that follow each passage.

This was the first week of middle school. The classes were so different–we had to change classes and rooms every time the bell rang. The lockers were little cubicles, and unfortunately, mine was on the bottom by the floor. The books for the classes were heavy and ripped my backpack. School was exciting, though, because there were so many new kids to meet and make friends with. The seating was assigned in all my classes, which forced me to talk to kids that were not already my friends. Everyone seemed to laugh and talk the whole class. It was hard for the teachers to keep us under control in the beginning. But somehow, they always knew how to make us behave ourselves and learn something important.

1. What is the main idea of this section? ____

____

Selling Door-to-Door

Selling door-to-door can be very exciting, but there are important precautions to take when selling. When walking around the neighborhood, be aware of moving cars and stray dogs so you can avoid them. Always remember to be courteous to everyone you talk to. If a child answers the door, be sure to ask for the parents to come to the door. Look at the person you talk to in the eye, and remember to smile. Never enter the house even if you are invited. Always thank people for their time when you leave. Most importantly, have a good time!

2. What is the main idea of this paragraph? ____

____

Mowing the Grass – A Tragedy

One sunny day, Allen went outside to mow the lawn for his parents. Quickly, he started the motor and began mowing. "I bet I can finish this whole lawn in under thirty minutes!" Allen said. Because he was mowing so quickly, Allen did not notice the large rock in the middle of the lawn. He did not think to clear the lawn of sticks and rocks before he started mowing. The rock entered his lawn mower with a *crunch* and broke apart the blade. Rock fragments pelted Allen in his shoes and ankles. Allen cried and spoke aloud, saying, "Ouch. My ankle really hurts. My new shoes are all messed up. Now I can't even mow the grass. I'll never mow the lawn so quickly again."

3. What is the main idea of this paragraph? ____

____

The men, for their parts, just like the Indians, impose all the work upon the poor women. They make their wives rise out of their beds early in the morning. At the same time, the men lie and snore till the sun has risen one-third of its course and lifted the fog. Then, after stretching and yawning for half an hour, they light their pipes, and under the protection of a cloud of smoke, venture into the open air; though if it were a little cold they return shivering into the chimney corner. When the weather is mild, they stand leaning with both their arms upon the cornfield fence and gravely consider whether they had best go and work a little with the hoe but generally find reasons to put it off until another time.

–Paraphrase from William Byrd's *History of the Dividing Line*

4. What is the main idea of this passage? ____

____

She was only 20 years old when she passed into eternity, her mummified body wrapped in fine linen and flower garlands. Carbon dating places the burial at 220 B.C. The mummy of a child lay at the foot of the coffin. When the woman lived, religious practices in Egypt were changing, influenced by contact with other Mediterranean peoples. But the inscriptions and the drawings on the mask, breastplate, and coffin reflect beliefs in physical resurrection and a ritual passage to life in the after-world. "Pure old-time Egyptian religion was doing well just before the Christian Era, thank you," states Dr. Griggs, "even here outside the Nile Valley." DNA studies should reveal the relationship between the woman and child and their ethnicity. The mummy will soon have an honored place in Cairo's Egyptian Museum.

– *National Geographic*

5. What is the main idea of this passage? ____

____

It's lovely to live on a raft. We had the sky, up there, all speckled with stars, and we used to lay on our backs and look up at them, and discuss about whether they was made, or only just happened–Jim he allowed they was made, but I allowed they happened; I judged it would have took too long to *make* so many. Jim said the moon could a laid them; well, that looked kind of reasonable, so I didn't say nothing against it, because I've seen a frog lay most as many, so of course it could be done. We use to watch the stars that fell, too, and see them streak down.

– Mark Twain, *Huckleberry Finn*

6. The main idea of the passage above is ____

____

Once there was a beautiful woman who lived in a pleasant valley on the earth. The rest of the world was filled with rocks and mountains. In this valley, summer was the ruling season, and honey and fruit were always available. Her only companions were the beaver and the doe. She was the reigning spirit of this world, and nothing ever grew old or died.

One morning the woman followed a scarlet butterfly to a remote waterfall where the butterfly disappeared. Realizing she was lost, the woman fell asleep from exhaustion. When she woke, a being like herself stooped down and lifted her off the ground. Clothed in a robe of clouds, the man being told her he saw her as he traveled across the sky.

Because he rescued her, the man being had broken the command of the Great Spirit. He would remain on earth and share her companionship. For many moons, they lived happily in the valley. The woman bore a child. Sad because he broke the law, the man sought the guidance and forgiveness of the Great Spirit. The Great Spirit took pity on the man and the woman. He opened up many more valleys and plains for the future inhabitants, but because of the broken command, the Great Spirit caused the man and woman to labor for their food. They would also suffer from cold, grow old, and die when their heads became white as the feathers of swans.

– A Catawba Myth

7. The main idea of this story is ____

____

One of the most famous prime ministers in British history was Sir Winston Churchill. When he attended Harrow public school as a teenager, however, he was known for mischief and poor grades. In fact, this man who was so admired for his speaking ability failed his English class at Harrow. If his father had not been so well-known, young Winston would probably have been expelled from school.

After finishing at Harrow school, Winston went on to college. Narrowly escaping death, he served very capably in the military in India and Africa. As a British prime minister during World War II, his moving speeches and strong leadership inspired his people to continue fighting against Germany despite the challenges.

In his last years as a prime minister, Winston Churchill was invited back to Harrow to speak at their graduation ceremony. The students looked forward to hearing the wisdom of this man of many accomplishments. After a long introduction by the headmaster, Sir Winston Churchill came to the podium. He gave a short but stirring speech. "Young men, never give up," he said. "Never give up! Never give up. Never, never, never, never."

8. What is the main idea of this passage? ______________________________________

____

Poaching the Giant Panda

Deeply in debt and desperately seeking a way out, Wu Hui Yuan of Shanghai decided to buy, then resell, a giant panda's pelt. His decision will cost him 12 years in a Chinese prison.

Wu went to Sichuan Province, home of the Giant Panda, and paid two men 30,000 yuan– about $5,500– for a panda skin. He returned home, had it photographed, and, with the help of his associate Wang Shu He, he lured a buyer to Shanghai's Peace Hotel. When the buyer turned over payment of 200,000 yuan, police swooped in and arrested both Wu and Wang. For his help, Wang will spend eight years in prison.

Giant pandas, which number only 1,000 or so in the wild, are at risk of extinction; Chinese poachers and traffickers face the death penalty if they are caught. Still, more than 200 people have been arrested for illegal dealings in panda skins.

Stuart Parkins of the World Wide Fund for Nature says that demand for the exotic pelts is strongest in Taiwan but exists also in Japan and Hong Kong. The going price is about $10,000.

9. The main idea is ____

____

American teen-age girls must find their own husbands, and no one else can do it for them.

This concept is very difficult for teenagers in India to understand as you can tell from the following interview with two Indian teen-age girls.

"Don't you want to be able to choose your own husbands?" I asked.

"No, Never!" the girls answered vehemently. Nisha, a very beautiful girl with wide, almond-shaped eyes went on to say, "I don't want to worry about whether I'll get married or not. I know I'll get married. I know my parents are a better judge of character than I am. I am too young to make such a decision. When my parents choose someone for me, I know it will be someone that will be able to support me, and someone that my family already likes and respects."

"What if I lived in America and I chose a boy my family didn't like? Before it was over, everyone might be against me. There might be bad feelings at home with my parents because of my choice, and if I argued with my husband, who would support me?"

It was Rasheed's turn. "It seems the American system would be very humiliating for me. I would have to spend a lot more time making myself beautiful and attractive and try to figure out ways to get boys to notice me. And if the boy I liked didn't notice me, maybe I would feel like a failure as a person. I would have to compete with other girls to be the prettiest–it seems so demeaning and stressful. And what if I were shy? Would I get married?"

"Possibly not," I answered honestly.

Nisha asked the hardest question, "In America, does the girl get to choose? Isn't it the boy who chooses anyway?" A good question.

10. The main idea is ____

____

Lobstergate

An electrifying discovery was made by New Hampshire Fish and Game officers. A worker at the Portsmouth power plant allegedly found his job offered some outstanding employee benefits– a steady supply of lobsters sucked into the plant through a cooling pipe.

"We were in shock, obviously," said state marine biologist Bruce Smith. During peak times, 50 to 80 lobsters were being taken. An officer caught the employee headed home with 28 lobsters for his freezer, which was stuffed with 508 more.

The plant lies four miles from the Atlantic Ocean on the Piscataqua River, salty and rich in lobsters. Sand buildup had raised the bottom of the river allowing lobsters to crawl into an intake pipe. They wound up on a screen that is washed every four hours. The suspect could be fined $30,000 and spend a year in jail.

11. What is the main idea of this passage? ________________________________

____

During the terrible Irish famine of 1847-1852, large numbers of Irish people immigrated to the United States. The most common route was Ireland to Liverpool, England and then to North America, usually to New York or Quebec, Canada.

The English and, sad to say, some Americans took great advantage of these poor immigrants, both upon leaving and arriving. Both governments looked the other way while ruthless businessmen brutalized and ripped off the immigrants.

When arriving at Liverpool, England, brokers would gather the starving immigrants and sell tickets at high prices and force them to stay in extremely crowded houses, also at high prices, until the ships were ready to sail. They promised safe and secure passage aboard good ships with plenty of food and water in route. They took the immigrants for as much as they could before letting them leave. There were plenty of laws regulating this traffic, but they were never enforced. The prejudice against the Irish was deeply seated in the culture of the time.

The ships, also called packets, were mostly old and small, a mere 180-250 tons. The immigrants called them "coffin ships" and for good reason. Thousands of the innocent died in route from disease, starvation, and brutal treatment. It was not uncommon for a ship to lose half its passengers during the trip over.

12. The main idea is ________________________________

____

Chapter 2

READING FOR DETAILS, PATTERNS OF IDEAS, AND WORD MEANING

Locating details is an essential skill for reading comprehension. Comprehension also includes understanding the **sequence of events** in a story or steps in a set of directions. Finally, you need to understand **cause-effect relationships** in a passage.

LOCATING DETAILS

Locating details is the ability to identify **facts, reasons,** and **examples** that support the main idea in a paragraph or passage. An easy way to understand details is to picture a table. The main idea is like the top of the table, and the details are like its legs. A table without its legs would be useless. Likewise, a main idea would not be understood without details and facts to explain it.

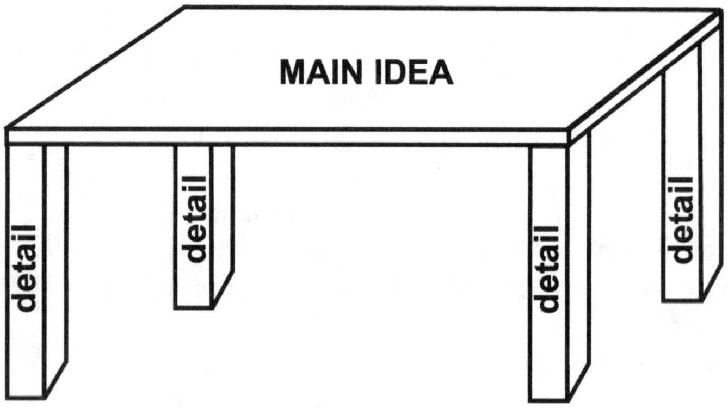

Many passages are organized around details and facts. The details are based on the 5 W's and H (who, what, when, where, why, and how). When you are asked to find a detail or fact, you should scan or look for a specific piece of information by reading the passage again. For example, if you were given a passage on armadillos, you may be asked: What is an armadillo? Where do armadillos live? How big are armadillos? Why are armadillos a nuisance? When you read a question containing one of the 5 W's or H, you will be looking for an answer with a fact or detail.

Tips for Locating Details

1. **Read the passage carefully.**
2. **Scan the passage to answer the questions with the 5 W's or H.**
3. **Match key words in your choice of answers with those in the passage.**
4. **Always confirm your answer by going back to the passage.**

For practice, read this paragraph. Use the Tips for Locating Details to answer the questions that follow.

During the early 1900s, Hollywood and New Jersey were competitors for the movie industry. New Jersey was desirable because so many actors and actresses worked on Broadway, which is near New Jersey. However, all filming had to take place outside where the light was strong enough. As a result, Hollywood, nestled in the hills of sunny southern California, became the better choice for year-round filming. By 1911, fifteen film companies had made their home there.

1. Where were movies made?

2. Why was Hollywood a better choice for making movies?

3. How many companies moved to Hollywood?

4. What made New Jersey popular for film makers?

Draw a table with six legs and label the main idea, the 5 W's, and H for the selection below. Compare your answers with those of your classmates or instructor.

Geronimo

Geronimo is the most famous of the Apaches. He and his small band of warriors, 12 women, and six children managed to resist 5,000 United States soldiers and perhaps 3,000 Mexican soldiers from 1881-1886.

He was a talker– not an orator of eloquence but a spokesman, a debater, a thrasher-out of ideas. With either revolver or rifle, he was one of the best Chiricahua marksmen.

What made Geronimo such a remarkable leader? His fearlessness in battle, his apparent ability to foretell future events, and his sharp intelligence all gave his advice deep authority. In addition, his refusal to give in when faced with hopeless odds inspired others.

Geronimo

By his family he was named Goyahkla, which is usually taken to mean "one who yawns." It was the Mexicans who started calling him Geronimo, perhaps for St. Jerome. The name came from a battle in which Goyahkla repeatedly ran through a hail of bullets to kill soldiers with his knife. When they saw the Indian warrior coming toward them, they began to yell out in desperation, "Geronimo!"

PRACTICE 1: LOCATING DETAILS

A. **5 W's and H.** On your own or in a group, read three to four news stories or short stories from your literature book. Make a chart listing the 5 W's and H for each selection. Then create questions based on these details for classmates to answer. See how many details they can recall.

B. **Creating Questions.** Bring in newspaper articles. Create questions for your classmates to answer based on the 5 W's and H. See how many details they can answer correctly.

C. **Pantomime.** Act out an experience that happened to you recently. Other students observe, take notes, and record the 5 W's and H. Then see how many can retell the event accurately.

SEQUENCE OF EVENTS OR DIRECTIONS

Questions dealing with a **sequence of events or directions** require you to make connections between events, observations, or instructions in a passage. The subject of these passages may be a historical event, a story, an editorial, a description, directions, etc. Passages can follow one of three logical orders: **chronological (time) order**, **order of importance**, or **spatial order**.

Tips for Answering Questions About Sequence of Events or Directions

1. **Skim the passage.** Look for key words that indicate a sequence of events or directions.
2. **Read the passage.**
3. **Read the question and scan the sequences to find the answer.**
4. **Try to match key words from the question with the events or directions in the passage.**
5. **Check your answer against the evidence in the selection.**

Chronological Order

The most frequently used method of ordering a paragraph is **chronological order.** Using this method, events are presented in time order starting from the first event, then going to the second event, third event, and so on.

Questions about events or directions are often worded a certain way. For example, if you were answering questions about the California Gold Rush, you might be asked these kinds of questions. Find the answers in a history book or encyclopedia.

1. What was California like **before** the gold rush?

   ____

2. **When** and **where** was gold discovered in California?

   ____

3. What was California like **during** the gold rush?

   ____

4. Which important events happened **after** gold was discovered?

   ____

Sequence questions usually contain **key words** that will help you locate the answers in a passage. These key words are listed below:

first	before	next	second	after	until	later	now
third	then	most important	finally	when	last	between	

For practice, read the following two passages. Use the <u>Tips for Answering Questions About Sequence of Events or Directions</u>. Then, answer the questions.

When the Pilgrims landed in November of 1620 in what is now Massachusetts, they needed to provide food and shelter if they were to survive. There were no stores and markets for buying things, and no houses for the Pilgrims to move into. They had to meet their own needs, and even the smallest hands contributed to that effort.

The Pilgrims overcame many hardships to establish a colony. The winter was long and cold, and much work had to be done for spring planting. Their hard work that first year was rewarded with a bountiful harvest in the autumn of 1621, and the Pilgrims celebrated the first Thanksgiving as a time of gratitude.

Over the next several years, Plymouth grew into a successful community of 180 colonists. By 1627 more than one-third of them were age 16 or younger. There were no schools, but the children were always learning. They learned by working.

1. What happened first in this story? ______________________________

2. What was the last event mentioned in the passage? ______________________________

   ____

3. What did the pilgrims do after the long, cold winter? ______________________________

4. List the main dates and events in the passage in chronological order. ________________

   ____

5. Underline the key words that guide the sequence of events in the passage.

Surviving a Home Fire

If a fire should occur during the night in your home, follow these steps for survival. First, roll out of bed. Next, crawl to the door, and feel the door. If it is hot, do not open the door. Or, if smoke or hot gases rush into the room when you open the door, close it and find another method of escape. If the door is not hot, then brace yourself against it very slowly. Toxic gases or fire may be on the other side. Third, if no smoke enters the room, open the door, covering your nose and mouth with a moist cloth. Then crawl quickly to safety. Most importantly, get out by the quickest, safest route. Finally, use an escape ladder, knotted rope, or a fire escape to leave your home. Or you may be able to climb out a window on the roof and drop to the ground. Then find a phone, and call the fire department.

– Shriners' Burn Institute, Cincinnati, Ohio

1. What should you do before opening the door? ______________________

2. When should you cover your nose and mouth with a moist cloth? ______________

____

3. What should you do after escaping from a burning house? ________________

____

4. In your own words, list the steps for escaping from a fire in your home. __________

____

____

5. Underline the key words that introduce the steps for escaping.

PRACTICE 2: CHRONOLOGICAL ORDER

A. Passage Analysis. Read the following passage. Review the list of key words for sequence on page 35. Then complete the activities.

There was no escape from the severe regimen Ida was compelled to follow. She had work to do; she had rules to observe. First, there was breakfast at seven-thirty sharp because the store had to be opened by her father at eight, which meant rising at seven; next, luncheon at twelve-thirty, so as to satisfy her father and her own noon recess hour which was completely filled in by this; finally, dinner always at six-thirty because there were many things, commercial and social, which fell upon the shoulders of William Zobel at night. And between whiles, from four to six on weekdays and later from seven to ten at night, as well as all day Saturdays, there was store duty in her father's store.

While other girls walked the streets arm in arm, or made pairs with young men of the region or elsewhere and were off to the movies, or to some party – and came in at what hours after – (didn't she hear them laugh and chatter at school and on their way home, afterwards) – she, because of her father's and later her step-mother's attitude, was compelled to adhere to the regimen thought advisable for her. No parties that kept her out later than ten at night at anytime – and then only after due investigation. Those she really liked were always picked to pieces by her step-mother and, of course, this somewhat influenced the opinion of her father.

– Theodore Dreiser, *Typhoon*

1. Underline the key words that provide clues to the story's sequence of events.

2. Retell the story in your own words with correct sequence of events.

3. In a small group or on your own, scramble the story's events. Work in pairs to put them back in the proper sequence. Then compare your answers with the events in the original passage.

B. Sequence Practice. Review some news stories or short stories from your literature book.

1. Underline the key words that reveal the sequence of events.

2. Retell or rewrite these stories in your own words.

3. Scramble the stories' events and then unscramble them again.

C. Pantomime or act out a personal experience or directions on how to do something. Then see how many can retell the events or directions correctly.

D. Giving Directions. Imagine you are helping someone who is lost find the principal's office, the cafeteria, the media center, the restroom, etc. Tell and then write the directions. What key words did you use? List two or three questions a person might ask about your directions.

Order of Importance

In this method of organization, details are organized either from least important to most important or vice versa.

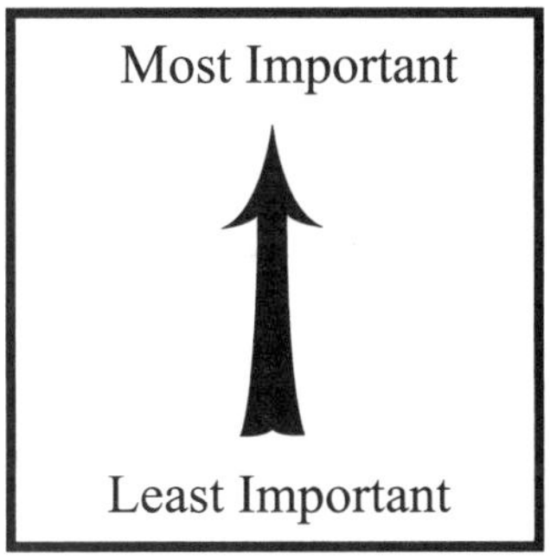

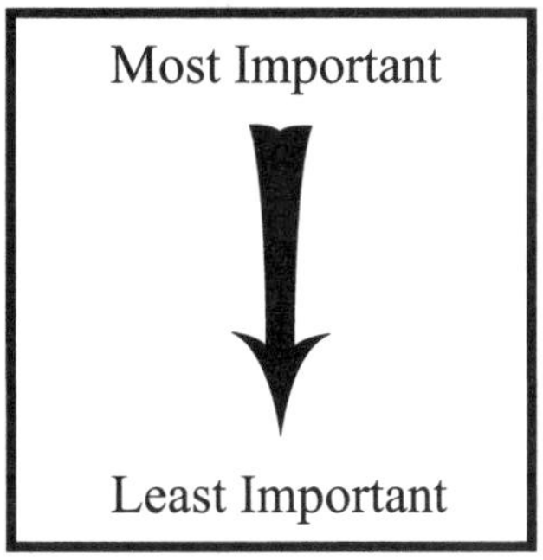

Examples: A politician's speech on his agenda.
A report on prioritizing your career goals.

Key Terms For Order of Importance

most importantly	least importantly
first	in addition
second	also
third	moreover
finally	then
most of all	least of all

Read the passage below, and decide the correct number order for the sentences.

1) Most importantly, I will push new legislation through Congress that will allow every citizen of our state the opportunity to obtain quality healthcare. 2) Finally, the people will be able to enjoy more freedom by abolishing the law which requires all pets to be registered with the state. 3) Third, I will make our streets safer by establishing more positions for police officers in our state. 4) In addition, I will initiate new legislation to reform government spending and pass the savings onto you, the people, in the form of middle and lower income tax credits. 5) As your new senator, I promise your lives will be better as a result of my work for you.

In this passage, the first sentence is 5 because it describes the main idea of the whole paragraph. The second sentence is 1 because it starts with the words **Most importantly**. The third sentence is number 4 because it starts with the words **In addition**. The fourth sentence has to be 3 because the word **Third** appears at the beginning of the sentence. The fifth sentence is 2 because the sentence begins with **Finally**, which is used in the last sentence of a paragraph.

PRACTICE 3: ORDER OF IMPORTANCE

Directions: Read the following paragraph, and rewrite the sentences in correct order by order of importance.

Least importantly, Shamie was looking for a way to smuggle her pet hamster, Juju, in to school because she wanted to bring a friend. Mostly, she was concerned about being accepted by her peers in the new school. Second, Shamie was concerned about maintaining her good academic performance from elementary school. Shamie had many questions in her head before she started her first day of middle school. Specifically, she was concerned with keeping her grades high in science. Next, Shamie was concerned with choosing the extracurricular activities she would join.

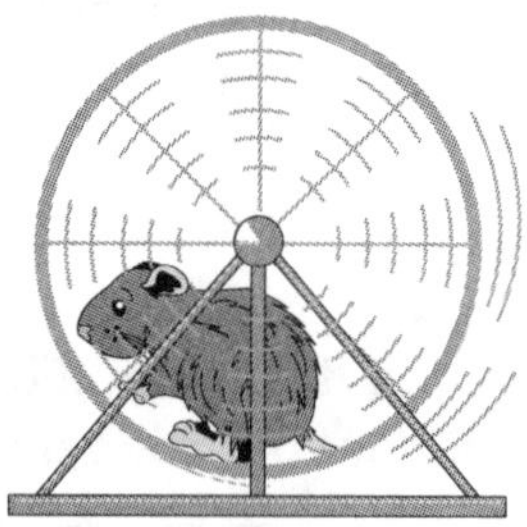

____

____

____

____

____

____

____

____

____

____

____

Spatial Order

When you describe a scene or a location, you can sometimes use **spatial order** to arrange your ideas in a paragraph. Imagine yourself holding a camcorder and moving the camera in every direction possible. You will see that you could order your observations from **top to bottom**, **left to right**, **clockwise**, **near to far**, **front to back**, **inside to outside**, **East to West**, **North to South**, **etc.**, and all of these directions *reversed* (i.e. **bottom to top**). Read the following description of a horse described in spatial order.

When I saw the horse, I knew I was looking at a creature of great athletic beauty and ability. The horse's head was finely shaped, as if sculpted by an artist. On either side of its head, the eyes were alert and far-seeing. The ears were pointed and moved attentively to the slightest sound. The horse's neck was crested in a proud arch and its muscular shoulders tapered down to powerful legs. The spine of the horse was perfectly aligned, and the back legs were unblemished and moved freely. The hindquarters of the horse were well-rounded and the horse's tail flowed like silk in the wind. In short, this horse was a magnificent animal.

The details of the horse in the passage above are organized clearly in a front to back order. First, the writer discusses the teeth, eyes, and ears on the horse's head. Second, the writer provides details about the front legs and shoulders. Third, the writer describes the spine and the back legs. Finally, the author tells us about the horse's tail.

Look at the picture of the horse on the right. Does it make sense from the description you just read? If not, what additional details or observations would improve the description?

PRACTICE 4: SPATIAL ORDER

Directions: Read the following sentences, and write the correct arrangement of the sentences on the line below.

________ On the second dive, the hunters found the shipwreck they had been looking for.

________ Raising their heads, the divers could see the front of a ship.

________ The divers looked down at the ocean floor and saw an old iron anchor and a skull.

________ This looked like the largest preserved shipwreck ever found.

________ At the limits of their vision, the divers could see a shark hungrily circling the mast of the ship.

________ The divers landed on the ocean floor and began looking in the opposite direction.

PRACTICE 5: SEQUENCE OF EVENTS EXTRA PRACTICE

For Extra Practice: Look at the pictures below. Create a story surrounding these pictures, and write it on the lines below. Make sure the sentences follow the order listed above the picture.

Chronological Order

Order of Importance

Spatial Order

CAUSE-EFFECT RELATIONSHIPS

Authors sometimes explain a topic by including the **causes** or **reasons** for an event and the **effects** or **results** of an event. Passages about **cause-effect relationships** may center on a story, a scientific topic, history, or a news event. Questions often require you to identify causes or effects discussed in a passage. **Review this passage, and then answer the questions that follow.**

The Popularity of New Shoes

Nike designed shoes appealing to joggers and 15-22 year olds. The results of Nike's efforts were an expanded market of 20 million walkers and joggers and 30% of the teenage and young adult buyers in the United States.

1. What **caused** an expanded market for Nike shoes? ______________________________

2. **Why** are Nike shoes so popular? ______________________________

3. What **effect** did Nike's designs have on joggers and 15-22 year olds? ______________________________

4. What were the **results** of Nike's new shoe designs? ______________________________

Cause-effect questions often contain **key words** that will guide you in scanning the passage to find the answers. These key words are listed below:

Causes	
why	basis
reason	due to
because	origin
source	cause

Effects	
affect	product
result	aftermath
consequence	therefore
outcome	effect

Tips for Answering Cause-Effect Questions

1. **Read the passage.**
2. **Look for key words that signal that the passage is about causes or effects.**
3. **Note any key words in the questions that suggest a cause or effect would be an answer.**
4. **Scan for the answer, and use the text to confirm your response.**

For practice: Read the following passage. Use the **Tips for Answering Cause-Effect Questions** as a guide. Then answer the questions that follow.

Pesticides in Our Food

Many Americans are unaware of how pesticides affect our food supplies. Health risks are the inevitable result. Pesticides can run off into groundwater and run off into nearby streams, where they are carried from their original dispersal site. This is how pesticides end up in drinking water, fish, and game. And because of wind, rain, and evaporation, residues routinely show up in animals in the remotest parts of the world. For example, if grain fields or rough lands are sprayed with pesticides, residues can show up in poultry, eggs, milk, and butter. The end result is that every food we eat carries pesticides as the inevitable consequence of spraying crops with these poisons. And human exposure doesn't even end there; residues are transferred from mother to child through the placenta and mother's milk.

– Citizen Action News, Summer 1995

1. What causes harmful residues in a newborn child? ______________________________

2. Why are residues found in animals in remote parts of the world? ________________
____

3. What effects do pesticides have on streams? ____________________________________
____

4. What are the results of pesticides sprayed on grain fields? ______________________
____

PRACTICE 6: CAUSE & EFFECT

A. Passages. Review 3-4 passages from a newspaper, magazine, or textbook that show cause-effect relationships. Articles on science, history, health, or news editorials might be good examples.

1. What causes and effects can you identify in the selections?
2. Underline key words that indicate the selections emphasize causes or effects.
3. Create questions based on these selections about cause-effect relationships. Exchange your questions with classmates and see how many they can answer correctly.

B. Personal Choices. Recall some important decisions you made recently. List 2-4 reasons and 2-4 results of your decisions. Share your lists with a partner, a small group, or your instructor. Do they agree that the reasons are causes and the results are effects of your decisions? Why or why not?

C. News Event. Discuss a recent news event about your school, community, or country. On your own or in a group, list all the possible causes and effects of that event. Each group should then decide on which ones they agree. The group shares its causes and effects with the class until the entire class can develop a final list it can agree on.

D. Graphic Organizer. Victor's teacher asked him to create a graphic organizer of a successful student. He identified three causes or reasons and three effects of being a successful student.

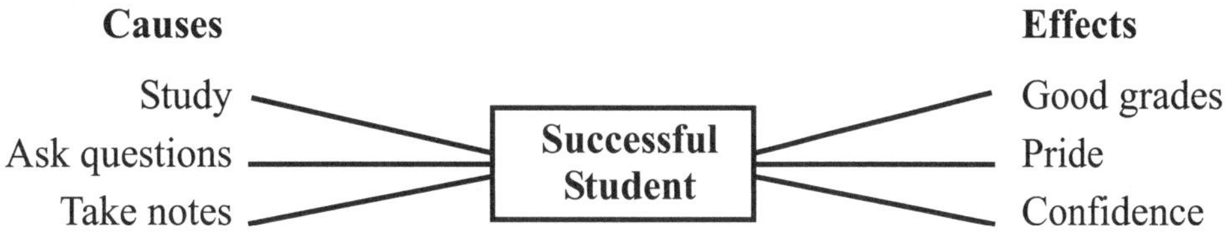

Using the above diagram as a guide, create cause-effect graphic organizers for the following topics:

river pollution	flooding	high school diploma
allergies	meeting a famous athlete	winning athletic team
moving to another town	exercise	prejudice

Share your graphic organizers with your partner or class. Choose your best one, and write a paragraph or essay on your topic.

WORD MEANING

Anything you read requires that you understand the meaning of words in sentences. Otherwise, written material would not make sense to you. Ultimately, the more words you know, the better you'll be able to comprehend written information. In this section, you will practice learning word meaning through context clues.

Now, let's choose the best response to the following sentences.

Green algae become dormant until rains revive them.

1. In this sentence, **dormant** means

A. larger.
B. dead.
C. smaller.
D. inactive.

Aerobic conditioning is low impact exercise that requires oxygen and is sustained for long periods of time.

2. In this sentence, **aerobic** means

A. hair.
B. skin.
C. light.
D. diabetic.

Many people believe that extraterrestrial creatures exist on other planets.

3. In this sentence, **extraterrestrial** means

A. beyond the earth.
B. tall.
C. scary.
D. friendly.

CONTEXT CLUES

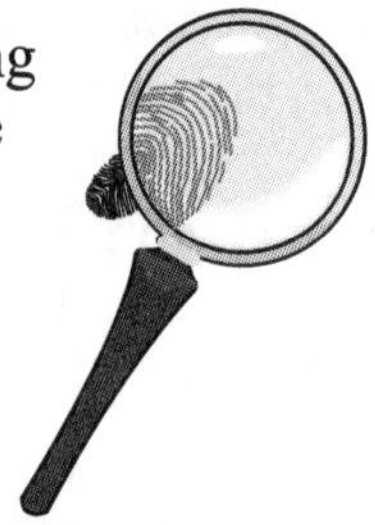

Using **context clues** is the most common strategy for unlocking the meaning of words you don't know. For example, if you chose D for question 1, you made use of the clause, "until rains revive them." This group of words suggests that dormant is not a "dead" state but an **inactive** one since the rains bring the algae back from a state of rest. In addition, the signal word, "until" tells us that **dormant** is the opposite of **revive.** Consequently, you use a **contrast clue** to determine the meaning.

In question 2, the answer should be C, light. In this example, you used a **definition clue.** The meaning of **aerobic** is explained in the phrase following "is," which becomes the signal word leading us into the definition. Low impact suggests light exercise.

For question 3, the answer would be A, beyond the earth. The phrase "exists on other planets" suggests that extraterrestrial creatures live on other planets beyond the earth.

Therefore, context clues help us determine the meaning of words from the way they are used in a sentence. By analyzing the phrases and signal words that come before or after the underlined word, you can often figure out its meaning.

Here are three main types of **context clues** with their signal words:

CONTEXT CLUES	**SIGNAL WORDS**
Comparison	also, likewise, resembling, too, both
Contrast	but, however, until, instead of, yet, while
Definition or Restatement	is, or, that is, in other words, which
Example	for example, for instance, such as, a dash or colon

PRACTICE 7: CONTEXT CLUES

Directions: Using context strategies, write the meaning above the boldfaced word from these sentences.

1. Pre-trial release is hard for those who cannot afford **bail**.
2. Strong **herbicides** are needed to eliminate weeds from the garden.
3. Henri said the ocean was very **tranquil**. I also thought the ocean was peaceful.
4. When a car **accumulates** weight, it will burn more gas.
5. At the sound of Lancelot's **clattering** footsteps, the hermit turned with a start.
6. **Residues** such as ammonia even show up in grain sprayed with **pesticides**.
7. While Greenland is labeled an island, Antarctica's larger size makes it a **continent**.
8. You could smell the freshly caught catfish **sizzling** over the fire.
9. **Mulch,** which is composed of grass clippings and leaves, keeps soil moist around trees and shrubs.
10. Instead of **incarcerating** youthful offenders, let's educate them so that they can hold well-paying jobs in the workplace.

PRACTICE 8: CONTEXT QUESTIONS

Choose the best meaning for the bold words in the following examples.

> Recently, Loganville celebrated the **centennial** of its founding in 1898.

1. In this sentence, **centennial** means

   A. victory.
   B. 100 years.
   C. place.
   D. time.

> Mr. Carver does not **tolerate** or permit talking during class.

2. In this sentence, **tolerate** means

   A. prevent.
   B. restrict.
   C. hear.
   D. accept.

> We were able to **apprehend** the thief.

3. In this sentence, **apprehend** means

   A. capture.
   B. chase.
   C. see.
   D. help.

> Sam is now **eligible** to play on the team. Vin is able to play too.

4. In this sentence, **eligible** means

   A. reluctant.
   B. qualified.
   C. irritated.
   D. pleased.

> The teacher **intervened** to prevent a fight between the girls.

5. In this sentence, **intervened** means

   A. yelled.
   B. came between.
   C. laughed.
   D. withdrew.

> Most mammals have strong **maternal** instincts to protect their young.

6. In this sentence, **maternal** means

   A. nesting.
   B. fighting.
   C. fatherly.
   D. motherly.

> Don't **distract** me when I'm studying. In other words, keep quiet.

7. In this sentence, **distract** means

   A. phone
   B. criticize.
   C. disturb.
   D. ask.

> The **finale** of the concert was the best part of the show.

8. In this sentence, **finale** means

   A. beginning.
   B. middle.
   C. end.
   D. singing.

> Can you **visualize** the day you will graduate from high school?

9. In this sentence, **visualize** means

   A. picture.
   B. place.
   C. remember.
   D. plan.

> Someone gave an **anonymous** gift to the homeless shelter

10. In this sentence, **anonymous** means

   A. amazing.
   B. enormous.
   C. urgent.
   D. unnamed.

Choose the best meaning for the bold words in the following phrases.

11. The **black** doorway
    - A. clear
    - B. ebony
    - C. hard
    - D. translucent

12. Her **thrifty** habits
    - A. dangerous
    - B. many
    - C. obvious
    - D. economical

13. A **foggy** day
    - A. misty
    - B. silvery
    - C. tired
    - D. clear

14. A familiar **rhythm**
    - A. spacing
    - B. harmony
    - C. beat
    - D. melody

15. The little **twerp**
    - A. thief
    - B. brave person
    - C. nerd
    - D. silly person

16. **Evade** the dentist
    - A. avoid
    - B. entertain
    - C. jump on
    - D. bite into

17. A **sarcastic** wit
    - A. sincere
    - B. snide
    - C. sordid
    - D. gracious

18. **Creeping** through
    - A. running
    - B. foraging
    - C. skipping
    - D. crawling

19. Have good **posture**
    - A. memory
    - B. ability
    - C. stance
    - D. growth

20. The **gracious** host
    - A. thankful
    - B. unhappy
    - C. polite
    - D. unremarkable

21. **Scrumptious** pie
    - A. rotten
    - B. delicious
    - C. beautiful
    - D. smelly

22. **Reiterate** your idea
    - A. repeat
    - B. explain
    - C. change
    - D. create

23. He looks **relaxed**
    - A. formal
    - B. casual
    - C. uptight
    - D. weird

24. A **raucous** sound
    - A. loud
    - B. soft
    - C. melodious
    - D. hoarse

25. Ed is **arrogant**
    - A. humble
    - B. conservative
    - C. proud
    - D. narcissistic

26. Her **tendency** is
    - A. work
    - B. plan
    - C. belief
    - D. habit

27. My dog **salivates**
    - A. drools
    - B. barks
    - C. howls
    - D. sits

28. Terri **procrastinates**
    - A. cries
    - B. delays
    - C. hasten
    - D. debates

PRACTICE 9: WORDS FROM PASSAGES

Read some passages from a newspaper or magazine. Underline words you don't know, and try to figure out their meanings from context. Write the sentence in which the word appears on a
3 × 5 card with the meaning on the back. With other students, form quiz panels to test

ANALOGIES

An **analogy** is a partial or limited similarity between groups of words or ideas. Two things, essentially different in nature, that possess something in common can make an analogy. We can express the relationship between the words with the symbol : which means "is to." The double symbol :: between the two sets of words means "as." Thus, the analogy **man : boy :: woman : girl** can be stated: **man is to boy as woman is to girl**. There are several ways that sets of words can have something in common. In fact, there are at least ten ways.

1. **cause - effect -** One word (cause) has an effect on the second word.
   Example: **cut : pain**
2. **size -** One word object is drastically different in size than another.
   Example: **elephant : hamster**
3. **shape -** Two word objects share the same shape in common.
   Example: **chessboard : square**
4. **time -** Two words measure increments of time.
   Example: **Thursday : Friday**
5. **similarities -**Two words have a similar meaning (synonyms).
   Example: **icy : freezing**
6. **opposites -** Two words have an opposite meaning (antonyms).
   Example: **darkness : light**
7. **part to whole -** One word is a category of the other word.
   Example: **leaves : branch**
8. **purpose or use -** Both words are used together in some action.
   Example: **needle : thread**
9. **object to action -** A word is paired with an action.
   Example: **basketball : dribble**

10. **worker and tool -** A type of worker is paired with a tool of his or her trade.
    Example: **doctor : stethoscope**

PRACTICE 10: ANALOGY QUESTIONS

Directions: Read the following statements, and fill in the blanks with the appropriate analogies.

1. Bubble is to sphere as can is to _______.

   A. will C. cylinder
   B. jar D. peanut butter

2. Studying is to school as singing is to _______.

A. playing
B. chorus
C. clapping
D. birds

3. Spoke is to wheel as bone is to _______.

A. body
B. muscle
C. cartilage
D. hard

4. Car is to driving as book is to _______.

A. worm
B. opening
C. talking
D. reading

5. Island is to ocean as mountain is to _______.

A. river
B. valley
C. cave
D. continent

6. Day is to month as month is to _______.

A. week
B. year
C. hour
D. century

7. Dragonfly is to eagle as minnow is to _______.

A. tadpole
B. shark
C. algae
D. goldfish

8. Bible is to preacher as scissors is to _______.

A. tailor
B. doctor
C. cutting
D. miner

9. Burn is to scar as pierce is to _______.

A. ear
B. through
C. hole
D. nail

10. Pen is to paper as brush is to _______.

A. tangle
B. push
C. away
D. canvas

11. Finger is to hand as tooth is to _______.

A. brush
B. tiger
C. mouth
D. tongue

12. Birth is to death as fire is to _______.

A. walking
B. ice
C. burning
D. melting

13. Fork is to knife as canoe is to _______.

A. oar
B. fish
C. water
D. jet ski

14. Marble is to bowling ball as CD is to _______.

A. baseball
B. cassette
C. Frisbee
D. light bulb

15. Minute is to second as day is to _______.

A. minute
B. hour
C. night
D. week

16. Prism is to triangular as lens is to _______.

A. square
B. elliptical
C. triangle
D. concave

17. Lens is to camera as wheel is to _______.

A. oven
B. motorcycle
C. computer
D. table

18. Sun is to moon as computer is to _______.

A. calculator
B. microchip
C. pencil
D. chaos

19. Brewing is to coffee as baking is to _______.

A. oven
B. hot
C. gas
D. cookie

20. Spinning is to dizzy as relaxing is to _______.

A. excited
B. ready
C. sleepy
D. confused

CHAPTER 2 REVIEW

Directions: Read the following passages, and answer the questions that follow.

Emily's Birthday

Emily was sitting with her family and friends in a restaurant when the hostess announced that Emily had a telephone call. Confused by who would be calling her at the restaurant, she left to go to the phone. While she was gone, her sister went to the car and brought in gifts and cards for Emily's birthday including the best gift of all, a toy poodle puppy. After finding out the caller wanted an Emily with a different last name, she returned to the table and was completely surprised. She couldn't believe her parents were going to let her have a puppy after all!

1. Do we know who was calling Emily? ______________________________

2. In the story above, who changed his/her mind? ______________________________

3. After the phone call, who got back to the table first? ______________________________

4. Why was Emily so surprised? ______________________________

Harriet "Moses" Tubman
$40,000 reward!!
for capture of Harriet Tubman
Slave Fugitive!

Slave owners around the South distributed posters like the above example because of one woman's efforts to help slaves escape to freedom. Her name was Harriet Tubman. Between 1844 and 1865, she rescued between 300-400 slaves from farms and plantations.

Using the Underground Railroad, Tubman guided them on the perilous journey to freedom. The Underground Railroad was a secret organization of Whites and Blacks that provided refuge and escape routes to the Northern states where slavery was abolished. Food, blankets, shelter, and transportation were available through this network. Like a real railroad, the "passengers" were the slaves, and the "station" was a house along the way. The "ticket" was a map or letter giving directions to the house, and the "conductor" was any person guiding the slave from one station to another. "Stations" connected the slave states of the South to Northern states and to Canada.

Sometimes Tubman and her passengers experienced great hardships. To avoid capture, they hid in snowy woods or rainy fields where they slept in the cold. Once on the journey, this 19th century Moses made sure no person would ever turn back from the challenges. "You must go on or die," she would tell everyone. She carried a pistol as a warning to anyone who would turn back, but she never used it. And no one was ever captured on her many rescue missions.

5. What was the Underground Railroad? ______________________________

____

Directions for Performing a Magic Trick

1. Show the audience the rabbit and the inside of the hat.
2. Place the rabbit inside the hat.
3. Wave your magic wand around the hat, and say, "Presto!"
4. Turn the hat upside down to demonstrate that the rabbit disappeared.

6. According to the magic trick above, when should you wave your magic wand?

____

Directions for a Science Experiment

1. Place a small amount of water in a glass dish.
2. Make a two inch diameter circle of sewing thread.
3. Float the thread on the water.
4. Sprinkle pepper on the water inside the circle.
5. Put one drop of a dish washing detergent in the circle.

7. According to the science experiment above, when should you sprinkle the pepper?

____

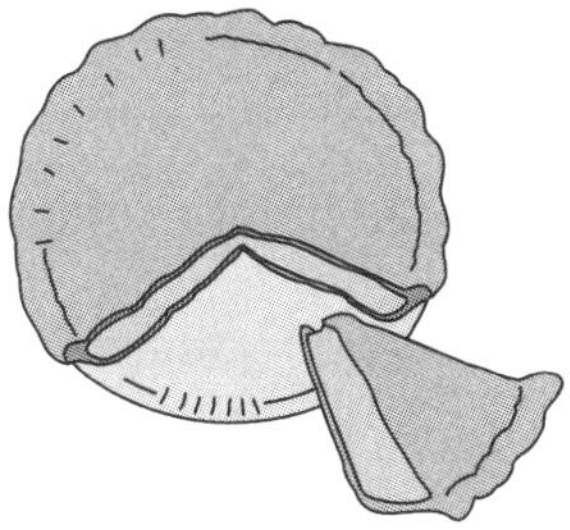

Pumpkin Pie

1	**pie crust**
2	**eggs**
H	**cup sugar**
21	**teaspoon cinnamon**
1	**teaspoon nutmeg**
1	**teaspoon salt**
1	**(16-oz.) can pumpkin**
1	**(12-oz.) can evaporated milk**

Heat oven to 425°. Prepare pie crust according to package directions for filled one-crust pie using 9-inch pie crust. In large bowl, beat eggs slightly. Add remaining ingredients; blend well. Pour into crust-lined pie pan. Bake at 425° for 15 minutes. Reduce oven temperature to 350°, and continue baking for 45 minutes or until knife inserted near center comes out clean. Cool. Store in refrigerator.

8. What must be done immediately before the ingredients are placed in the pie pan?

____

Seahorses Make Great Fathers

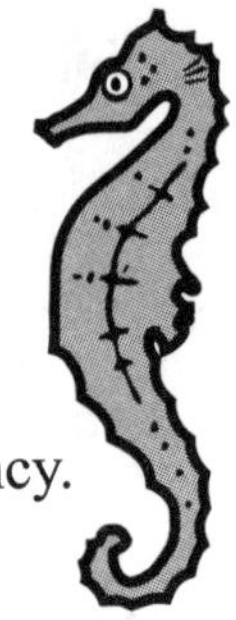

From start to finish, a male seahorse does all the parenting. His is indeed a real pregnancy, closely resembling that of mammals, including humans. Just as a woman provides her fetus with oxygen, transfers nutrients, and regulates conditions in the uterus, a seahorse does no less for the babies in his pouch. Remarkably, the hormone prolactin, which stimulates milk production in women, also governs seahorse pregnancy. Perhaps this explains a tantalizing note in the March 1753 issue of *Gentleman's Magazine*: "The ladies make use of them (seahorses) to increase their milk."

Males of the smallest species have fewer than ten offspring. Then there was James from the Caribbean – surely the world record holder for "most young in one pouch." His pouch was only half a tablespoon in volume, but in it were packed 1,573 babies; end to end they would have stretched more than 12 yards.

9. What causes the male seahorse to sustain the babies in his pouch? ____________________

Sea Adventure

Four men in an open life boat caught glimpses of the steamer sinking into the sea . . .

A seat in this boat was not unlike a seat on a bucking bronco, and, by the same token, a bronco is not much smaller. The craft pranced and reared and plunged like an animal. As each wave came, and she rose for it, she seemed like a horse leaping a fence outrageously high. A singular disadvantage of the sea lies in the fact that after successfully surmounting one wave, you discover there is another behind it just as important and just as nervously anxious to do something effective in the way of swamping boats.

"Good thing it's an on-shore wind," said the cook. "If not where would we be?"

"That's right," said the correspondent.

The busy engine master nodded his assent.

Then the captain in the bow chuckled in a way that expressed humor, contempt, tragedy, all in one. "Do you think we've got a show, now, boys?" said he.

Whereupon the three went silent, save for a little hemming and hawing. To express any particular optimism at this time they felt to be childish and stupid, but they all doubtless possessed this sense of the situation in their mind. A young man thinks doggedly at such times. On the other hand, the ethics of their condition was decidedly against an open suggestion of hopelessness. So they were silent.

"Oh well," said the captain, soothing his children, "we'll get ashore all right."

But there was that in his tone which made them doubt, so the engine master said, "Yes, if this wind holds!"

The cook was bailing water, "Yes! If we don't break apart in the surf."

– Stephen Crane, "Open Boat"

10. What caused the four men to be together? ________________________________

11. What does the word optimism mean in the story above? ______________________

Life is but a Dream

Steve got up one Saturday morning, barely awake. He stumbled into the kitchen and grabbed some orange juice. His roommate, Jeff, came in a little later. Jeff said, "Man, that was a strange dream I had last night."

"What did you dream, Jeff?" Steve said.

"Well, I dreamed that you and I were at a gas station. We found some fire hoses and were dousing each other with water. Then, you jumped into your pickup truck and wrecked it in the woods."

"That's pretty weird," Steve muttered. "You know, I had a similar dream last night. Only in my dream, I was driving my truck, and it slipped and spun out of control on a patch of ice."

Just then, the phone rang. Jeff picked it up. "Hello," he said.

"Hi, is this Steve?" the woman asked.

"Just a second," Jeff said and handed the phone to Steve.

"Hello?" Steve said.

"Hi, my name is Allison. I work with your girlfriend, Jenny. She just had a small seizure and wants to know if you can pick her up."

"OK," Steve said. "I'm on my way." After he hung up, Steve told Jeff what had happened and jumped in his truck.

"Rats," Steve said, "I'm almost out of gas." Steve pulled into a gas station near his apartment and fueled up. After paying the attendant, he went on the road. It was a four-lane road with no divider lane. It was raining, so he had to drive carefully. Driving in the left lane, Steve suddenly had to slam on his brakes, as the car in front of him was stopping to make a left turn. The truck began to skid forward. Quickly, Steve turned the wheel to the right. Because he was hydroplaning, the truck went to the left instead of the right, directly into oncoming traffic. Steve braced himself as he hit a smaller white sedan in a head-on collision.

Steve opened his eyes in shock at the scene before him. The front of his truck was bashed in past the radiator. Luckily, Steve was wearing his seat belt and was unhurt. The car Steve hit was smashed in to the engine, and the engine was on fire. The driver in this car was also unhurt because his airbag had opened. He got out of his vehicle, the police came, and fire trucks were called in to put out the fire. Totally freaked out, Steve called Jeff back at the apartment from a pay phone. "Jeff," he said, "I think that maybe <u>you</u> were supposed to pick up Jenny today…"

12. The outcome of this story suggests that ____

    ____

13. The main reason Steve drove his truck Saturday morning was because ______________

    ____

14. Who is the main character in this story?____

15. Based on the lesson learned in this story, how is Steve likely to change? ______________

    ____

16. What event caused Steve's truck to collide with another car? ______________________

    ____

For questions 17-21, number the statements in the correct order by order of importance.

17. _______ In conclusion, the people of our city would very much appreciate this necessity for our city and our health.
18. _______ Third, property values will rise as the stench in the land surrounding the river will disappear.
19. _______ In addition, the city will gain back its federal funding when the plant is built.
20. _______ This is primarily needed because untreated sewage currently entering our river is a serious health risk to humans and wildlife.
21. _______ The new sewage treatment plant is a much needed project for our city.

For questions 22-26, number the statements in the correct spatial order.
Hint: There are two possible answers.

22. _______ On his left hand side, Hank saw that the people had begun exiting the plane in an orderly fashion.
23. _______ The jet had cooled enough to allow Hank to enter the smoking cabin of the airplane.
24. _______ Hank was very relieved that the accident did not cause anyone to be hurt.
25. _______ To his right, Hank noticed that the pilot and the crew were smiling and thankful to be alive.
26. _______ Straight ahead, Hank noticed that the wide screen on the television had melted from the fire.

Select the word or phrase that matches the meaning of the underlined word.

27. At one time, computers were <u>massive</u> machines.

A. complex
B. rare
C. large
D. small

28. I felt so <u>inadequate</u> I almost wanted to leave.

A. strong
B. helpless
C. cool
D. ridiculous

29. The video <u>depicts</u> a real volcanic eruption.

A. releases
B. ignites
C. avoids
D. shows

30. <u>Fatigue</u> is more common in adults than in children.

A. weariness
B. energy
C. joy
D. disease

31. Headache, nausea, and fever are <u>symptoms</u> of the flu.

A. principles
B. causes
C. purposes
D. signs

32. Studies of volcanoes provide unique opportunities to <u>decipher</u> how the earth was formed.

A. feel sorry for
B. disapprove
C. figure out
D. exaggerate

33. Her whispers were <u>inaudible</u> in the crowded mall.

A. heard
B. spoken
C. unheard
D. loud

Solve the following analogies.

34. <u>Danger</u> is to <u>security</u> as <u>peace</u> is to _______________.

35. <u>Bee</u> is to <u>hive</u> as <u>bird</u> is to ______________.

36. <u>Cheetah</u> is to <u>mammal</u> as <u>iguana</u> is to _______________.

37. <u>Justice</u> is to <u>unbiased</u> as <u>injustice</u> is to _______________.

38. <u>Social studies</u> is to <u>education</u> as <u>baseball</u> is to _______________.

Chapter 3

INFERENCES, CONCLUSIONS, GENERALIZATIONS, PREDICTIONS, AND SUMMARY

An **inference** is information not directly stated in a passage. You have already learned how to locate main ideas and details, but this information is generally stated directly in the passage. However, a skillful reader should be able to combine background knowledge plus facts and details from the passage and make inferences about the information presented.

We make inferences often in our daily lives. For example, if you notice two dogs wagging their tails as you walk toward them, you would infer that they are friendly and eager to meet you. The dogs don't say anything, but their behavior suggests they are friendly. If you observe your football coach jumping for joy after an interception, you might infer that your team gained some yards and a chance to score a touchdown. Even though no words are spoken, the actions speak for themselves.

Types of inference questions you may be asked to answer are listed below:

1. **Inferences and Generalizations**
2. **Conclusions**
3. **Predictions**
4. **Summary**

INFERENCES AND GENERALIZATIONS

When you draw an **inference**, you are making an educated guess based on facts and details in a passage. By reviewing various ideas and details in a selection, you can infer information that is not directly stated in a passage.

The following is a passage in which the topic must be inferred. Notice how the details in the paragraph contribute to the inference.

> These storms occur over land and are the most violent of all atmospheric disturbances. They are highly localized and, therefore, do not affect large areas at one time. The actual path of destruction of these storms is rarely more than 100 yards in width. They take the form of a rotating column of air that extends down to the land from a thundercloud. They happen most frequently in the Midwestern states and in the southeastern part of the United States.

Can you infer the topic of this passage? If you decided that the author was describing **tornadoes**, you were right. The facts and details provided all of the clues. Such information included the following:

- storms occurring over land
- the violence and localized nature of the storms
- a narrow path of destruction
- a rotating column of air
- storms common in the Midwest and the Southeast

You could also draw other inferences about the selection. For example, you could infer that tornadoes cause great damage to people and property. The passage also suggests that since tornadoes emerge from thunderclouds, they occur during unstable weather such as thunderstorms.

Now reread the above selection. Think of two other inferences you could make about the information. Then, write your inferences on the spaces provided.

Inference ____

____

Inference ____

____

A **generalization** is a specific type of inference in which you apply knowledge in a passage to new situations that are related. You can make generalizations from your reading as well as from your daily life.

Let's read a simple example to see how generalizations work. Then, answer the questions, that follow.

> Many students must deal with stress in their daily living. The sources of this stress may be academic, emotional, or physical. Many students develop positive ways to cope with this stress.

1. According to the passage, which of the following situations would most likely create stress?
   A. Taking a summer vacation
   B. Studying for a final exam
   C. Eating your favorite breakfast

2. Based on the passage, which of the following would be a positive way of coping with stress?

   A. Staying up all night
   B. Missing your final exam
   C. Talking with friends about a problem

The answer for (1) is B. Studying for a final exam is a specific, academic source of stress. You applied what you learned about stress to a related situation. For question 2, the best answer is C. Talking with your friends about a problem is a specific, positive way of coping with stress. The other choices are negative ways of coping with stress and would be incorrect applications of the information you read. Therefore, both answers are valid generalizations applied to new, related situations.

Now review the previous passage on tornadoes on page 56. Then choose the correct generalizations from the passage.

1. According to the passage, which of the following states would most likely have tornadoes?

   A. New York
   B. Arizona
   C. Mississippi
   D. Connecticut

2. Based on the passage, which of the following generalizations is true?

   A. A funnel-shaped cloud over water would be called a tornado.
   B. A tornado would rarely destroy a big city.
   C. The worst tornadoes have occurred in the Southeast.
   D. Carrying an umbrella will protect you against tornadoes.

Answers: 1 (C), 2 (B). Both answers are valid generalizations based on the information in the passage. Mississippi is the best answer because it is a specific state in the Southeast. Tornadoes are confined to small local areas, so big cities would be less affected.

PRACTICE 1: INFERENCE AND GENERALIZATION

Directions: Read the following passage. Then, choose the best inference or generalization for each question.

Turning his head swiftly, the youth saw his friend, Jim, running in a staggering and stumbling way toward a little clump of bushes. His heart seemed to wrench itself almost free from his body at this sight. His friend made a noise of pain. He and the tattered man began a pursuit. There was a singular race.

When he overtook the tall soldier, he began to plead with all the words he could find. "Jim–Jim–what are you doing–what makes you do this way–you'll hurt yerself."

The same purpose was in the tall soldier's face. He protested in a dulled way, keeping his eyes fastened on the mystic place of his intentions.

"No–no –don't touch me–leave me be–leave me be– "

The youth, aghast and filled with wonder at the tall soldier, began quaveringly to question him. "Where yeh goin', Jim? What you thinking about? Where you going? Tell me, won't you, Jim?"

The tall soldier faced about as upon relentless pursuers. In his eyes there was a great appeal. "Leave me be, can't yeh? Leave me be fer a minute."

– Stephen Crane, *The Red Badge of Courage*

1. Based on the passage, we can infer that

   A. the tall soldier has been wounded.
   B. the youth has been injured.
   C. the youth is trying to arrest the tall soldier.
   D. the tall soldier wants to walk home.

2. The passage suggests that

   A. the youth is angry with the tall soldier.
   B. the youth is trying to help the tall soldier.
   C. the youth is indifferent toward the tall soldier.
   D. the youth is trying to bring the tall soldier back to camp.

3. Which of the following events is likely to happen?

   A. The tall soldier will run away from his pursuers.
   B. The youth will convince the tall soldier to return to camp.
   C. The tall soldier will tell the youth what he is thinking.
   D. There is not enough information to make a determination.

4. Based on the passage, which of the following generalizations is true?

   A. One soldier out of three will be injured in a war.
   B. Tall soldiers are more likely to survive a war.
   C. We must choose whether or not to respond to another person.
   D. Tall soldiers are more helpful than young soldiers.

PRACTICE 2: MORE INFERENCES AND GENERALISATIONS

Directions: Read some passages from newspapers or magazines. What inferences can you make from the information? State any generalizations you can make as well. Cite facts or details to support your inferences and generalizations. Share your passages and inferences and generalizations with other students. Is there agreement about the inferences and generalizations?

CONCLUSIONS

Drawing a conclusion is a common type of inference skill. When you draw a conclusion, you form a judgement or opinion based on the details in a passage. S. I. Hayakawa once said that conclusions are "statements about the unknown made on the basis of the known." To draw conclusions, use all the facts and clues present in the passage.

Look at the picture of a fish with a hook. Check the most logical conclusions that can be drawn from this picture.

_______ 1. The fish will bite the hook.

_______ 2. The fish will not bite the hook.

_______ 3. The fish is waiting until bait is placed on the hook.

Here is an explanation of the answers:

1. This is not a logical conclusion. Anyone knows that a hook must have bait before a fish will bite.

2. This is a logical conclusion. A fish rarely bites a bare hook even though it may be curious about this strange object in the water.

3. This is a logical conclusion. Fish may wait nearby until bait is placed on the hook. This is particularly true in areas where people fish frequently.

For further practice, read the following paragraph, and then answer the question.

At a signal from the captain, the propeller had been disengaged and the fins placed vertically; then the *Nautilus* had shot up at a terrifying speed, like a balloon being carried into the atmosphere. It cut through the water with a loud quivering noise. We could see nothing. In four minutes we had covered the four leagues between us and the surface, and after leaping into the air like a flying fish, we came hurtling back down onto the water, making it splash up to a prodigious height.

– Jules Verne, ***20,000 Leagues Under the Sea***

Based on this paragraph, we can conclude that

A. the Nautilus was descending into the ocean.
B. the Nautilus was a flying fish named by the captain.
C. the Nautilus rose out of the ocean with great force.
D. the Nautilus raced across the ground at amazing speeds.

To choose the best answer for this question, you should first read the paragraph carefully, paying special attention to the facts and details. Secondly, the question requires you to draw the right conclusion, so you need to narrow your choices to responses that contain stated information from the paragraph. You also should eliminate responses that do not contain facts or details from the passage.

Following this process of logic, you will disregard A. Rather than descending, the author says the Nautilus "shot up" and leapt "into the air like a flying fish." B would be eliminated because the passage does not mention the captain naming the Nautilus after a flying fish. The Nautilus is compared to a flying fish, but this is different from the B response. Choice D is not appropriate because the Nautilus "cut through the water" and made a splash. Therefore, the best answer is C. The facts and details about cutting through water and covering "four leagues between us and the surface," lead us to the conclusion: the Nautilus "shot up" and rose out of the ocean with great force.

PRACTICE 3: CONCLUSIONS

A. Reading for Conclusions. Read the following passages. Check only the valid conclusions. Then, cite evidence to support your answer.

SLEEPING

Some people think they don't move at all while they sleep. They believe that they go to bed and never change position. Not true. Studies show that everybody makes at least 8 to 12 major posture shifts a night. Insomniacs may double or triple that.

Which is a valid conclusion?

______ 1. Insomniacs shift positions less often than regular sleepers.

______ 2. Insomniacs shift positions more often than regular sleepers.

Evidence for your choice____

____

HURRICANES

Hurricanes are cyclones caused by very low barometric pressure. Their characteristic center, or eye, is an area of relative calm encircled by powerful winds and storms. Once a tropical cyclone reaches winds of 74 mph, it is technically called a hurricane. The National Hurricane Center in Miami, Florida keeps track of storm formation using all types of monitoring devices to determine location and wind velocity. The center then broadcasts information needed by local weather officials to track the progress of the storm and to take the proper steps to warn citizens and visitors of a hurricane's approach.

Which is a valid conclusion?

_______ 3. A storm with winds of 80 mph is classified as a hurricane.

_______ 4. A storm becomes a hurricane when it reaches winds of 73 mph.

Evidence for your choice ____

____

FLIGHT

When Orville Wright made the first powered airplane flight in 1903 at speeds of 50 kilometers (31 miles) per hour, the significance of his achievement was barely recognized. Yet in little more than half a century following that historic event at Kitty Hawk, astronauts succeeded in orbiting the Earth at speeds measured in thousands of miles per hour and set foot on the moon.

Which is a valid conclusion?

_______ 5. Orville Wright was widely praised for the first powered airplane flight in 1903.

_______ 6. Orville Wright was a pioneer of the Space Age.

Evidence for your choice ____

____

B. Passage Practice. Reread several passages from newspapers and magazines. What conclusions can you draw from the information? Cite facts or details to support your conclusions. Share your passages and conclusions with other students. Is there agreement about the conclusions?

C. Create Riddles. Cut pictures of people, places, or objects from magazines or newspapers. Each student writes the name of each item in the corner of the picture. Exchange your pictures around the room. Then each person writes a riddle of five clues for each picture. The students in the class number their papers. Then students take turns reading each riddle, and everyone writes the answers on paper. The student solving the most riddles wins a prize.

D. Riddle Game. The instructor makes a list of familiar objects for several class teams. Each student must clearly describe one of the objects to his or her team without naming it. If the team guesses the object in 3 minutes, it receives a point. The team with the most points wins.

E. Popular Games. Practice drawing conclusions by playing **Clue** (board or video version), **Charades, Where in the World is Carmen Sandiego?**, or popular detective games. These games are available at retail stores.

F. Guilty or Not Guilty? Attend a real trial or observe one on television or video. Form groups of juries. What are the facts in the case? What conclusions can be drawn from the information? Is the person guilty or not guilty?

G. **Read Riddles.** On your own or with a group, read from Aesop's **Fables** or a book of riddles. Cover the moral or solution to the riddle, and see if you can guess the answer from the information presented.

PREDICTIONS

Another type of inferring is called **making predictions. Predictions** involve thoughts or actions than could continue beyond the passage. Sometimes predicting is referred to as **applying ideas.** In other words, you may be asked to relate the information in the passage to a new situation not mentioned in the passage. Once again, clues and facts in the passage will guide your predictions.

To illustrate what predicting is, look at the following signs that are often seen along highways and interstate roads.

You know that the first sign portrays a deer crossing the road. Therefore, you could predict that you should drive with more caution because you could hit a deer up ahead. The second sign is a symbol for two roads intersecting. As a driver, you should apply this knowledge by slowing down since other cars could be crossing the road ahead of you. In both cases, you are making predictions based on information and applying it to new situations.

For further practice, read the following paragraph and then answer the questions.

Many people believe that Africa is full of jungles populated by wild beasts and primitive people with strange customs. From books and movies, others imagine hunters in loincloths throwing spears at elephants and zebras. However, Africa is quite different from what people believe. For example, much of Africa is not jungle but mostly desert or grasslands. You would find less wildlife than expected, and most of these animals live on reserves. Besides small villages, Africa contains large modern cities like Lagos, Nigeria, and Nairobi, Kenya. And instead of hunters in loincloths many Africans dress just like Americans.

1. According to the passage, if you visited Nairobi, Kenya, how would the men most likely be dressed?

   A. in dashikis
   B. in pants and shirts
   C. in robes
   D. in loincloths

2. If cities in Africa grow larger, what will probably happen to the wildlife?

   A. Wildlife will be seen only in zoos.
   B. Wildlife will become extinct.
   C. Wildlife will be seen only in its natural habitat.
   D. Most wildlife will be seen only in reserves.

To answer question 1, you would look for any facts in the passage that will support your prediction. Since the last sentence states that "many Africans dress just like Americans," the best answer would be B. Since American men generally wear pants and shirts, many Africans in large cities would probably dress the same way. Men in dashikis (A), robes (C), or loincloths (D) would be less commonly seen, especially in a modern city like Nairobi, Kenya.

The clearest clue for question 2 is sentence 5 in the paragraph. Less African wildlife is now living in jungles and grasslands. Consequently, a logical prediction would be that as cities get bigger, reserves will probably be the only place you will see wildlife like elephants and zebras. Therefore, D is the best answer. The passage never mentions wildlife in zoos (A) or wildlife becoming extinct (B). C would not be a choice because the passage states that fewer animals now live in the wild. Future growth would reduce the wild animal populations even further.

Tips For Answering Questions About Conclusions and Predictions

1. **Read the passage twice.**
2. **Read the question and answer choices.**
3. **Choose your answer based on the stated facts or clues in the passage.**

PRACTICE 4: PREDICTIONS

A. **Reading for Predictions.** Read each passage. Then check only the valid predictions. Cite evidence from the passage to support your answer.

Sea Lions Put Fishermen in a Tangle

To sport fishermen of Washington State, a California sea lion feasting on a steelhead salmon is a most unwelcome visitor. Eleven years ago, a small but feisty band of marine mammals began arriving from California waters every fall to gorge on steelhead and other salmon species at Chittenden Locks in Seattle. Repeated efforts to repel or relocate the hungry invaders have met with little success. Now their appetites may cost some sea lions their lives.

"The sea lions could mean the end of this steelhead run," says Joe Scordino of the National Marine Fisheries Service. "Since 1983, the run has fallen from 2,575 steelhead to just 70 last year. In past years, sea lions have taken as much as 65 percent of the returning fish. At this point, every fish they remove is one too many."

Thirty to sixty sea lions cruise the area. About six at a time stake out the locks' fish ladders and waylay steelhead en route to Lake Washington, where they spawn in its tributaries. The run starts in December and peaks in February and March.

Under an amendment to the Marine Mammal Protection Act, Washington State officials are seeking control measures that include killing 10 to 15 sea lions during the next three years. Scordino says no West Coast aquarium will accept the animals; all are males that weigh 600 to 900 pounds.

Which is a valid prediction?

______ 1. If the number of sea lions is reduced, the steelhead population should increase.

______ 2. Extra sea lions will be donated to aquariums or zoos.

Evidence for your choice ____

____

COCAINE

Some 3,000 people a year die in the United States after using cocaine. But the drug has another deadly side. In the rain forests of Bolivia, Columbia, and Peru, hundreds of illegal coca farms are contaminating rivers and streams with millions of gallons of toxic chemicals.

Which is a valid prediction?

______ 3. Water pollution will increase once cocaine is declared illegal.

______ 4. Cocaine will destroy more people and the environment as it spreads to other countries.

Evidence for your choice ____

____

B. **Videos.** On your own or as a class, view a video that you have not seen before. For the first 20 minutes or so, jot down some of the events and traits of the major characters. Then stop the video periodically, and try to predict what the characters will do next.

C. **Short Stories.** With a partner or in a group, read a high interest short story to the others. Pause at critical points, and see if the others can anticipate the events. Stop just before the climax. Have the other students write an ending. Then read the actual ending, and ask which ending was preferred.

D. **Practice Passages.** Review passages from other chapters in this book. Make predictions from the information. Point out facts and details to support your predictions.

MEANING OF A PASSAGE

The **meaning** of a passage is a sentence that contains the message in a passage. It is a concise insight gained from reading a selection.

Directions: Read this passage and choose the best meaning.

The youth gave a shriek as he confronted the thing. He was, for moments, turned to stone before it. He remained staring into the liquid-looking eyes. The dead man and the living man exchanged a long look. Then the youth cautiously put one hand behind him and brought it against a tree. Leaning upon this he retreated, step by step, with his face still toward the thing. He feared that if he turned his back the body might spring up and stealthily pursue him.

– Stephen Crane, *Red Badge of Courage*

Which of the following statements is the best meaning for the passage?

A. The living and the dead form bonds of love.
B. Death should not be feared.
C. Never speak badly about the dead.
D. Confronting death can be terrifying.

In choosing your answer, you must determine which statement best expresses the message or meaning in the passage. It should be a statement that most appropriately applies to the events described in the selection. Therefore, the correct answer is D.

While the other choices contain general truths, they do not apply specifically to this passage. For example, (A) focuses on love between the living and the dead while the details in the passage convey fear and dread. Likewise, (B) ignores the fear so apparent in the description. Finally, (C) is incorrect because the youth never speaks badly about the dead person. His shock is so great that all he can do is shriek in fear.

Tips for Finding the Meaning

1. Read the passage carefully.
2. Reread the passage for details.
3. Choose the statement that best expresses the meaning of the passage.

PRACTICE 5: MEANING OF A PASSAGE

Directions: Read each passage. Then, select the best meaning.

1. We need to remember as well as to celebrate the end of World War I. We need to remember the dead and the wounded, the widows and orphans, the destroyed and broken homes, farms, and businesses. We need to remember these casualties of war. We must prevent another such war from happening.

– from a newspaper editorial about World War I

A. Widows and orphans should remember the dead and wounded.
B. War is part of the human condition.
C. Remember those who were lost or wounded in the war.
D. We must prevent war in the future.

2. An old male elephant was dying in the African wilderness. A group of elephants from his herd gathered around this male, trying to get him to stand up. They tried to stroke him with their trunks, raise him with their tusks, and put food in his mouth. Nothing seemed to work, so the herd left. However, a mother and her calf remained, standing with their backs to the dead elephant. The mother tried to touch the dead elephant with one foot. Then the herd returned and began circling the dead companion. After a time, they gathered tree branches and grass clumps, scattering these items on or around the body.

A. Elephants often die alone in the wilderness.
B. Some animals perform rituals to mourn their dead.
C. Death is a fact of life in the African wilderness.
D. The elephant population in Africa is declining because they are hunted and killed.

3. A man was going down from Jerusalem to Jericho, when he fell into the hands of robbers. They stripped him of his clothes, beat him, and went away, leaving him half dead. A priest happened to be going down the same road, and when he saw the man, he passed by on the other side. So too, a Levite, when he came to the place and saw him, passed by on the other side. But a Samaritan, as he traveled, came where the man was; and when he saw him, he took pity on him. He went to him and bandaged his wounds, pouring on oil and wine. Then he put the man on his own donkey, took him to an inn and took care of him. The next day he took out two silver coins and gave them to the innkeeper. "Look after him," he said, "and when I return, I will reimburse you for any extra expense you may have."

– The Bible

A. Robbers can be dangerous on the roads.
B. Try to avoid areas where there is crime.
C. Innkeepers take good care of their customers.
D. A good neighbor loves those in need.

4. 

It was market-day. The narrow window of the jail looked down directly on the carts and wagons drawn up in a long line, where they had unloaded. He could see, too, and hear distinctly the clink of money as it changed hands, the busy crowd of whites and blacks shoving, pushing one another, and the haggling and swearing at the stalls. Somehow, the sound, more than anything else had done, wakened him up,–made the whole real to him. He was done with the world and the business of it. He let the tin fall, and looked out, pressing his face close to the rusty bars. How they crowded and pushed! And he,–he should never walk that pavement again!

– Rebecca Davis, *Life in the Iron Mills*

A. We can do little to change past mistakes.
B. The world is filled with crowds of friendly people.
C. Criticizing the world helps us feel better.
D. Jail is a place to relax and enjoy the world.

5. As the old man walked the beach at dawn, he noticed a young man ahead of him picking up starfish and flinging them into the sea. Finally, catching up with the youth, he asked why he was doing this. The young man explained that the stranded starfish would die if left until the morning sun.

"But the beach goes on for miles, and there are millions of starfish," commented the old man. "How can your effort make any difference?"

The young man looked at the starfish in his hand and then threw it safely in the waves. "It makes a difference to this one," he said.

– Anonymous

A. The morning sun will kill stranded starfish.
B. Starfish must be saved from extinction.
C. Saving even one life can make a difference.
D. Saving millions of starfish is a waste of time.

6. Whenever the white man treats the Indian as they treat each other, then we will have no more wars. We shall all be alike–brothers of one father and one mother, with one sky above us and one country around us, and one government for all. Then the Great Spirit Chief who rules above will smile upon this land, and send rain to wash out the bloody spots made by brothers' hands from the face of the earth. For this time the Indian race is waiting and praying. I hope that no more groans of wounded men and women will ever go to the ear of the Great Spirit Chief above, and that all people may be one people.

– The Words of Chief Joseph

A. Mutual respect and fairness will unite people together.
B. The Great Spirit Chief rules over heaven and earth.
C. Unity comes from the Great Spirit.
D. The White Man's government belongs to the Indian race.

7. In 1964, Disney Productions bought a chunk of central Florida woodland about the size of San Francisco and began transforming it into a super attraction. Opened in October, 1971, Disney World drew 12 million visitors in 1972, more people than live in the state of Florida and twice as many as the number of foreigners who toured the United States that year.

Beneath the Magic Kingdom is an area called Utilidor. Here overhead pipes funnel utilities, including a waste removal system that vacuums trash with a 60 mile per hour "whoosh."

Utilidor houses a huge wardrobe center where seamstresses maintain more than 100,000 costumes. A computer keeps the bears dancing in time, coordinates the groans of the ghouls, and even sniffs the air in the Hall of Presidents to warn against fire.

A. Disney World has an impressive array of costumes.
B. An area the size of San Francisco has been transformed into Disney World.
C. Disney World is a super attraction with state-of-the-art equipment.
D. Waste tunnels funnel trash at 60 miles per hour.

8. It was cold and drafty in the second floor apartment. The place was converted from an old farmhouse. It had a kitchenette with a small refrigerator and hot plate just to the right of the entrance. The door had opened to a large room serving as the living room and dining room with a small alcove in the back for a bedroom and a tiny bathroom that used to be a hall closet. It was sparsely furnished in "early attic" furniture. That's all Jake needed right now. He was trying to make it on his own.

Jake had gotten a job at a gas station doing small repairs and maintenance to cars. The job didn't pay much, but it kept food on the table and put a roof over his head, with a little left over to take in a movie when he had time. Jake had also gotten a little federal grant money and a student loan to pay his books and tuition at the University. He was finally back in school.

Jake was working toward a degree in sociology. He wanted to help kids like himself, kids who had taken a wrong turn along the way, or were mixed up or in trouble. He wanted to lead them back to a path of success and then give them the push to go forward down the right road. He wanted to be there for at least one kid even though no one was there for him.

A. Jake faces an easy climb up the ladder of success.
B. Jake enjoys repairing cars and is trying to open his own garage.
C. Jake lives in a farmhouse and works at a gas station.
D. Jake works and goes to school to give others the help he didn't have.

9.

Allie was quite bright, and after a few years, her job was just that, a job. Allie wanted a career. So she went back to school at night while she worked. After graduating, she got a position with a company as a computer programmer. It was challenging, and Allie was good at it. Allie was promoted within two years and transferred to the corporate headquarters in South Carolina.

Moving to another state was difficult. Allie didn't know anyone, and she was young, 28 years old. All the people in her work group were men in their 40s who were already married. Allie decided to pour herself into her work for a while and try to get promoted and transferred again. Allie worked hard, and it paid off. They offered her a promotion and a transfer to Fort Worth, Texas. There was only one problem. She was in love.

A. Working hard brings happiness.
B. Education results in better job opportunities.
C. Choosing between a career and a relationship is a challenge.
D. In today's society, promotions occur more often than in the past.

10. Dr. Haim Ginott in *Between Parent and Teenager* told this story: Jean walked along the beach with her mother. She asked, "Mom, how do you hold a husband after you've found him?"

Her mother gave her a silent lesson in love. She scooped up two handfuls of sand. One she squeezed hard. The more she squeezed, the more sand escaped. The other she held lightly, and the sand remained.

Jean said, "I see."

A. Learn the dangers of love.
B. Learn the principles of sand science.
C. Learn the many meanings of love.
D. Learn the difference between love and possessiveness.

PRACTICE 6: MEANING OF A PASSAGE

Directions: Read the following passage. Then write two different statements that would summarize the meaning of this passage. Compare your responses with your group, class, or instructor.

> It rained. The procession of weary soldiers became a bedraggled train, despondent and muttering, marching with churning effort in a trough of liquid brown mud under a low, wretched sky. Yet the youth smiled, for he saw that the world was a world for him, though many discovered it to be made of oaths and walking sticks. He had rid himself of the red sickness of battle. The nightmare was in the past. He had been an animal blistered and sweating in the heat and pain of war. He turned now with a lover's thirst to images of tranquil skies, fresh meadows, cool brooks – an existence of soft and eternal peace.
>
> – Stephen Crane, *Red Badge of Courage*

1. ______________________________

____

2. ______________________________

____

PRACTICE 7: MEANING STATEMENTS

Directions: On your own or in a group, review 6 passages found in this book. Write a meaning statement for each one. Then compare your answers with the class or the instructor.

CHAPTER 3 REVIEW

Read the following passages, and answer the questions that follow.

500 Pound Alligator

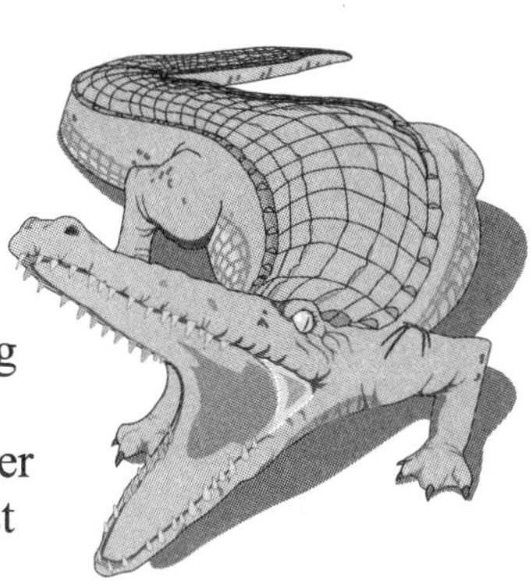

Pensacola, Fla. - For the past 20 years, hunting dogs have been disappearing in the Blackwater River State Forest. Their owners thought people were stealing their expensive animals.

The thief, it turns out, was a 500-pound alligator that turned a game trail into his private diner, grabbing dogs as they ran across Coldwater Creek in pursuit of foxes or deer.

Their barking apparently was his dinner bell. At least six hunting dogs met their fate in the gator's jaws.

One of the final victims was Flojo, Rufis Godwin's $5,000 Walker fox-hunting hound. The dog disappeared a few weeks ago in the forest about 45 miles northeast of Pensacola. The last Godwin heard of her was her bark as she chased an animal, probably a deer.

Four days later, Godwin was using a tracking device to search for Flojo's electronic collar when he caught a faint signal. The beeps were very weak until he pointed his receiver at a deep swamp hole.

Jamie Sauls, who was with Godwin, also received signals from a collar worn by a dog he had last seen several weeks earlier. They also got a response from a third collar that had been on another friend's dog.

"When we walked up to this hole, all of a sudden the boxes went to beeping wide open," Godwin recalled in a telephone interview from his home in Chumuckla. "So we knew then we were dealing with a gator."

The 10-foot, 11-inch reptile was captured Aug. 15 by state-contracted gator hunters.

1. Summarize the meaning of above passage.____

____

____

During the 1880s and 1890s, Andrew Carnegie was a prominent leader in the steel industry and one of the richest men in the world. With his money, he established 1,681 libraries in urban centers across the United States. In 1956, the Library Services Act gave libraries strong federal support.

2. What would have likely happened if Andrew Carnegie had not promoted libraries in urban areas?

____

____

Can Snakebites be Healthy?

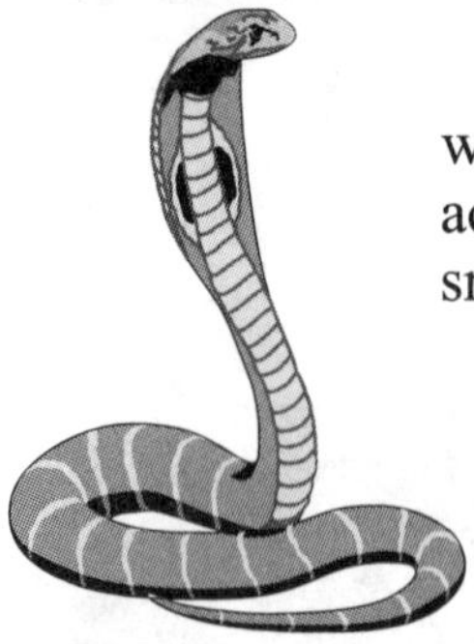

Bill Haast, an 85 year old Floridian, has developed a reputation as a man with an acquired immunity to snakes. Playing with a cobra is an everyday activity with Mr. Haast, who has been bitten no less than 162 times by venomous snakes.

He began his experimentation with snake venom in 1948 by injecting himself with small amounts of rattlesnake venom. Over the years, he has built up the dosage. He believes the snake venom has kept him healthy. He has not once been sick since he began injecting himself with venom.

He had his near death experiences, though. In 1958, Haast was bitten by a blue krait, an Asian snake which has venom many times more poisonous than a cobra's. It has been known to kill elephants. During his one day ordeal, Haast realized that something as powerful as venom must have something useful for medicine. In the late 1970s, Haast produced a drug called PROven which mirrored the effects produced by his own immunity to snake bites. The drug has been used to treat rheumatoid arthritis and MS (multiple sclerosis). Over 7,000 patients have been treated with this high-demand drug.

He recently purchased a house for snake-keeping in southwestem Florida. Daily he collects venom from over 400 snakes and sells it to laboratories. His own blood is so full of antibodies that it is used as an antidote for victims of snakebites.

3. Summarize the meaning of this passage. ______________________________________

____

____

4. Based on this passage, what is likely to happen if Bill is bitten again by a poisonous snake?

____

____

What I Lived For

An honest man has hardly need to count more than his ten fingers, or in extreme cases he may add his ten toes, and lump the rest. Simplicity, Simplicity, Simplicity! I say, let your affairs be as two or three, and not a hundred or a thousand; instead of a million count half a dozen, and keep your accounts on your thumbnail. In the midst of this chopping sea of civilized life, such are the clouds and storms and quicksands and thousand-and-one items to be allowed for, that a man has to live, if he would not founder and go to the bottom and not make his port at all, by dead reckoning, and he must be a great calculator indeed who succeeds. Simplify, Simplify. Instead of three meals a day, if it be necessary eat but one; instead of a hundred dishes, five; and reduce other things in proportion.

–Henry David Thoreau, *Walden*

5. Based on this passage, we can conclude that the writer's philosophy is ______________

____

Explore America's Hands-On Museum of Space Travel

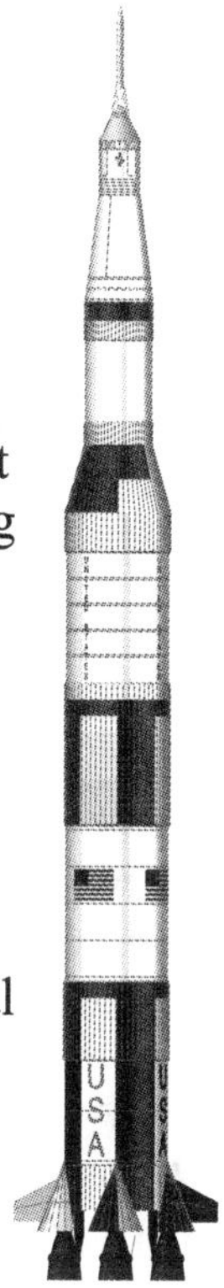

Pilot a spacecraft to the moon's surface. Fire lasers at the speed of light. Feel the force of triple gravity in a spinning moonship. Leap 15 feet high on the zero gravity machine. It's all part of a 21st century adventure of space travel and adventure at The Space and Rocket Center.

Sixty action exhibits involve you in an educational and entertaining experience in which you're an astronaut for the day. You'll see and touch rockets and spacecrafts that have made the fantastic journey into space, watch demonstrations of astronauts' training equipment and meet Baker, the monkeynaut who pioneered space travel.

From the early days of flight to the Space Shuttle and tomorrow's explorations beyond the stars, The Space and Rocket Center offers first-hand experience with the challenges of man in space.

United States Space Camp

Young people from all over the world come to Huntsville for a unique, educational experience. Boys and girls build and launch model rockets, train like astronauts, try on a space suit, and fly a simulated Space Shuttle mission, complete with shuttle cockpit and mission control. From astronaut training with authentic NASA equipment to receiving their wings at week's end, there's no other experience like it on earth!
(Open March through November, Huntsville, Alabama)

6. From the information presented, we can conclude that ______________________________

____

____

7. Based on these articles, who do you think is the intended audience? __________________

____

From an editorial —

In today's Morning News, we heard the Surgeon General's latest report about smoking among young people. Three million teenagers smoke a billion packs of cigarettes every year, and the numbers are growing. The average age to start smoking is now 14! years of age.

What can we do to prevent adolescent smokers from becoming adult smokers? One way is to ban cigarettes from vending machines which are easily accessible to children. Another strategy is to restrict ads featuring glamorous, sexy, and awesome images of smokers portrayed on billboards, appealing to teenagers.

Eliminating the special coupon promotions for tee-shirts and hats on cigarette packs would also reduce smoking. When young people do not hear about or see cigarettes everywhere, they will pay more attention to the health risks associated with cigarette smoking. Smoking-related illnesses kill over 400,000 smokers annually.

Therefore, education and legal action will protect our young people from the smoking habit!

8. What summarizes the writer's viewpoint? ____

____

9. What does the writer claim is the leading cause of teenage smoking? ________________

____

Harry Houdini

In the summer of 1912, a man was chained and then nailed into a wooden box. Then the box was bound with rope and steel cables and lowered into the East River. Minutes passed as the audience waited to see what would happen. Fearing for the man's life, many gasped for breath themselves. Suddenly, the man emerged from the water, unharmed and freed from his chains. His name was Harry Houdini.

Houdini spent a lifetime performing escapes that left his audiences astonished and clamoring for more. Dangling upside down from a crane, he could wrestle himself out of a straightjacket in minutes. He could be handcuffed and lowered into a steel drum secured with padlocks and filled with water. Three minutes later, he would emerge alive and well.

How did Houdini accomplish his feats? Besides being a master of illusion, he also possessed two unique talents. His body was flexible and muscular which allowed him to untie knots with his fingers and teeth. He also trained himself to hold his breath under water for up to four minutes. Besides that, he could pick apart any lock or chain in the world. In fact, he often showed people from his audience that he could open locks they brought to him. In this way, he proved that the ones he picked were not fake. In 1901, he was handcuffed to a pillar by police who would return in an hour to free him. He escaped before they left the room. In 1903, German police accused him of cheating and encouraging criminals. He escaped in the courtroom and won the case.

10. Which statement above is a conclusion drawn by the author? ______________________

____

____

11. What generalization could accurately describe Houdini's abilities? ________________

____

Moon

Through space exploration, scientists have constructed a history of the moon dating back to its infancy. Rocks collected from the lunar highlands date about 4.0 to 4.3 billion years old. It's believed the solar system formed about 4.6 billion years ago. The first few million years of the moon's existence were so violent that few traces of this period remain. As a molten outer layer gradually cooled and solidified into different kinds of rock, the moon was bombarded by huge asteroids and smaller objects. Some of the asteroids were the size of small states like Rhode Island or Delaware, and their collisions with the moon created huge basins hundreds of kilometers across.

The catastrophic bombardment died away about 4 billion years ago, leaving the lunar highlands covered with huge overlapping craters and a deep layer of shattered and broken rock. Heat produced by the decay of radioactive elements began to melt the inside of the moon at depths of about 200 kilometers (124 miles) below its surface. Then, from about 3.8 to 3.1 billion years ago, great floods of lava rose from inside the moon and poured over its surface, filling in the large impact basins to form the dark parts of the moon called maria or seas. Explorations show that there has been no significant volcanic activity on the moon for more than 3 billion years.

12. From this passage, we can generalize that ______________________________

____

13. Based on this article, what is likely to happen if an asteroid hits the moon's surface?

____

____

The Wild Pitcher

It is the last game of the championship. Tamara, the girl who is always picked last when forming teams, sits on the bench and cheers her team, the Rockets, against the visiting team, the Panthers. Earlier in the game, Louise, the star pitcher of the Rockets, sprained her arm in the opening pitch. Now, in the last inning with a one run Rockets advantage and bases loaded, her replacement, Jenny, also sprained her arm. In a desperate move, Dalia, the coach of the Rockets, told Tamara, "Try your best honey. Just try not to break your hand when you throw the ball." Tamara stumbled clumsily to the mound and readied her first pitch. All she had to do was strike out this one hitter and the game was won. The Rockets fans closed their eyes in fear of what Tamara would do. She threw the ball so strangely it seemed to spin in spirals, yet it passed through the strike zone of the hitter, and she missed it. Tamara continued to throw like this, and by the time the third out was called, the fans stood up and shouted, "Tamara, Tamara, Tamara!"

14. The lesson to be inferred from this story is ______________________________

____

15. Based on this story, what is the coach most likely to do with Tamara? _______________

____

Chapter 4

FACT AND OPINION

Being able to distinguish a fact from an opinion is an important reading skill. A **fact** is a true statement that can be proven by observation, statistics, or research. An **opinion** is a judgment or viewpoint about a person, place, event, or idea. An opinion may not really be true, even though the author may want you to believe it is. Now, let's look at some examples of fact and opinion.

1A. Fact: Many vegetables contain vitamins and minerals that are essential for health.

1B. Opinion: Vegetables are easy to cook and delicious.

2A. Fact: Oprah Winfrey was born in Kosciuska, Mississippi on January 29, 1954.

2B. Opinion: The Oprah Winfrey Show is my favorite talk show on television.

Statement **1A** about vegetables' health benefits is a **fact** because researchers have proven that vegetables contains important vitamins and minerals. However, the phrases describing vegetables as "easy to cook and delicious" in statement **1B** are **opinions.** They express a viewpoint, since not all people think vegetables are delicious or easy to cook.

Statement **2A** about Oprah Winfrey is a **fact** because official birth records indicate the place and date of her birth. On the other hand, statement **2B** is clearly an opinion since the phrase "my favorite" describes one person's belief about the Oprah Winfrey Show.

For practice, read the following paragraph. See if you can distinguish the factual statements from those that are opinions.

> **1)** Viola Clay is 110 years old. **2)** She has a 73 year old grandson on Social Security. **3)** According to her 92 year old daughter, Tillie, Viola is delightful, charming, and civil most of the time. **4)** At precisely 2 p.m. every day, Tillie visits her mother at the Forest Hills Nursing Home. **5)** She brings some cake or cookies to share. **6)** "When she gets cranky, I know it's time to leave," her daughter says. **7)** According to birth records, Viola has outlived 22 presidents of the United States. **8)** "It's hard to believe, but my mother's older than the Statue of Liberty," Tillie whispers to her friends.

On the spaces below, write the sentence numbers for the fact and opinion statements.

Facts: ______________________________

Opinions: ______________________________

Tips for Identifying Facts and Opinions

1. **Facts state information based on observation, statistics, or research.**
2. **Opinions express a personal viewpoint or belief about a person, place, event, or idea.**

Hint 1: Opinions contain adjectives like **best, worst, favorite, dishonest, etc.**

Hint 2: Opinions sometimes include phrases such as **I feel, I think, my view, my opinion, etc.**

PRACTICE 1: FACT OR OPINION

Directions: For the following statements, write **F** next to facts and **O** next to opinions. Be able to support your answers.

1. ______ Frog legs are light, tender, and tasty!
2. ______ Alabama joined the Confederate States of America on February 8, 1861.
3. ______ The United States Department of Agriculture recommends that Americans eat 3 to 5 servings of vegetables each day.
4. ______ Our dog is a comical creature the size of a basketball.
5. ______ Ralph Nader is an outstanding candidate for president.
6. ______ Wayne Beecham was charged yesterday with armed robbery of the Hays Convenience Store on Palm Boulevard.
7. ______ I think that people in small towns are friendly.
8. ______ Highway speed limits vary from state to state.
9. ______ Tom Glavin is still one of the hottest pitchers in baseball.
10. ______ A used car often costs less than a new car.
11. ______ The Backstreet Boys will be on channel 32 tonight at 8:00 p.m.
12. ______ The best lunch in the restaurant is spaghetti with meatballs.
13. ______ Atlanta, Georgia was the site chosen for the 1996 summer Olympic games.
14. ______ Everyone attending the Olympic games had a good time.
15. ______ The temperatures at the equator are warmer than those at the North Pole.

PRACTICE 2: READING FOR FACTS AND OPINIONS

Directions: In the following paragraphs, write an **F** in front of statements that are facts and an **O** in front of statements that are opinions. Be able to defend your answers.

Lost Sea

1) The Lost Sea in Sweetwater, Tennessee is the largest underground lake in the world. **2)** The temperature inside the cavern remains at 58 degrees all year long. **3)** Many interesting rooms exist inside the cavern. **4)** In one room, you can see rare cave flowers called anthodites. **5)** Every second of the tour is a fascinating experience you'll never forget.

1.______ **2.**______ **3.**______ **4.**______ **5.**______

Wilderness Adventure

1) In the evening, we pitched our tent near Miry Creek. **2)** Our hunters killed a large doe and two bears. **3)** No one loves bear better than men of the woods. **4)** I don't think this is a proper diet for us because we may get sick. **5)** However, we have subsisted plentifully on the bounty of this land. **6)** We arrived at Coggins Point about four in the afternoon and then went on to Westover. **7)** My happiness was complete when I learned my family prospered in my absence.

– adapted from the *Diaries of William Byrd*

1.______ **2.**______ **3.**______ **4.**______ **5.**______ **6.**______ **7.**______

PRACTICE 3: CREATE FACTS AND OPINIONS

Directions: On your own or with a partner, think of two persons, places, things, and ideas. Then write a statement of fact and a statement of opinion about each one. Review your statements with a teacher or other students. Revise them based on their feedback.

PRACTICE 4: FIND FACTS AND OPINIONS

Directions: Find five facts and five opinions in newspaper or magazine articles, ads, and editorials. Underline them, and then share them with your instructor or classmates for feedback.

PRACTICE 5: LOCATING FACTS AND OPINIONS

Underline all of the **facts** in **Amazing Achievements**. Then underline all of the **opinions** in **Dr. North.**

Amazing Achievements

Around the world are many amazing architectural achievements. One such structure is the Taj Mahal in India. The Emperor Shah Jahan built this magnificent monument in memory of his wife. Constructed of pure white marble, this building took 20,000 workers 20 years to finish. Sadly, the emperor executed the architect of this structure, so he could never design a more beautiful place.

A similar fate awaited the architect of the impressive St. Basil's Cathedral in Moscow, Russia. Ivan the Terrible ordered this vividly painted church to be built from precious stones. After this structure was completed, he had the architect blinded, so no one could duplicate this masterpiece.

Even more astonishing was the task of building the Great Pyramid Of Egypt over 4,500 years ago. It contains enough stone to construct a 10 foot high wall around Spain. For 30 years, over 4,000 men hauled stones weighing 16.5 tons each. Nearly 2,300,000 of the stone blocks were needed to build the Great Pyramid.

Dr. North

So Dr. North left his secret mark upon the neighborhood—as all of us do, for good or for ill, upon our neighborhoods, according to the strength of that character which lives within us. For a long time I did not know that it was he, though it was not difficult to see that some strong good man had often passed this way. I saw the mystic sign of him deep-lettered in the hearthstone of a home; I heard it speaking bravely from the weak lips of a friend; it is carved in the plastic heart of many a boy. No, I do not doubt the immortalities of the soul; in this community, which I have come to love so much, dwells more than one of John North's immortalities – and will continue to dwell. I, too, live more deeply because John North was here.

He was in no outward way an extraordinary man, nor was his life eventful. He was born in this neighborhood: I saw him lying quite still this morning in the same sunny room of the same house where he first saw the light of day. Here among these common hills he grew up, and save for the few years he spent at school or in the army, he lived here all his life long.

In old neighborhoods and especially farm neighborhoods people come to know one another – not clothes knowledge, or money knowledge–but that sort of knowledge which reaches down into the human springs of human character.

CHAPTER 4 REVIEW

Directions: For each of the following sentences, write F if it expresses a fact or O if it expresses an opinion.

______ 1. With outstretched wings, a bald eagle sweeps over the nest and presents the youngster with food in its beak.

______ 2. These blue flowers are the most beautiful on the face of the earth.

______ 3. The new album from this heavy metal band is totally obnoxious.

______ 4. Andrew Wiles has solved a mathematical equation that has riddled mathematicians for centuries.

______ 5. George Washington was the first president of the United States.

______ 6. It takes a brave man to wear a tie that looks like that.

______ 7. I think that is the best movie that came out last year.

______ 8. Spending more money on the space program is more important than spending money on cancer research.

______ 9. Neither New York nor Atlanta has a chance to win the World Series next year.

______ 10. Beth knew the song because she heard it so many times on the radio.

Directions: Read the following passage. For each sentence, write F if the sentence is a fact, and write O if the sentence is an opinion.

King Buck

11) Buck was neither house dog nor kennel dog. 12) The whole world belonged to him. 13) He usually plunged into the swimming tank or went hunting with the judge's sons. 14) He was the king – king over all creeping, crawling, flying things of Judge Miller's place, humans included. 15) During the four years since his puppyhood, he had lived the life of a king. 16) He had been fed three times a day and was allowed to roam the countryside. 17) Hunting and other outdoor delights had kept down the fat and hardened his muscles. 18) Buck's love of water had been a help and a health preserver. 19) His massive frame was given a bath two times a week. 20) He seemed to be one of the happiest, most contented dogs alive.

– Jack London's *Call of the Wild*

11. _____	16. _____
12. _____	17. _____
13. _____	18. _____
14. _____	19. _____
15. _____	20. _____

Chapter 5

READING GRAPHIC AIDS

Graphic aids present complex information in a simplified, visual format. In this chapter, you will read and answer questions about graphic aids.

SCHEDULES

Schedule - information arranged in a timetable with dates and times. Schedules may contain departure and arrival times such as a bus or plane schedule. They may also include programs or meeting times like a television schedule or a class schedule.

OAKDALE BUS SCHEDULE

Weekdays gray and white — Saturday and Sundays gray only

OUTBOUND from downtown (Bus sign reads Oakdale) — INBOUND from Oakdale Mall (Bus sign reads Downtown)

1st & Hyatt	10th & Lake	18th & Miami	25th & Water	Oakdale Mall	Oakdale Mall	25th & Water	18th & Miami	10th & Lake	1st & Hyatt
6:10	6:18	6:22	6:28	6:35	6:40	6:47	6:53	6:57	7:05
7:10	7:18	7:22	7:28	7:35	7:40	7:47	7:53	7:57	8:05
8:10	8:18	8:22	8:28	8:35	8:40	8:47	8:53	8:57	9:05
9:10	9:18	9:22	9:28	9:35	9:40	9:47	9:53	9:57	10:05
10:10	10:18	10:22	10:28	10:35	10:40	10:47	10:53	10:57	11:05
11:10	11:18	11:22	11:28	11:35	11:40	11:47	11:53	11:57	12:05
12:10	12:18	12:22	12:28	12:35	12:40	12:47	12:53	12:57	1:05
1:10	1:18	1:22	1:28	1:35	1:40	1:47	1:53	1:57	2:05
2:10	2:18	2:22	2:28	2:35	2:40	2:47	2:53	2:57	3:05
3:10	3:18	3:22	3:28	3:35	3:40	3:47	3:53	3:57	4:05
4:10	4:18	4:22	4:28	4:35	4:40	4:47	4:53	4:57	5:05

1. T or F The gray areas are for weekends only.
2. When does the 9:18 bus from 10th & Lake arrive at the Oakdale Mall? ________________
3. Where does the 12:53 bus pick up passengers? ________________________________
4. How many minutes does it take to travel from 1st and Hyatt to 25th and Water? __________
5. Where would you be if you left the Oakdale Mall at 8:40 and noticed the time was 9:05?

   ____

6. T or F The Oakdale Mall is closer to 10th and Lake than it is to 18th and Miami.
7. When is the earliest you can catch an inbound bus at 18th and Miami on Sunday? ________

TABLES

Table - a way to present data and statistics. It is a concise way to present a large quantity of information using rows and columns to organize the information.

Carefully read the table below. Then answer the questions that follow.

LIFE INSURANCE RATES

MONTHLY RATES SMOKERS					MONTHLY RATES NON-SMOKERS				
Issue	$100,000		$250,000		Issue	$100,000		$250,000	
Age	Male	Female	Male	Female	Age	Male	Female	Male	Female
40	22.56	17.58	50.22	37.58	**40**	12.98	12.62	26.08	25.25
41	23.38	18.79	52.12	40.68	**41**	13.04	12.71	26.31	25.46
42	24.21	20.06	54.22	43.79	**42**	13.15	12.81	26.50	25.72
43	25.07	21.31	56.29	46.93	**43**	13.21	12.89	26.72	25.92
44	25.89	22.48	58.38	50.06	**44**	13.31	12.99	26.91	26.10
45	27.15	23.42	61.52	52.16	**45**	13.39	13.05	27.15	26.31
46	28.79	24.21	65.70	54.26	**46**	13.81	13.16	28.20	26.51
47	30.12	25.13	68.84	56.32	**47**	14.62	13.22	30.26	26.75
48	32.18	25.91	74.05	58.47	**48**	15.54	13.31	32.36	26.95
49	34.25	27.18	79.28	61.62	**49**	16.32	13.42	34.42	27.16
50	37.18	28.82	86.53	65.71	**50**	17.16	13.82	36.52	28.20

1. What is the monthly rate for a $250,000 policy for non-smoking males who are 44 years of age? ______

2. If a 47 year old female smoker wanted a $100,000 policy, what would be her monthly payment? ______

3. What is the monthly rate for a $250,000 policy for a 46 year old, male, non-smoker? ______

4. If a smoker is paying $68.84 for a $250,000 policy, what age and sex is the person? ______

5. What is the monthly rate for a $100,000 policy for non-smoking females who are 47 years of age? ______

6. Looking at the insurance rates for men and women of the same age, which group has higher rates, smokers or non-smokers? ______

7. Looking at the insurance rates of men and women of the same age, which rates are lower, men's rates or women's rates? ______

8. If a smoker is paying $22.48 for a $100,000 policy, what age and sex is the person? ______

9. If a 48 year old non-smoking male wanted a $250,000 policy, what would be his monthly payment? ______

10. What is the monthly rate of a $100,000 policy for a 42 year old male smoker? ______

LINE GRAPHS

Line graphs can present a large quantity of data in a small space. Be sure to read the title of the graph and the horizontal and vertical headings as well as the key.

Study the line graph below, and answer the questions that follow.

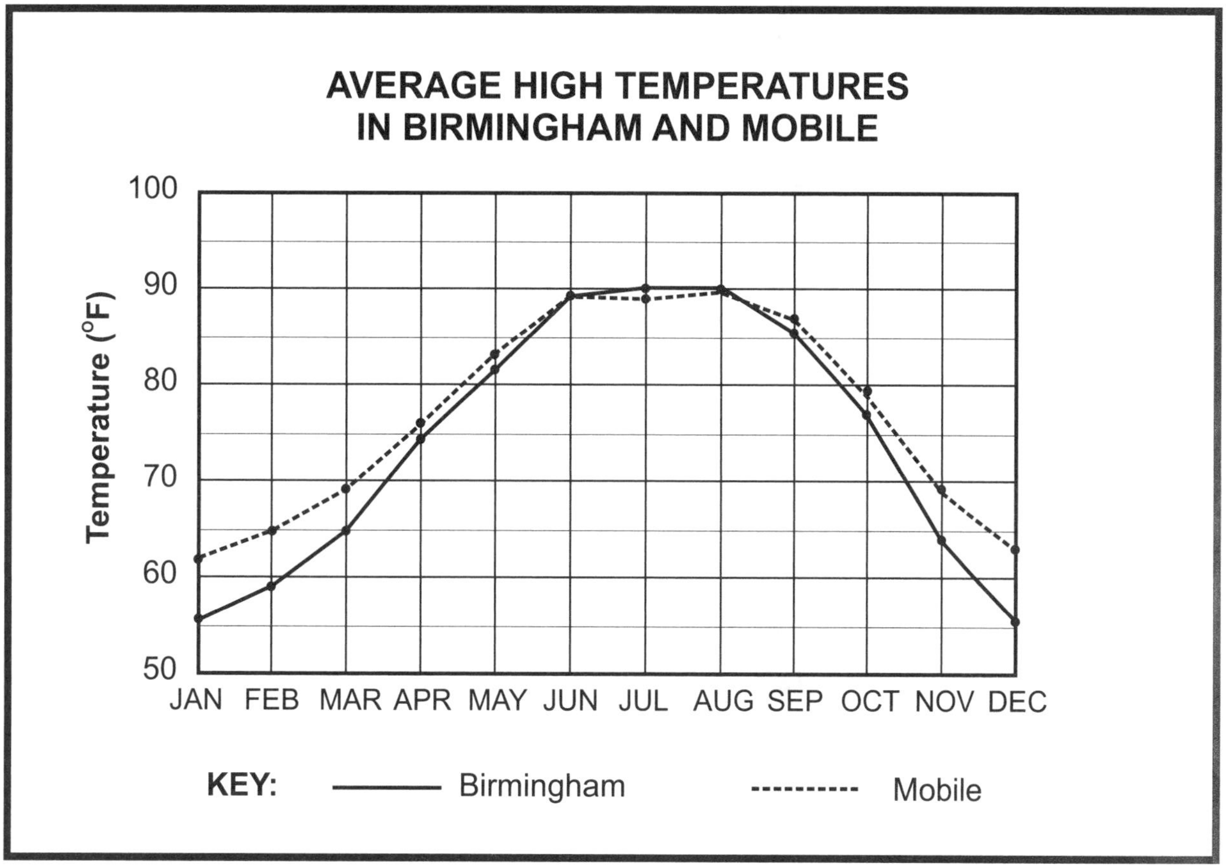

1. What is the average high temperature in Birmingham for the month of July? __________
2. How many months is the average temperature the same in both cities? __________
3. What are the 2 coldest months in Mobile? __________, __________
4. What are the three coldest months in Birmingham? __________, __________, __________
5. In which month is the average high temperature 65° in Birmingham? __________
6. What is the average high temperature in Mobile for the month of April? __________
7. In which two months is the average high temperature 69° in Mobile? __________, __________
8. Are the degrees in the above graph in Celsius, Fahrenheit, or Kelvin degrees? __________
9. If you disliked cold weather, would it be better to live in Birmingham or Mobile? __________
10. What is the average high temperature in May for the city of Mobile? __________

BAR GRAPHS

Bar graphs are another way of presenting data. **Study the bar graph below, and then answer the questions that follow.**

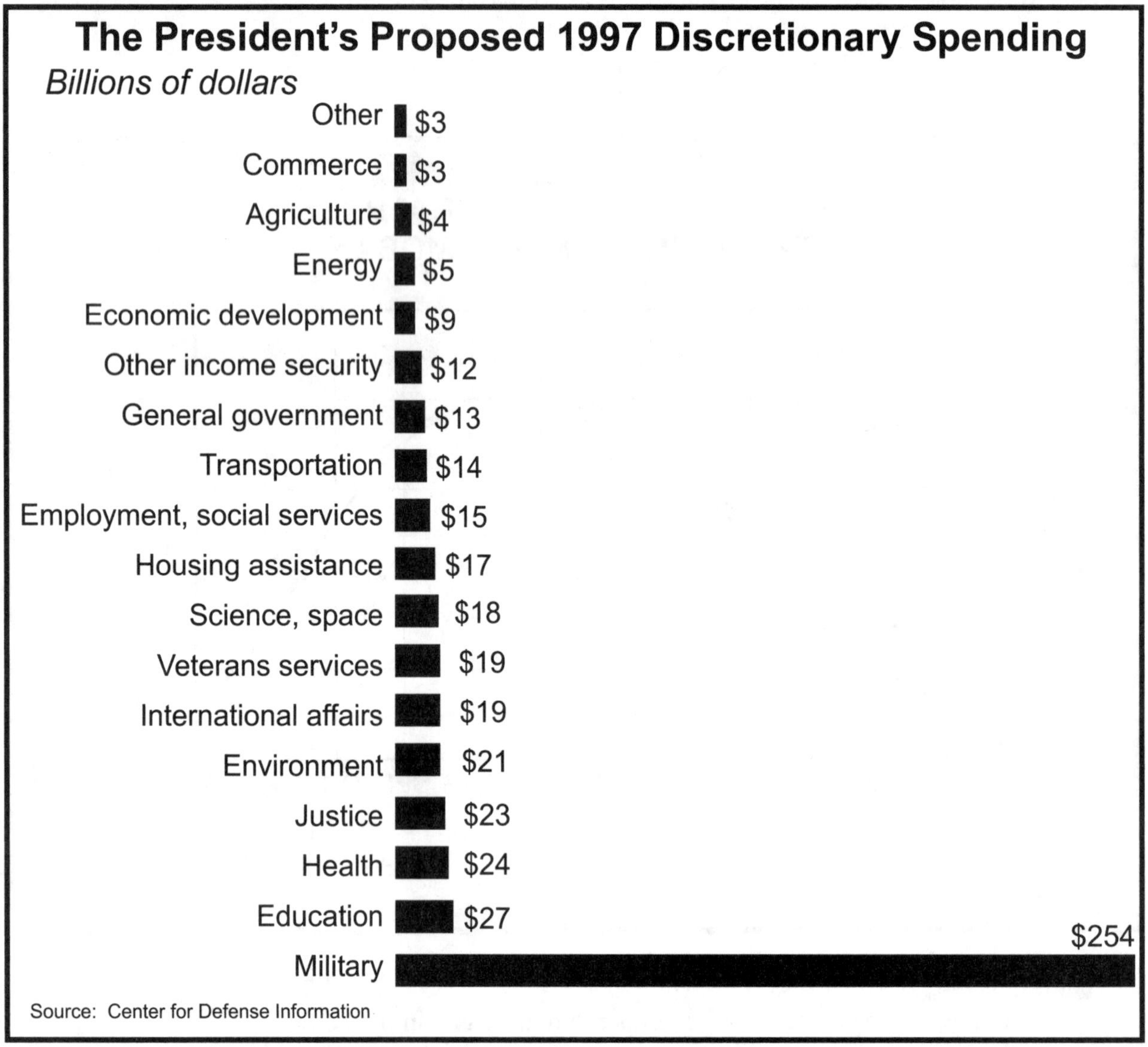

1. How much money did the president propose be spent on the military? __________
2. How much more does the president propose Congress spend on Agriculture than on Commerce? __________
3. Which two departments does the president propose funding at the sum of $19,000,000,000? __________ , __________
4. How much does the president propose spending on transportation? __________
5. How much does the president propose that the Department of Justice receive? __________
6. What is the source of information for the graph above? __________
7. What conclusions can you draw from this bar graph? __________

SYMBOL GRAPHS

Sometimes, graphs use symbols or pictures to represent data.

Study the graph below, and answer the questions that follow.

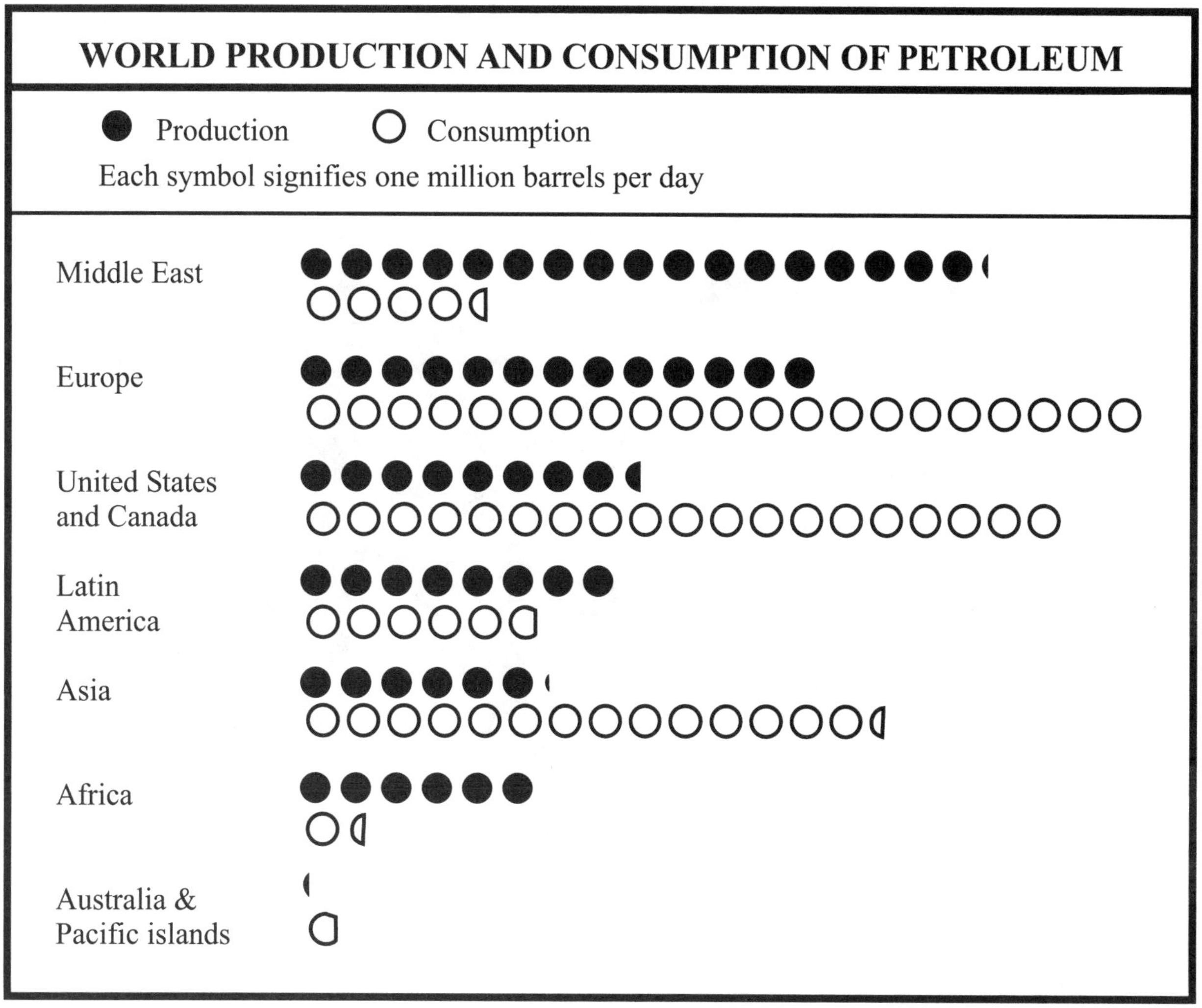

1. What part of the world consumes the most oil? __________
2. How many parts of the world produce more oil than they consume? __________
3. How many parts of the world consume more oil than they produce? __________
4. How many more barrels of oil does Europe produce daily than Africa? __________
5. How many barrels does the Middle East produce every day? __________
6. Which three areas of the world consume more than twice as much oil as they produce? __________

____

____

MAPS

A **map** is a flat drawing of all or part of the earth. A **globe** is a model of the earth shaped like a ball or sphere. North, south, east, and west are called **cardinal directions**. North is usually at the top of a map or globe, south is at the bottom, east is to your right, and west is to your left.

Maps and globes also contain a symbol to help you find directions. This symbol is called a **compass rose** like the one shown on the world map below. A compass rose shows the four cardinal directions. It may also show the **intermediate directions** (in-between directions). These intermediate directions are **northeast (NE), northwest (NW), southeast (SE), and southwest (SW)**.

Now practice finding directions on the world map shown below.

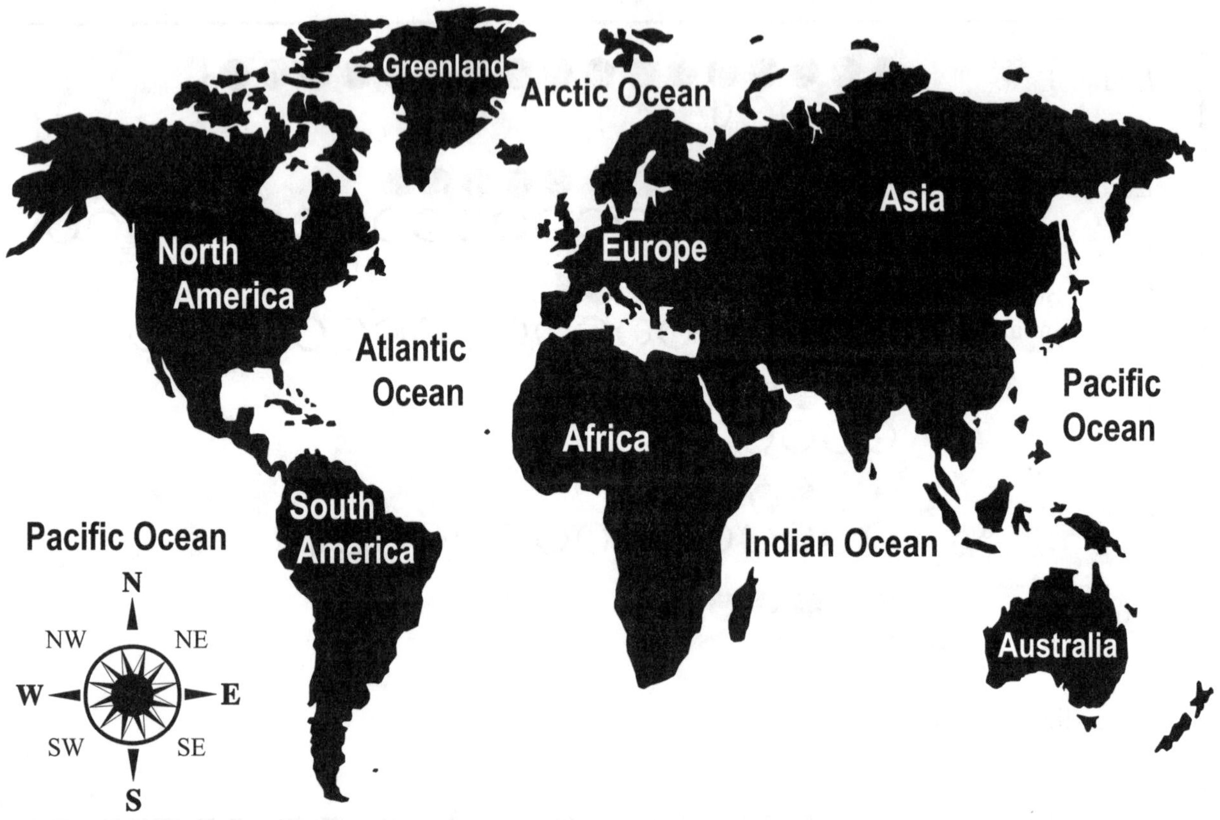

1. Which continent is south of Europe? __________
2. Which ocean is north of Europe? __________
3. Which continent is east of Europe? __________
4. Which continent is west of Europe? __________
5. What ocean is northwest of Australia? __________
6. What continent is southeast of Asia? __________
7. What direction is Africa from South America? __________
8. What direction is South America from Europe? __________
9. What island is northeast of North America? __________
10. Which ocean lies east of Asia? __________

READING A HISTORICAL MAP

A **historical map** shows places and events from the past. The purpose of this kind of map is to help us understand and interpret historical events.

Study the historical map below. It shows how the German submarine U 20 sank American and British ships during World War I. **Then answer the questions that follow.**

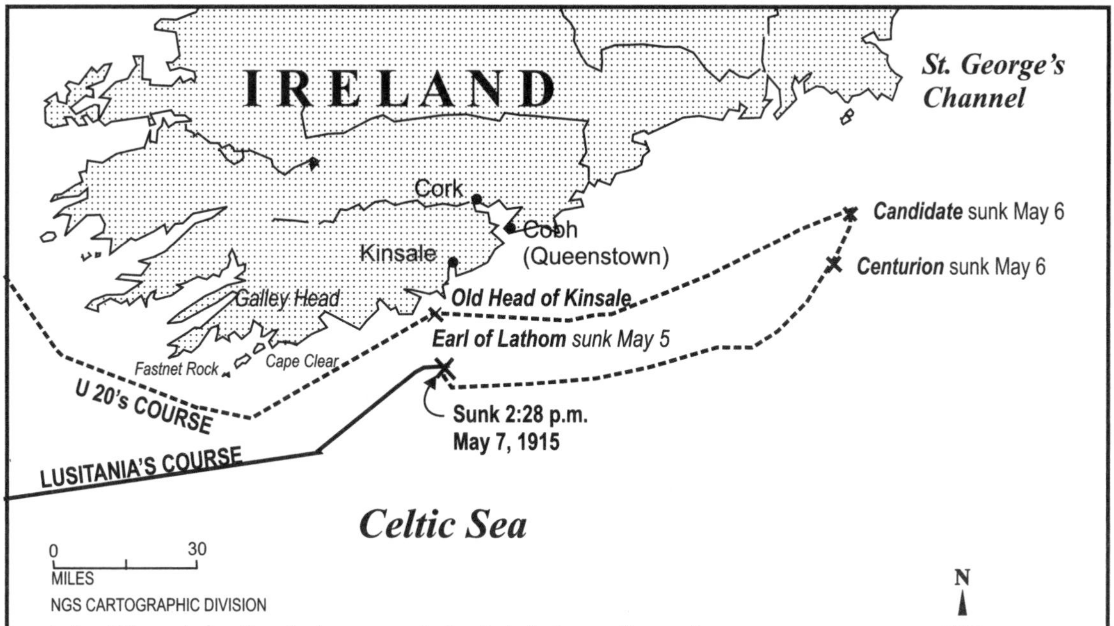

In the 48 hours before the attack on the *Lusitania*, the German submarine U 20 had sunk three ships off Irelands's southern coast. Yet Captain Turner, who had received warnings by wireless from the British Admiralty, took only limited precautions as he approached the area. To save fuel en route, as Cunard had instructed, the *Lusitania* was using just three of her four boiler rooms; when attacked, she was making only 18 knots.

1. Which line shows the U 20's course? ______________________________

2. In which direction was the U 20 moving right before it sank the *Candidate*? __________

3. Name the ships that the U 20 sank. ______________________________

____

4. When was the *Lusitania* sunk? ______________________________

5. In which body of water was the *Lusitania* sunk? ______________________________

6. Why was the *Lusitania* traveling so slowly? ______________________________

7. Which ship sank the closest to land? ______________________________

8. In which direction was the *Lusitania* moving when it was sunk? ______________________________

9. In which direction was the U 20 moving when it sank the *Lusitania*? ______________

READING A GRID MAP

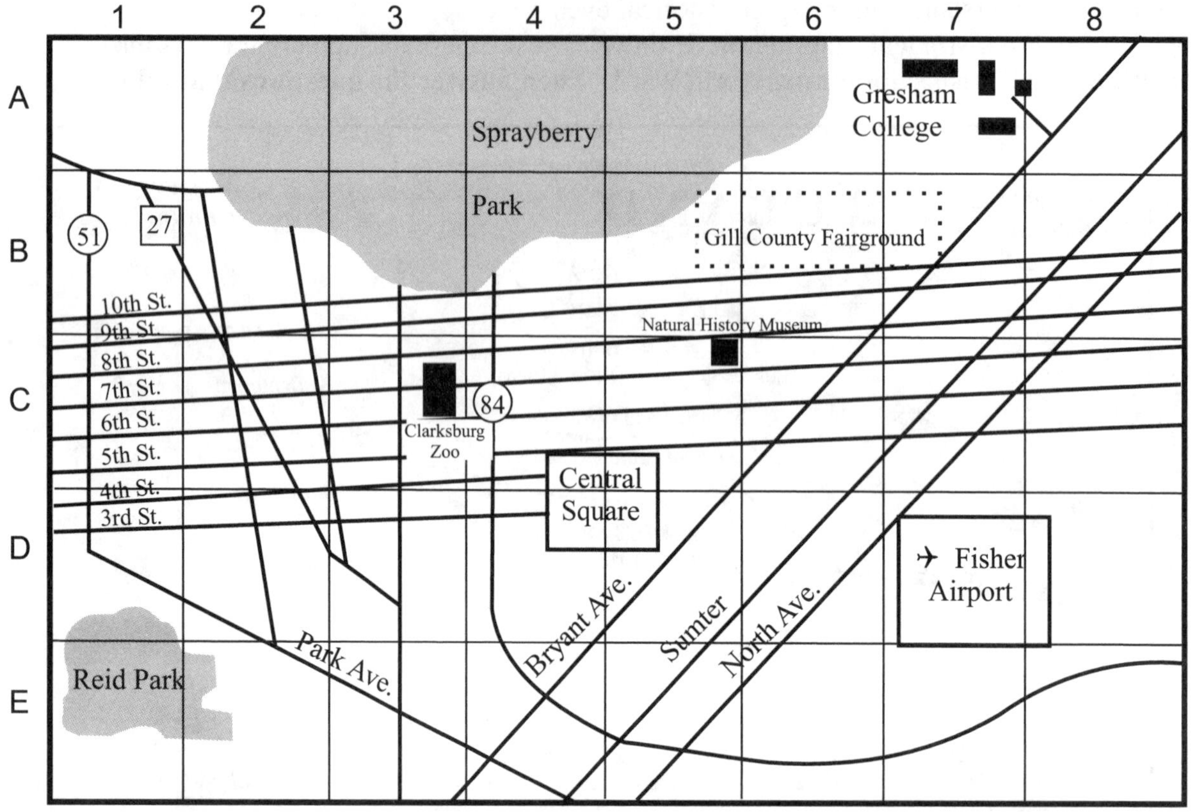

A **grid** is a pattern of lines drawn to make rows and columns on a map. These lines divide the map into squares. Each square can be identified by numbers and letters. The numbers appear on the top of the map, and the letters are located on the left side of the map.

Look at the letters on the side of the map above. The letters identify the rows of squares. The numbers label the columns of squares. If you were asked to locate Reid Park on the map, you would look to see which row and column it is in. Most of Reid Park is at the intersection of row E and column 1. Therefore, the answer is E-1.

Identify the row and column for each of the following places.

1. Gresham College ____________________
2. Fisher Airport ____________________
3. Natural History Museum ____________________
4. The center of Gill County Fairground ____________________
5. The intersection of Bryant Avenue and 6th Street ____________________
6. What is the location of 10th Street and Highway 27? ____________________
7. Where is Clarksburg Zoo? ____________________

DEGREES OF LATITUDE AND LONGITUDE

World maps and globes contain two sets of lines that form a grid around the earth. This grid helps us locate places. Horizontal lines that run parallel around the earth are called **lines of latitude**. The 0^0 line of latitude is the **equator.** It divides the earth into the **Northern Hemisphere** and the **Southern Hemisphere**. Lines of latitude are numbered 0^0 to 90^0 north and 0^0 to 90^0 south. The United States is in the Northern Hemisphere because we are north of the equator.

The second set of lines on the global grid is **lines of longitude**. The 0^0 line of longitude is the **prime meridian** which goes through Greenwich, England. It divides the earth into the **Eastern Hemisphere** and the **Western Hemisphere**. Lines of longitude are numbered from 0^0 to 180^0 east and 0^0 to 180^0 west. The United States is in the Western Hemisphere because we are west of England. The latitude measurement for a location is always listed first, followed by longitude.

Now look at Mexico's lines of latitude and longitude. Then answer the questions about this part of the globe. Example: Monterrey is located at 27^0 N 102^0 W.

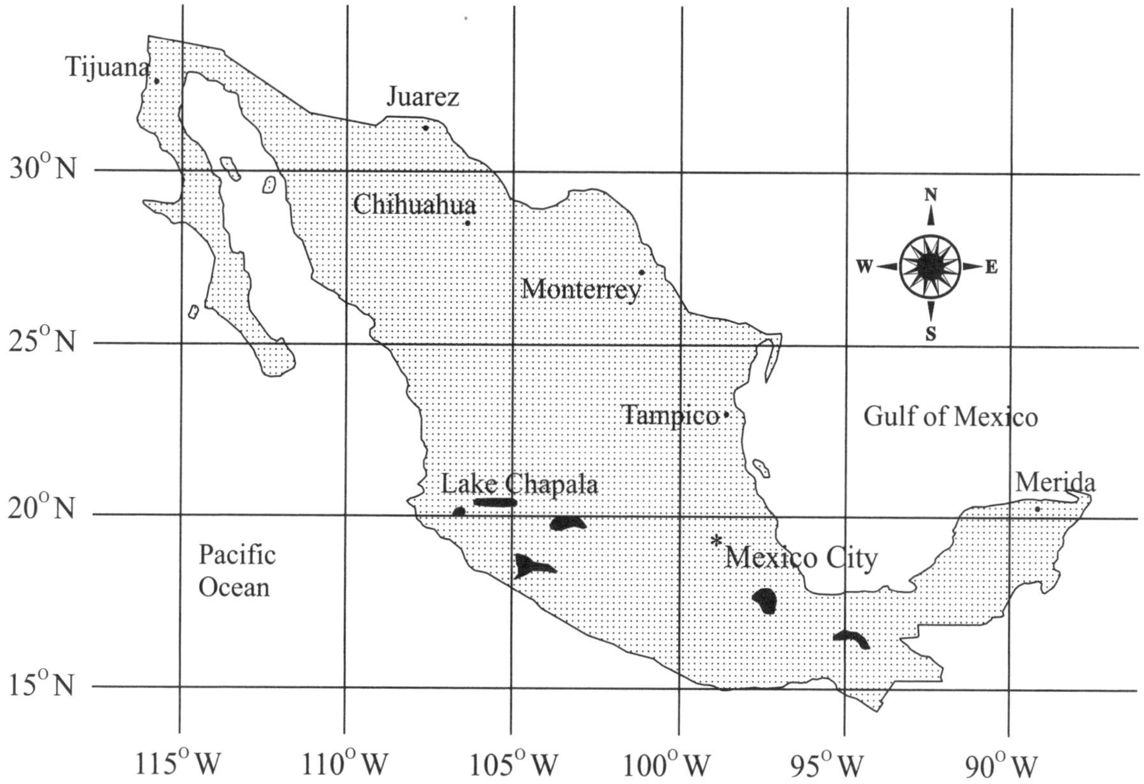

1. What body of water is at 105^0 W longitude? ______________
2. Is Mexico north or south of the equator? ______________
3. Is Mexico east or west of the Prime Meridian? ________________
4. Estimate the longitude of these cities: Monterrey _____________, Chihuahua ____________, Mexico City _______________.
5. Estimate the latitude of these same cities: Monterrey _____________, Chihuahua ______________, Mexico City ______________.
6. Estimate the latitude and longitude of Juarez ______________, Tampico ______________, and Merida ______________.
7. What city lies at latitude 34^0 N and longitude 116^0 W ? ____________________

READING A WORLD MAP

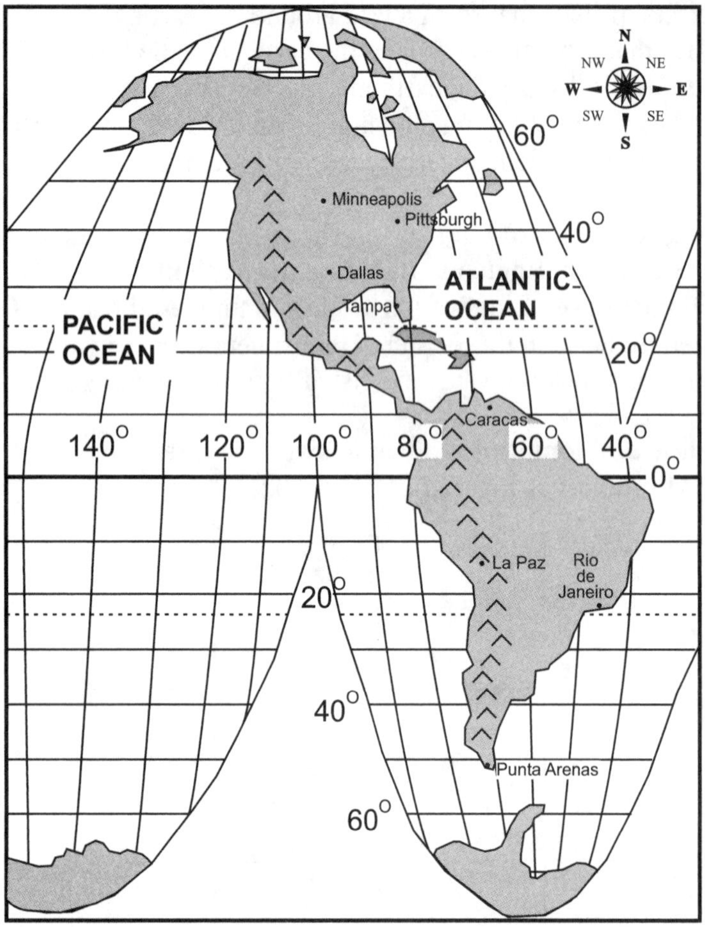

When reading a world map, it is important to remember that the warmest part of the earth is near the **equator** at 0° latitude. The coldest part of the earth is at the north and south poles. Also, the higher the altitude, like the top of a mountain, the cooler the temperature. Seasons in the Northern and Southern Hemispheres are opposite. For example, when it is summer in the United States, it is winter in Chile.

The latitude line at 231°N is called the **Tropic of Cancer**. The latitude line at 231°S is called the **Tropic of Capricorn**. These lines are denoted by dashes on the world map. Between these two lines of latitude is the area of the world that is called the **tropics**. The tropics grow fruits such as pineapples, coconuts, bananas, and mangos that do not grow well anywhere else. In addition, there is no noticeable change of seasons at these latitudes.

Use the world map above to answer the following questions.

1. Which city labeled in the southern hemisphere would tourist most likely find sunny, warm beaches? ____________
2. Which city labeled in the southern hemisphere would likely have the coldest winter temperature? ____________
3. If you flew from Dallas to Minneapolis, which direction would you be going? ____________
4. Which city labeled in the northern hemisphere would have the coldest average temperature in the winter? ____________
5. Which city is located 40°N 80°W? ____________
6. If you flew from Dallas to Rio de Janeiro, in which direction would you travel? ____________
7. If you flew from Pittsburgh to Punta Arenas in July, would you need to pack warm clothing? ____________
8. Which city would likely have a cooler climate, La Paz or Rio de Janeiro? ____________

ROAD MAPS

Reading a **road map** requires paying close attention to the key. The **key** gives information about what all the symbols mean. Reading the key will help you find the location of airports, railroads, camp sites, and more. In addition, most state maps will have little numbers on the roads showing you how many miles it is between towns. By adding the numbers together, you can determine the distance between two towns.

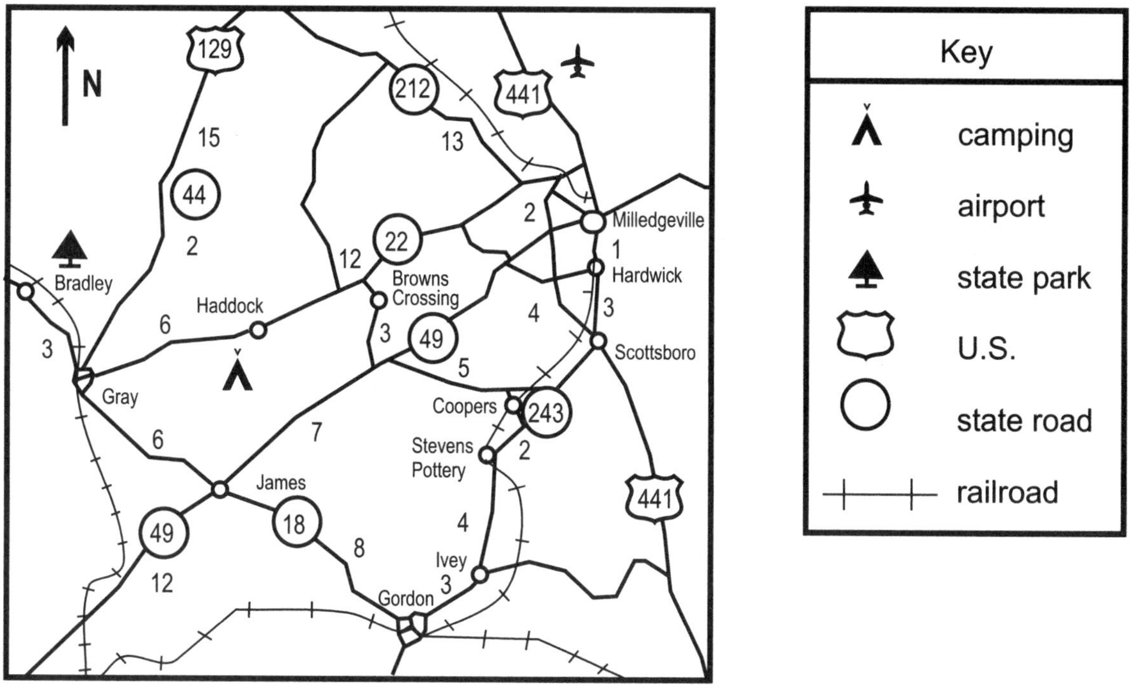

Directions: Carefully read the map and key above to answer the following questions.

1. How far is it from Milledgeville to Scottsboro traveling US 441? ____________

2. How far is it from Coopers to Stephens Pottery ? ____________

3. Is it shorter to go from Gordon to Brown's Crossing through James or Coopers? ____________

4. Which highway is closest to the airport? ____________

5. Where would this sign be found? | Haddock ⟶ 6 |

   A. At the intersection of State Roads (18) and (49).

   B. At the intersection of State Roads (212) and (49).

   C. At the intersection of State Roads (18) and (243).

   D. At the intersection of State Roads (18) and (22).

6. In which town can a train switch from a north-south track to an east-west track? ____________

7. How many miles apart are Gray and Gordon on state route (18) ? ____________

8. Which town is closest to a camping area? ____________

9. Which town is closest to a state park? ____________

10. What is the shortest route to take from Scottsboro to Gordon? ____________

ECONOMIC MAPS

An **economic map** shows resources and products of a country. These resources and products provide an income and standard of living for the people. **Study the following map of Australia, and then answer the questions.**

MAJOR MINERAL DEPOSITS AND AGRICULTURAL PRODUCTS IN AUSTRALIA

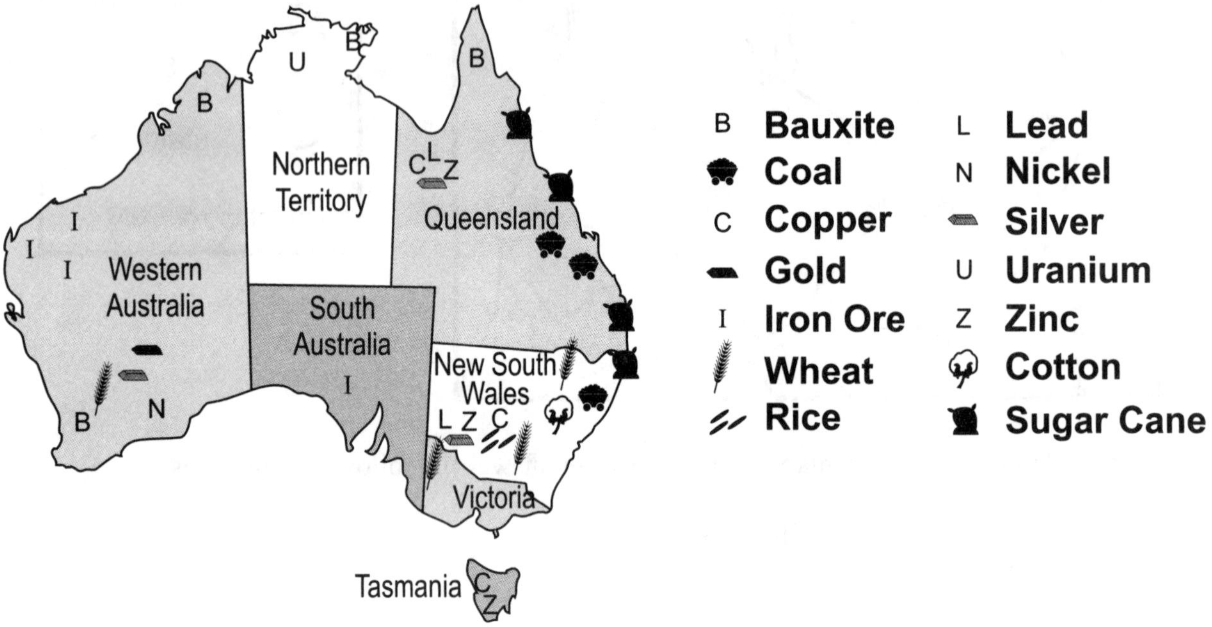

1. Based on this map, which agricultural crop is most prolific in New South Wales? ____________

2. Based on this map, which mining industry is the largest in Western Australia? ____________

3. Which region of Australia contains the most minerals? ____________

4. Which three provinces in Australia show no agricultural development? ____________

____

5. Which provinces have mines for precious metals (gold or silver)? ____________

____

DIAGRAMS

Sometimes a **diagram** can be used to explain a concept more clearly than an explanation written in paragraph form. The diagram below shows the earth's water cycle.

EARTH'S WATER CYCLE

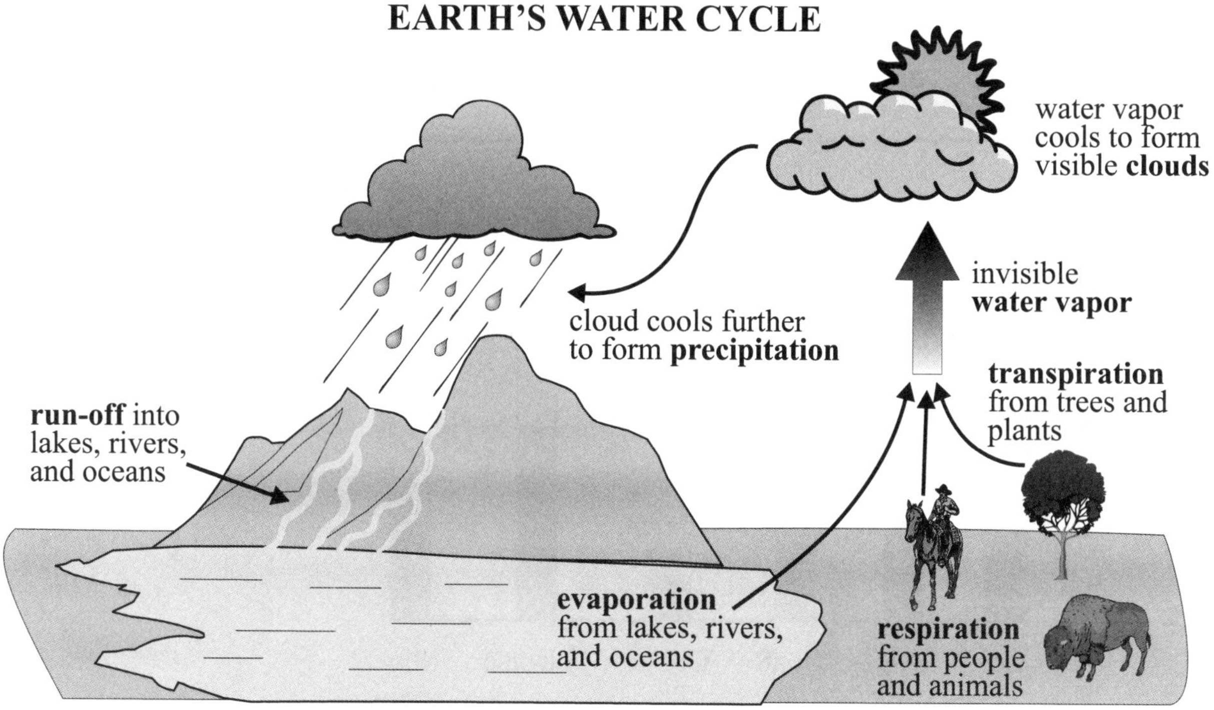

Directions: Study the diagram, and answer the questions below.

1. In what 3 ways does water get from the ground to the sky? ______________________

 ____

 ____

2. How are clouds formed? ____

 ____

3. What must happen to water vapor before it is visible? ______________________

 ____

4. Define precipitation. ____

 ____

5. What must happen to clouds before precipitation can occur? ______________________

 ____

6. Describe how the respiration of people and animals becomes rain. ______________

 ____

7. When you blow on a cool glass or mirror, what do you see? ______________________

CHAPTER 5 REVIEW

Directions: Use the schedules, tables, maps, graphs, and diagrams presented to answer the questions that follow.

LIFE SPAN OF DOMESTIC ANIMALS

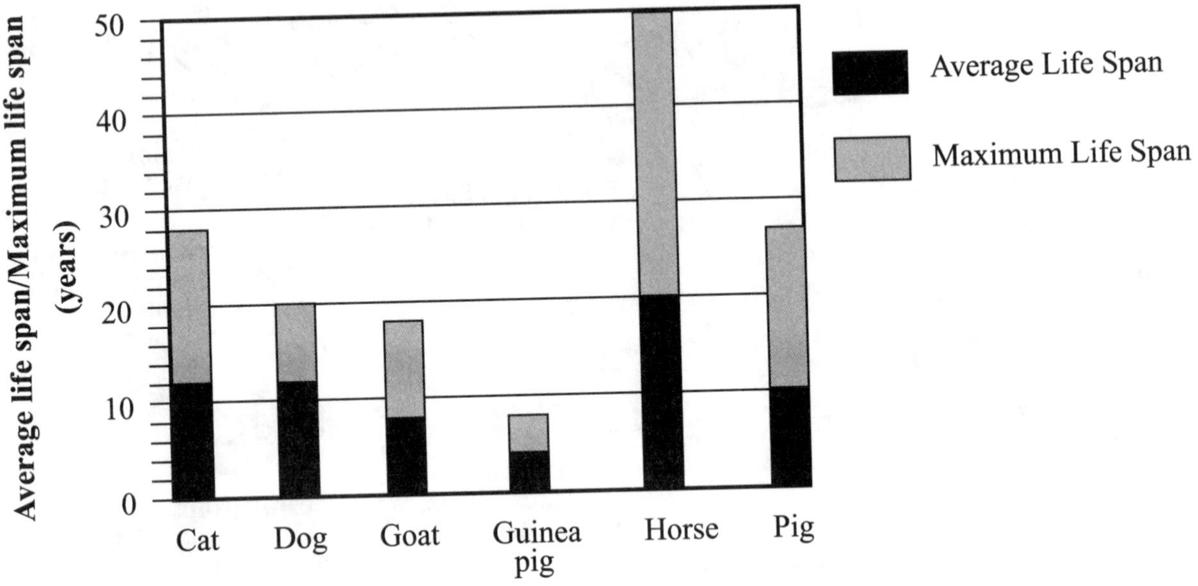

1. Which animal has the longest maximum life span? ____________

2. What is the average life span of a Guinea pig? ____________

3. Which animal lives longer on average, a dog or a pig? ____________

4. What is the maximum life span of a cat? ____________

5. How many more years does the average horse live than the average goat? ____________

6. Which animal has a maximum life span of 8 years? ____________

7. Which two animals are closest in maximum life span? ____________

8. Which two animals are closest in average life span? ____________

9. Which animal has an average life span of 20 years? ____________

TEAM STATISTICS
2001-02 Houston Rockets

Player	Mins./ Game	Field Goal %	Free Throw %	Rebounds/ Game	Assists/ Game	Avg. Pts./ Game
Mobley	42.1	43.8	85.0	4.10	2.5	21.7
Francis	41.1	41.7	77.3	7.00	6.4	21.6
Thomas	34.5	47.8	66.4	7.20	1.9	41.1
Williams	23.3	41.9	78.4	3.40	1.4	9.4
Griffin	26.0	36.6	74.4	5.70	.7	8.8
Rice	30.3	38.9	80.0	2.40	1.6	8.6
Norris	24.4	39.8	75.1	3.00	4.9	8.1
Cato	25.6	58.3	58.2	7.00	.4	6.6
Willis	16.6	44.0	74.7	5.80	.3	6.1
Torres	16.5	39.6	78.1	1.90	.6	6.0
Collier	14.6	43.2	75.0	3.30	.4	4.2
Morris	16.3	38.4	64.3	3.10	.9	3.8
Brown	10.1	42.6	75.0	1.10	1.8	3.1
Langhi	12.8	39.2	72.7	2.00	.4	3.1

10. When Rice attempted a free throw, what percent of the time did he score? ________________

11. Who had the highest average of assists? ________________

12. Which two players scored the lowest number of points? ________________

    ____

13. Who made the highest percentage of field goals? ________________

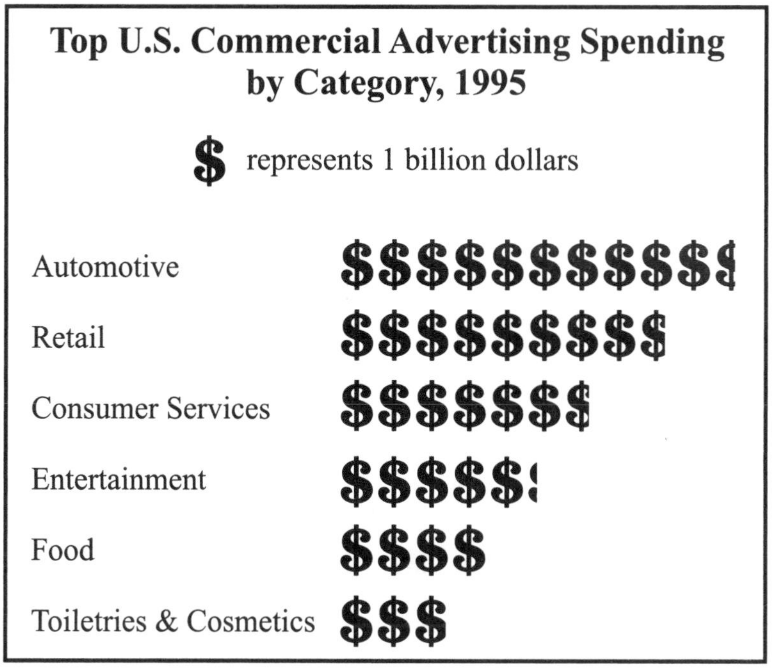

14. How much money was spent on food advertising?

    ____

15. How much money was spent on automotive advertising?

    ____

16. Was more money spent on entertainment or for retail stores?

    ____

17. What category spent the most on advertising?

    ____

CIRCULATION OF THE HEART

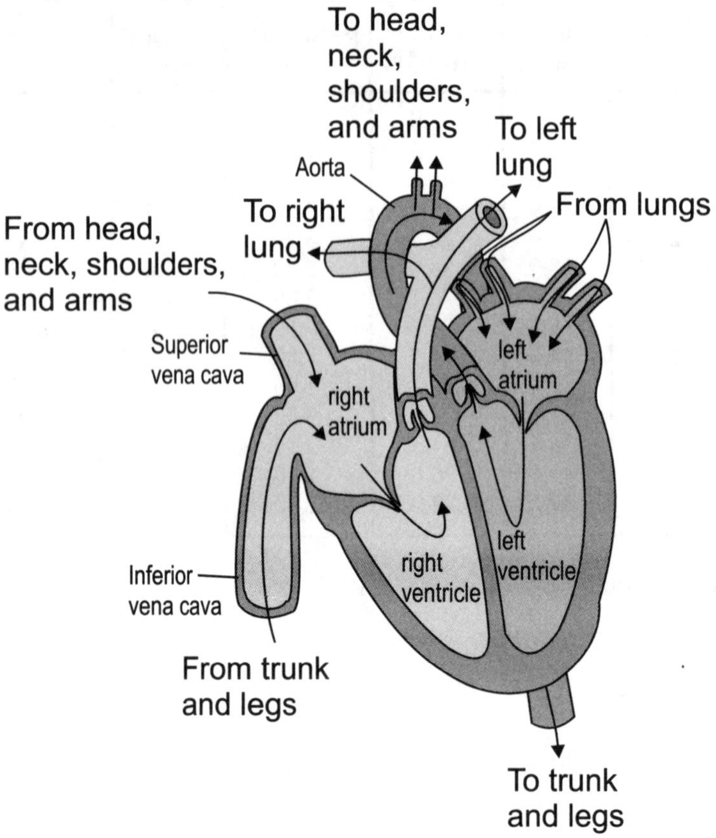

The human heart has 4 chambers.

18. Where does the blood go when it leaves the right atrium? ________________

19. Which chamber does blood coming from the lungs enter? ________________

20. Through which vessel does blood travel to get from the trunk and legs to the right atrium? ________________

21. Which vessel carries blood from the left ventricle to the neck and head? ________________

22. Where does blood go that leaves the left atrium? ________________

23. Which vessel carries blood from your head and neck to your right atrium? ________________

24. Where does blood go next when it leaves the right ventricle? ________________

AVERAGE TEMPERATURES FOR TAMPA AND MIAMI

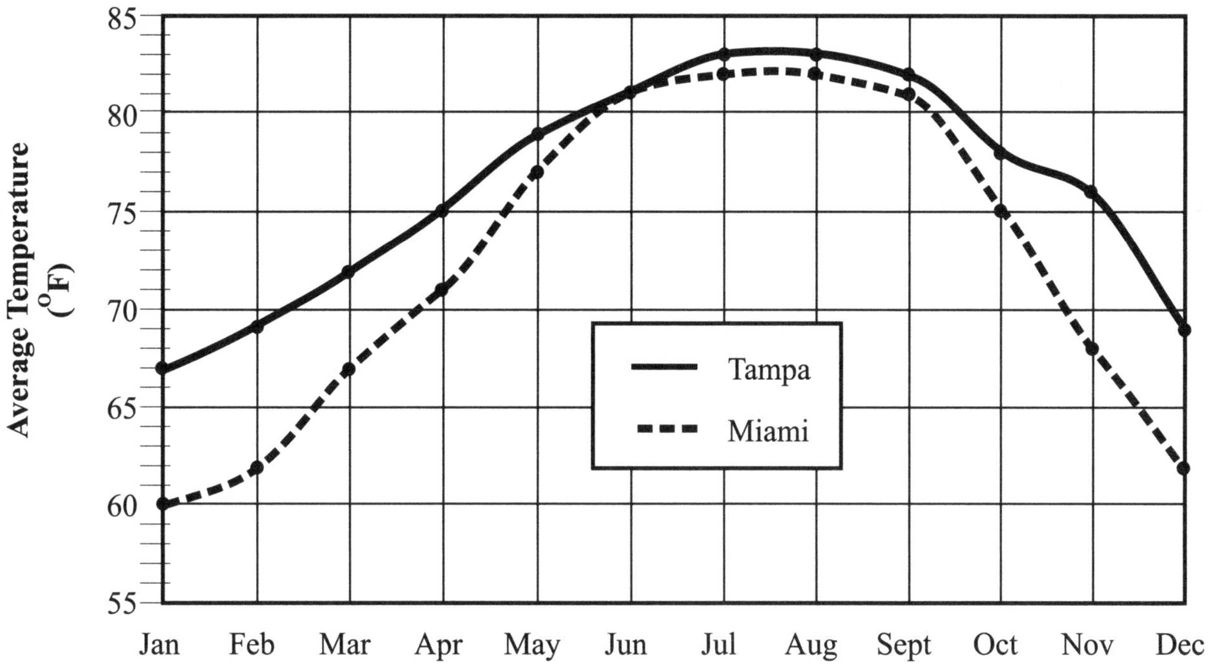

25. In which month is the average temperature in Miami and Tampa the same? ______________

26. What is the average temperature of Tampa in August? ______________

27. Between which two months does the average temperature fall the fastest in Miami? ______________

and ______________

28. What is the lowest average temperature for Miami during the coldest month of the year? ______________

29. For how many months of the year is the average temperature above 80°F in Tampa? ______________

30. During how many months of the year does the average temperature fall below 70°F in Miami? ______________

31. What is the average temperature in Miami in the month of March? ______________

ROAD MAP

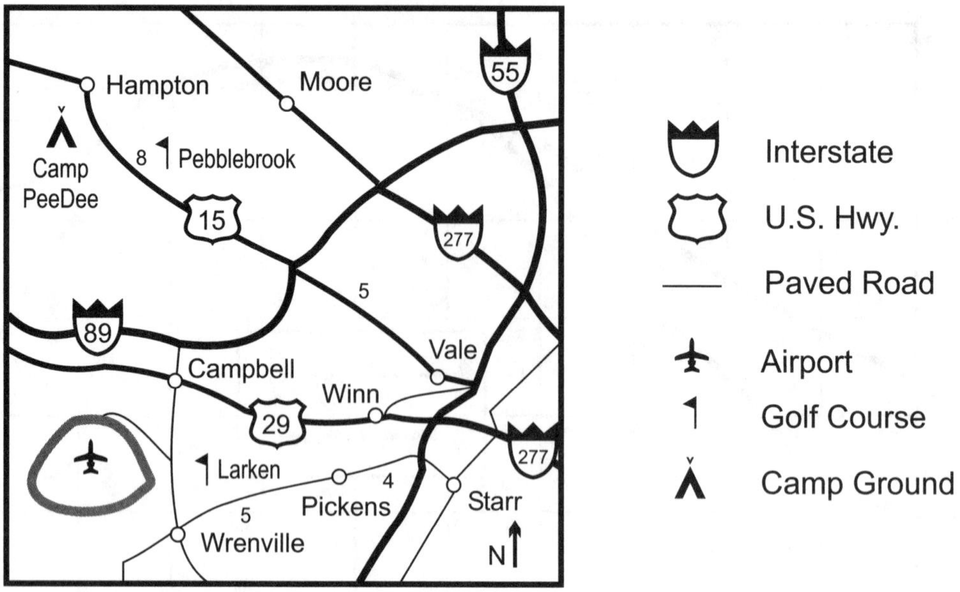

32. How many miles is it from Vale to Hampton? __________

33. If you are in Pickens, which direction is the Larken golf course? __________

34. What kind of road is closest to the campground? __________

35. Which interstate highway is closest to Vale? __________

36. How many miles will you drive to go from Pickens to Wrenville? __________

37. Which highway do you use to drive from Interstate 89 to Pebblebrook? __________

38. If you are in Campbell, which direction is Vale? __________

39. If you are in Wrenville, which direction is Campbell? __________

40. How many golf courses are on the map? __________

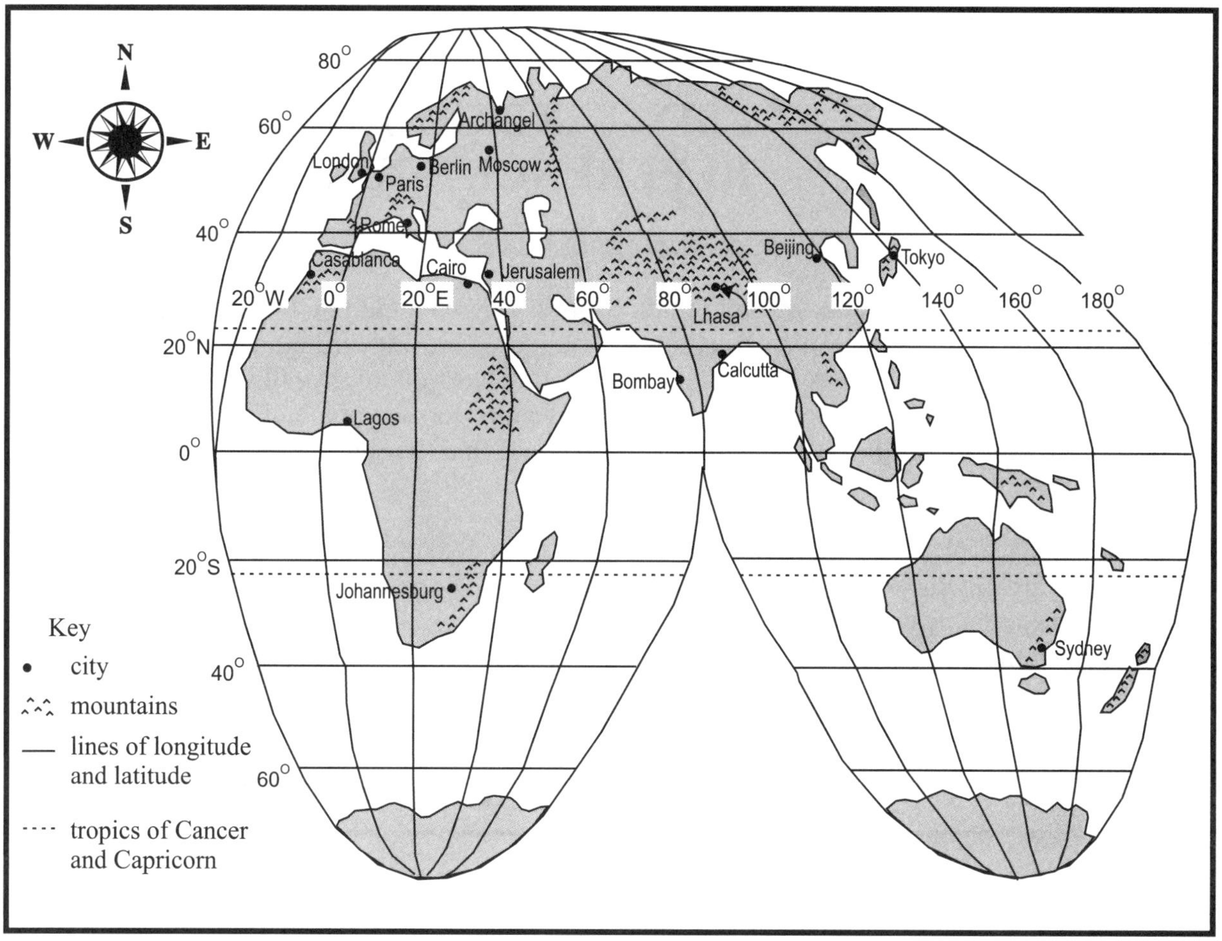

41. Which city would have cooler temperatures, Cairo or Lhasa? ________________

42. Which city would have a warmer average temperature, Bombay or Beijing? ________________

43. What is the latitude of the city of Lagos? ________________

44. What is the longitude of the city of Johannesburg? ________________

45. If you were in Rome, which direction would Beijing be? ________________

46. If you were in Moscow, which direction would Jerusalem be? ________________

47. Which city is located at 19°N, 87°E? ________________

48. Which city is located at 34°S, 151°E? ________________

49. Which city is located at 52°N, 1°W ________________

50. If you were on an airplane traveling from Sydney to Johannesburg, what direction would you be going? ________________

Chapter 6

USING AND CHOOSING REFERENCE SOURCES

If you were thinking about getting running shoes, where would you buy them and how much would you pay? If you're a smart shopper, you would browse through the newspaper ads for a shoe sale. Or you might scan the phone directory. Then you might call some stores near you to check prices and shoe sizes available. If you decided to shop at a mall or shopping center, you'd probably look over the mall directory, so you could find the shoe stores that carry the brand you want.

The ability to choose and use reference sources is an essential life skill in today's society. Whether you are buying shoes, doing research in the library, or reading a schedule or diagram, you will face situations where you will need the right resources. Obtaining and using the information from these sources can help you answer questions or complete a task in school, at home, or on the job.

LEARNING AND USING REFERENCE SOURCES

In this part of the chapter, you'll learn about important reference sources. You'll also practice answering questions about these sources. Here are the main ones:

Alphabetizing	**Glossary**
Thesaurus	**Encyclopedia**
Telephone Directory	**Reader's Guide to Periodical Literature**
Sections of a Book	**Dewey Decimal System**
Table of Contents	**Card Catalog**
Index	**Newspaper Index**
Bibliography	**Newspaper Ad**

Review the **Tips for Reference Sources** at the end of this section. Study the definition and example for each reference source. Then answer the questions about each one.

ALPHABETIZING

When lists of words are organized in some manner, the most common method of organization is **alphabetical order**. When words are alphabetized, they are arranged from the letters A - Z in the alphabet.

Many times, words in alphabetical order will begin with the same letter. In these cases, use the second letter of the word to decide which will go first. If the second letter is also the same letter, use the third letter, etc.

Example: **r**aw - first letter	l**e**mon - second letter	Ha**r**ding - third letter
sail	l**o**an	Ha**s**cal

All reference sources list their topics by alphabetical order. Telephone books and dictionaries post two guide words at the top of each page. Any entry can be found by simply looking for the entry between the guide words.

Example: Realtors - Temporary are guide words. Telephone is a word you could find on that page.

Other reference sources alphabetize by putting the first letter of the volume or drawer in which you will find all words starting with that letter or letters. Encyclopedias and card catalogs use this system.

Example: The letters N - O are listed on the front of a card catalog drawer. The subject oriental can be found in this drawer.

One reference source, the directory, alphabetizes by putting the last names of persons or the names of companies on a large sign. The names are placed in alphabetical order from top to bottom.

Example:

	Room Number
Atley & Company	106
Durham Foundation	210
Hands On Office Products	113
Lip Saver Technologies	302
Narcotics Recovery Counseling Service	111
Penn & Schuman Message Center	205
Vibrant Voices, Inc.	303

** If you wanted to add Car Care, Inc. to the directory, it would have to be placed between Atley & Co, and Durham Foundation.

PRACTICE 1: ALPHABETIZING

Directions: Select the correct answer.

1. If you are looking for the entry aggravation in the dictionary, which words could you find at the top of the page?

   A. afraid - against
   B. agriculture - ajar
   C. aflame - agrarian
   D. agree - amount

2.

ARTS & SCIENCES BUILDING

	Office Number
Dr. Greg Ainsley	105
Dr. Vicky Greene	206
Dr. Steve Loxley	203
Dr. Richard Planter	312
Dr. Laura Shannon	113
Dr. George Tinley	109
Dr. Sarah Vanderbilt	308

Dr. Zell Manford, a new faculty member in the Arts & Sciences Building, will have his name added to the above alphabetized building directory between

A. Dr. Steve Loxley and Dr. Richard Planter.
B. Dr. Richard Planter and Dr. Laura Shannon.
C. Dr. Vicky Greene and Dr. Steve Loxley.
D. Dr. Greg Ainsley and Dr. Vicky Greene.

3. If you are looking through the card catalog for the word zoology, which drawer would you look in to find the card?

A. A
B. W - Z
C. N - O
D. Q - R

4. If the guide words Furniture - Garage were at the top of a page in the yellow pages, which listing could be included on that page?

A. Flooring
B. Fender Repair
C. Garbage Collection
D. Futons

5. If you were looking for the word roundhouse in the dictionary, which words would you find at the top of the page?

A. roar - runt
B. ranch - rill
C. rat - roadhouse
D. rouse - rust

6. If you are looking in the J-K encyclopedia, which of the following articles will you find?

A. Catholicism
B. Indiana
C. Lithuania
D. Jakarta

7. If you are looking for the name Gulianni in the white pages of the telephone book, which guide words could be listed at the top of the page?

A. Guthrie - Gylord
B. Goethe - Gusman
C. Goodrum - Guff
D. Gunther - Guy

Atwater National Bank

	Suite No.
Ms. Nancy Birch	524
Mr. Phillip Dorman	213
Mrs. Gail Keckley	406
Ms. Monique Givens	106
Mr. Randall Landover	301
Mr. Jay Pickard	227
Mrs. Terri Tyler	408
Mr. Dan Williams	505

8. Mr. Al Sharpe, a newly hired CPA (certified public accountant), will have his name added to the above alphabetized building directory between

A. Mr. Randall Landover and Mr. Jay Pickard.
B. Mr. Jay Pickard and Mrs. Terri Tyler.
C. Mrs. Terri Tyler and Mr. Dan Williams.
D. Mrs. Gail Keckley and Ms. Monique Givens.

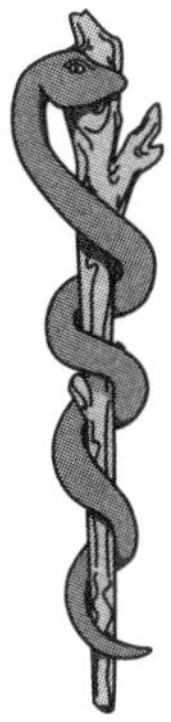

Fairview Health Clinic

	Suite No.
Mrs. Amanda Chadwick, LPN	105
Dr. Ray Fiorio	213
Mr. Trent Hesnor, RN	113
Dr. Colleen Lebont	201
Ms. Patricia Mason, RN	302
Dr. Enrique Petrarch	109
Mrs. Joan Quincy, LPN	212
Dr. Evelyn Spinnaker	307
Mr. Bill Thornton, LPN	311

9. Dr. Tad Ross, a new general practitioner in the Fairview Health Clinic, will have his name added to the above alphabetized directory between

A. Dr. Colleen Lebont and Ms. Patricia Mason, LPN.
B. Dr. Enrique Petrarch and Mrs. Joan Quincy, LPN.
C. Dr. Evelyn Spinnaker and Mr. Bill Thornton, LPN.
D. Mrs. Joan Quincy, LPN and Dr. Evelyn Spinnaker.

10. If the guide words <u>graft - grubby</u> were at the top of a page in the dictionary, which entry could be included on that page?

A. gross
B. graduation
C. grudge
D. graceful

THESAURUS

THESAURUS - a book containing lists of synonyms and antonyms in alphabetical order. A thesaurus improves writing and one's knowledge of words.

Thesaurus Entry

88. HEIGHT

NOUNS:

1. height, tip, stature, elevation
2. top, highest point, ceiling, zenith
3. hill, knoll, volcano, mountain

VERBS:

4. heighten, elevate, raise, rear, erect
5. intensify, strengthen, increase, advance
6. command, rise above, crown, surmount

ADJECTIVES:

7. high, towering, exalted, supreme

Antonyms: depth, descent

Directions: For Questions 1-3, circle the word that would best provide a synonym for the italicized word in each sentence below. Then answer questions 4-8.

1. With a *height* of 20,320 feet, Mt. McKinley is an impressive sight. **stature** **top** **elevation**
2. The *high* skyscraper stood in the center of the city. **exalted** **supreme** **towering**
3. The frequent thunder *heightened* our fears for Latasha's safety. **intensified** **erected** **crowned**
4. T or F **Increase** is the same part of speech as heighten.
5. T or F A mountain is lower than a hill.
6. What part of speech is **height**? ______________________
7. What are the antonyms for **height**? ______________________________________
8. List the synonyms for **high**. ____

TELEPHONE DIRECTORY

Telephone Directory - a book listing names, addresses, and phone numbers of persons, businesses, or organizations in alphabetical order. The phone directories provide a network for locating information. The white pages contain home phone numbers and sometimes business numbers. The yellow pages contain listings for businesses and organizations. In some cities, there are now blue pages for government listings.

STEPHEN'S SEAFOOD RESTAURANT

Family owned and operated
Open Daily for Lunch and Dinner
Major Credit Cards Accepted

Stephen's Seafood Restaurant
3822 Vista Drive Surf City............ 684-3210

Stone's Oyster Grill
112 Breeze Road North Beach...... 823-9434

Strike's Burgers
3340 Shore Blvd. Surf City 684-3288

Sub Stop
725 Ocean Road Coraltown 459-4666

Sunshine Diner
Rib and Shrimp Specials
2941 Vista Drive Surf City 683-7443

Supper Club
Fine Cuisine
603 Breeze Road North Beach 824-6000

Tastee Yogurt
810 Ocean Highway Linnville 572-8420

1. What is the phone number for the Sunshine Diner? ____________________
2. Where is Stephen's Seafood Restaurant located? ____________________
3. T or F The phone number for Strike's Burgers is 684-3288.
4. T or F Stephen's Seafood Restaurant is open on Mondays.
5. What is the main attraction at the Supper Club? ____________________
6. T or F Only two restaurants serve seafood.
7. How many restaurants are there in Surf City? ____________________
8. Where could you go to eat in Coraltown? ____________________
9. T or F The address of Stone's Oyster Grill is 1112 Breeze Road North Beach
10. What is served at the Sunshine Diner? ____________________

PRACTICE 2: TELEPHONE DIRECTORY

Directions: On your own or in a group, review telephone directories. List the various kinds of information you find. In groups, see how many of the following you can find:

an attorney's phone number
emergency numbers
the name of a hospital, church, and park
state government offices
the phone number for your nearest post office
long distance dialing directions
the address of a steak restaurant
a local radio and television station
the address of the closest movie theater
area code for New York City and Dallas

SECTIONS OF A BOOK

Each textbook will include each of several sections to help the reader acquire knowledge. Listed below is each of the sections of a book found when reading from front to back.

Title Page - This page displays the title of the book, the name(s) of the author(s), edition (if the book has been published before), copyright (date the book was published), publishing company, and place of publication.

Preface - This section provides an explanatory statement about the book, telling the book's history, purpose, or plan.

Table of Contents - This section lists all the parts of the book including the introduction, the chapter titles, chapter subheadings, and page numbers indicating where each chapter begins, as well as the additional material pages.

Appendix - This part of the book contains additional material that is not essential to the text itself. This material includes charts, documents, tables, illustrations, and/or photographs. The appendix is located at the end of the text.

Glossary - This section is a dictionary of the specialized terms at the end of a book. Definitions are written in a clear and brief manner; they are also arranged in alphabetical order. The glossary contains all the terms and words that were boldfaced or italicized in the text of each chapter.

Index - This part appears at the end of the book and contains the most important topics, headings, and subheadings discussed in the textbook. The index items are arranged alphabetically with their page number reference and include important people, places, events, locations, equations, and/or books.

Bibliography - This section contains the references or citations the author(s) used while writing their book. Each reference includes the title of the work, the name(s) of the author(s), the date of publishing, publishing company, location of the publisher, and page numbers.

PRACTICE 3: SECTIONS OF A BOOK

Directions: Read the following questions, and select the best answer based on the information above.

1. Which part of the book would you use to locate a table referred to in the book?

   A. bibliography
   B. appendix
   C. title page
   D. glossary

2. The preface is the part of the book that gives

   A. the introductory statement of the book.
   B. the citations of authors who wrote the textbook.
   C. the publisher's name and address.
   D. the chapter subheadings.

3. Which part of the book is used to find the sources used in writing the book?

A. table of contents
B. appendix
C. bibliography
D. title page

4. Which part of the book would you use to locate the definition of "paleontology?"

A. index
B. glossary
C. bibliography
D. preface

5. The <u>table of contents</u> is the part of the book that gives a list of

A. the author's name and publisher.
B. the title of the book.
C. the key words and definitions.
D. the chapter names and starting page numbers.

6. Which part of the book is used to find the name of the publishing company for the book?

A. title page
B. index
C. appendix
D. bibliography

7. Which part of the book would you use to locate the page number for a reference on the word "self-actualization?"

A. index
B. table of contents
C. glossary
D. bibliography

8. The <u>appendix</u> is the part of a book that gives information about

A. chapters and page numbers.
B. contributing author's names.
C. tables, charts, and graphs referenced in the book.
D. the definition of a particular word found in the book.

9. Which part of the book is used to find the introduction to the book?

A. preface
B. glossary
C. table of contents
D. bibliography

10. Which part of the book is used to find the page number for the beginning of chapter 5?

A. appendix
B. glossary
C. preface
D. table of contents

TABLE OF CONTENTS

Table of Contents - a listing of chapters and topics. A table of contents appears in the front of a book and provides an overview of the content and organization of a book.

Sample Table of Contents

1. In which chapter would you find information on Life expectancy? ____________________

2. On which page does the section on Religion start? ____________________

3. If you wanted to find statistics about marriage and divorce, on which page of the book would you look? ____________________

4. Which chapter would you read if you wanted to find out how much money is spent on health? ____________________

5. In which chapter would you find facts about immigration? ____________________

6. What is the last page dealing with Insurance coverage? ____________________

INDEX

Book Index - an alphabetical list of topics in a book with page numbers. The index generally contains every topic mentioned in a book and tells you which pages discuss the topic. An index appears at the end of a book.

SAMPLE INDEX

1. On which pages are deserts discussed?____________________________
2. Where would you read about the loudest noise? ________________________
3. On which page is a major city in Italy mentioned? ______________________
4. What are New Zealand's two famous attractions? _______________________
5. Where would you find out more about the Nile River? ____________________
6. On which pages is nectar discussed? ____________________________
7. In what country can you find diamonds? __________________________
8. On what page would you find information about nickel? ___________________
9. Look up six topics in another book index. List each topic and the page numbers about the topic here.

____________________ ____________________

____________________ ____________________

____________________ ____________________

BIBLIOGRAPHY

Bibliography - a list of writings about a particular author or topic. The writings consist of books or periodicals in alphabetical order by author's last name. A periodical is a magazine such as **National Geographic** or **Reader's Digest.** If the source is a magazine, the title of the article is in quotation marks. The name of the magazine is underlined. Titles of books are also underlined.

Read the sample bibliography below, and answer the questions that follow.

SAMPLE BIBLIOGRAPHY

Burnett, Frances Hodgson. The Secret Garden. New York: TDA, 1988.

Byars, Betsy. The Summer of the Swans. New York: Scholastic, 1970.

Keller, Helen. The Story of My Life. New York: Dell, 1965.

Reagan, C. & Stoner, G. "Great Stories For Children." Children Today 23 (1998): 76-77.

Sterling, Dorothy. Freedom Train. New York: Scholastic, 1954.

Verne, Jules. 20,000 Leagues Under The Sea. New York: Bantam, 1962.

Zeller, Hellen. "Games Children Play." Social Issues 11 (1997): 331-334.

1. Which listing in the bibliography is listed first? ______________________
2. Who is the author of *Story Of My Life*? ______________________
3. Which publishing company published the book by Jules Verne? ______________________
4. Which magazine has an article about children playing games? ______________________
5. Which book was published in 1962? ______________________
6. Where was *The Secret Garden* published? ______________________
7. How many sources listed are magazine articles? ______________________
8. Which book is the story of Helen Keller? ______________________
9. Which article has two authors? ______________________
10. Who is the author of The Summer of the Swans? ______________________

GLOSSARY

Glossary - an alphabetical list of specialized words with their definitions. The glossary is placed at the end of a book. Glossaries are found in science, social studies, literature, math books, and many others as well.

Sample Glossary Page

monogamy - marriage to one person at a time.

monopoly - one company dominating a particular market such as cars or telephones.

monotheism - belief in one God.

mores - standards of conduct that are held by a particular culture.

multiculturalism - respecting and accepting many cultures.

national health service - health care for all citizens regardless of income.

nationalism - one nation having more rights than another nation.

net financial assets - what we own minus what we owe.

nuclear family - a group consisting of two parents and their children.

occupation - a job for pay.

1. What is belief in one god called? ________________________
2. True or False. Volunteering to care for pre-school age children is an occupation.
3. True or False. Arriving at school on time is an example of a more.
4. True or False. A savings account is part of net financial assets.
5. Affordable medical care is called ________________________.
6. True or False. Racism is part of multiculturalism.
7. What is being married to one person called? ________________________
8. True or False. Nationalism occurs when everyone in the world is treated equally.
9. True or False. A single father with two children is a nuclear family.
10. When does a company become a monopoly? ________________________

    ____

ENCYCLOPEDIA

Encyclopedia - a reference work containing articles on a variety of subjects such as people, places, historical events, science, and technology. The articles are arranged alphabetically in volumes. Specialized encyclopedias on art, music, law, technology, and literature are also available in libraries.

Sample Encyclopedia Page

CAVY, *KAYvee,* is the common name for several related South American *rodents* (gnawing animals). Common cavies are called *guinea pigs.* Other cavies include *maras (Patagonian hares) and mocos.* Most cavies have fat bodies, short legs, and stiff, bristly hair. Maras have long, thin legs. A few kinds of *domesticated* (tamed) guinea pigs have long hair. All cavies eat plants or seeds.

CAYENNE PEPPER, a hot spice made from a plant called capiscum frutescens.

CAYMAN ISLANDS, A British dependency, located about 200 miles (320 kilometers) northwest of Jamaica in the Caribbean Sea. The three islands that make up the Cayman Islands are named Grand Cayman, Little Cayman, and Cayman Brac. They range over 100 square miles (259 square kilometers), and have 14,000 persons. The capital and largest city, Georgetown, is on Grand Cayman, the largest island.

CAYUGA INDIANS. See Iroquois Indians.

CAYUGA LAKE. See Finger Lakes.

CBR WARFARE. See Chemical-Biological-Radiological Warfare.

1. In what volume would you find more information on Cayuga Lake? ____________________
2. What is the common name for guinea pig? ____________________
3. What is another name for the Iroquois Indians? ____________________
4. Where are the Cayman Islands? ____________________
5. How many islands make up the Cayman Islands? ____________________
6. What kind of food do maras eat? ____________________
7. What does CBR stand for? ____________________
8. What is capiscum frutescens? ____________________

READER'S GUIDE TO PERIODICAL LITERATURE

Reader's Guide to Periodical Literature - contains articles from popular magazines. These articles are indexed alphabetically by subject and author. Volumes are published annually. To find an article on the topic you desire, consult a list of magazines your library receives.

Sample Reader's Guide

Key
Ja=January
F=February
Gov Quarterly=Government Quarterly
Am Games=American Games
Am Toys=American Toys

PASSPORT
Avoid rush: order passports early. T. Kelly. il *Gov Quarterly* 48:22-24 F '94
See also Immigration

PASSWORD
New twist to an old game. O. Vinson. il *Am Games* 14:6-7 Ja '94

PASTA
Choose the new pastas. L. Fideli. il *Cooking Today* 28:14-17 F '94
Pasta is healthy. R. Stokes, MD. il *Wellness* 6:9-11 Ja '94
See also macaroni, spaghetti

PASTE
Washable pastes for kids. il *Am Toys* 34:60-64 Ja '94
Pastes for wallpaper projects. B. West. il *Decorator* 41:18-22 F '94
See also cement, glue

PASTOR
The pastor is a good shepherd. il *Religion and Society* 64:28-33 F '94
See also minister, priest

1. On which pages would you find the pasta article by R. Stokes? ______________________

2. Who is the author of "Washable Pastes for Kids"? ______________________________

3. What other topic in the **Reader's Guide** deals with passports? ______________________

4. What is the volume and date for the pastor article? ______________________________

5. Which article discusses a word game? ______________________________________

PRACTICE 4: ENCYCLOPEDIA AND READER'S GUIDE

A. Encyclopedia. Write the key word or heading you would use to find the following information. It would be helpful to look in the index of your encyclopedia set to start. Then mention the page where you found the information, and answer the question.

1. Where and in what year did Columbus make his second voyage to the New World?
2. Describe the Zulu culture.
3. How do you care for a baby?
4. How large do leatherback sea turtles get?
5. What were the teachings of Mahatma Gandhi?
6. Which vitamins are found in beef?
7. Teaching chimpanzees American Sign Language.
8. How did jazz music start?
9. Name the seven wonders of the world.
10. Where did Joseph Stalin die?
11. What are the cures for sea sickness?
12. List four famous American humorists.
13. Explain how a telescope works.
14. How do microwave ovens work?
15. What products come from pine trees?

B. Reader's Guide Exercise. Visit a library after thinking about some topics to research. Possible topics might include the following: **AIDS, tooth decay, manatees, Atlanta Braves, computers, generation X, erosion, bass fishing, peaches.** Find two articles on each topic. Then make a copy of one article, and share it with the class. Write down the author's name, title of the article, name of the periodical, volume, page numbers, and the date of publication.

DEWEY DECIMAL SYSTEM

Many libraries use the **Dewey Decimal System** to organize their books and make them easy to find. The numbering system is divided into the 10 categories listed below.

Section Numbers	Category	Examples
000 - 099	General Works	encyclopedias
100 - 199	Philosophy	psychology, ethics
200 - 299	Religion	mythology, world religions
300 - 399	Social Sciences	law, government, economics, education
400 - 499	Languages	dictionaries, grammars
500 - 599	Science	astronomy, biology, chemistry, physics, math
600 - 699	Technology	medicine, business, engineering, farming, homemaking
700 - 799	Arts & Recreation	dance, painting, music, hobbies
800 - 899	Literature	poetry, plays, short stories, novels
900 - 999	History	biography, geography, travel

Use the chart above to determine what section or category you would use to find the following books.

1. Which section would have a book about a United States president? ____________
2. Which category would have a book about Buddhism? ____________
3. Which category would have a book about shooting stars? ____________
4. Between what numbers would you find a book about painting with acrylics? ____________
5. Which category would have a book about what to see in India? ____________
6. In which section would you find a book about the causes of storms? ____________
7. In which section would you find the book <u>The Mystery of the Missing Necklace</u>? ____________
8. In which category would you find a Spanish-English/ English-Spanish dictionary? ____________
9. Which section would have a book about starting your own business? ____________
10. In which category would you find a book on Freud's contributions to modern psychology? ____________

CARD CATALOG

Card Catalog - alphabetical listing of books in a library found on a computer system or in a cabinet. The card catalog consists of an **author card, title card,** and a **subject card** for each book. On the **author card,** the name of the author is at the top. On the **title card**, the title of the book is at the top, and on the **subject card,** the subject of the book is at the top. Each **catalog card** contains the following information: the author's full name, the title of the book, place of publication, name of publisher, date of publication, number of pages, and brief facts about the book. The **call number** is listed at the bottom of the card. In many libraries, the card catalog is now on microfilm or in a computer.

Subject Card

Famous Americans - Biographies

Palacios, Argentina, 1953- comp.
Standing Tall: The Stories of Ten Hispanic Americans.
New York: Scholastic, Inc, 1994.
234 pp.

Includes Selected Bibliography and Sources
1. Famous Americans - Biographies I. Title
HA 922.43TS4

1. How many pages does the book contain? ____________________
2. Who is Argentina Palacios? ____________________
3. Under what subject is the book classified? ____________________
4. What is the book's call number? ____________________
5. Where and when was the book published? ____________________
6. What is the book about? ____________________
7. What is the book's title? ____________________
8. What company published the book? ____________________

NEWSPAPER INDEX AND NEWSPAPER AD

Newspaper Index - an alphabetical list of sections in a newspaper. This index helps you locate articles on a particular topic.

Sample Newspaper Index

Sections	
Main News	A
Editorials	B
Travel	C
Sports	D
Entertainment	E
Obituaries	F
Advertisements	G
Classified Ads	H

Main News/Front Page - the page where the most important news items are printed.

Editorial Section - the section where the editor's or publisher's opinion on some subject are printed.

Travel Section the section where information about different areas of the world and prices of travel are printed.

Sports Section - the section where the latest sports events and famous sports players are discussed.

Entertainment Section - the section where the latest movies, theater performances, and musical concerts are posted and discussed.

Obituaries - the section where funeral notices and brief biographies of the deceased are posted.

Advertisements - public notices or announcements recommending certain products or services.

Classified Section - the section where notices of employment opportunities, homes for sale, apartments for rent, lost and found, etc. are posted.

Tell which section you would look for the following articles.

1. Where would you find an article about a major earthquake in China? ________________
2. Where would you find news about the state basketball playoffs? ________________
3. What would you find in the obituaries? ________________
4. Where would the movie listings appear? ________________
5. Where would you find the time and place of a movie you want to see? ________________

6. Where would you look for the cheapest plane fare to New York? ____________________

7. Where would you look to find the details on the time for a funeral? ________________

8. Where would you find the editors' opinions on the latest government crisis?___________

9. Where would you find the department store sales this week? ______________________

10. What would you find in the classified section? _________________________________

11. What would you expect to find on the front page?_____________________________

NEWSPAPER AD

Newspaper (Classified) Ad - a notice designed to promote a product, service, or business. Newspaper ads vary in size, shape, and color and are often created to increase sales or to offer employment.

> Fine dining restaurant in Liberty now hiring hostess, cooks, servers, and bussers. Will work around your school schedule. Jobs pay between $5 - $8 per hour. Ask for Sandra or Keva. Apply at 461 Whistle St. or phone 889-4200.

12. What is the address of the restaurant? ______________________________________

13. When are the workers needed? ____

14. Whom should you speak with about the positions? ______________________________

15. Since the employer works around a school schedule, who is the main audience for the ad?

    ____

PRACTICE 5: NEWSPAPER/MAGAZINE AD

A **magazine** is a publication issued weekly, semimonthly, monthly, or quarterly which contains nonfiction articles or fictional stories from different contributors. Magazines also publish current information on the latest events and trends around the world.

For homework, each student finds an ad in a newspaper or magazine and then develops four questions about it. Students bring their ads and questions to class, and exchange them with other students. Answers are given after students reply to the questions.

QUESTIONS ABOUT REFERENCE SOURCES

TIPS FOR QUESTIONS ABOUT REFERENCE SOURCES

1. **Skim through the reference source.**
2. **Read the reference source two or three times.** Become familiar with the format and organization of the reference.
3. **Read the question carefully.**
4. **Scan the reference source to find your answer.**
5. **Confirm your answer by reviewing the evidence in the source.**

CHOOSING THE RIGHT REFERENCE SOURCES

In the first part of this chapter, you learned about important **reference sources**. Then you practiced answering questions about them.

Let's say that you are doing a report on cowboys. Several sources may give some information about cowboys, but only a few sources will give you enough material for a report. For example, a **dictionary** will give you a definition of cowboy. A **bibliography** might list some books about cowboys. The *card catalog* can help you locate the books about cowboys if you have any in your library. You might even locate a **map** of states where cowboys live. However, only one or two reference sources will provide enough information for a report. Most likely this information will come from longer articles in an **encyclopedia** or from the **Reader's Guide to Periodical Literature**.

Based on the above example, you can see that choosing the right reference source means: 1.) Knowing the right source to use; 2.) Practice using each reference source.

In the chapter review and chapter test, you'll be identifying the best resource for obtaining information on a particular topic or problem. Before you start answering the questions, review the main reference sources from this chapter.

CHAPTER 6 REVIEW

Directions: Read each question. Then choose the appropriate source for finding the information.

1. Which source will help Tyrone fix his computer?

   A. encyclopedia
   B. dictionary
   C. card catalog
   D. telephone directory

2. Sonya wants to write to Michael Jordan of the Chicago Bulls. Where would she look?

   A. dictionary
   B. thesarus
   C. **Reader's Guide**
   D. index

3. Josh found a gold watch in the woods with no identification. Where would he find the owner?

   A. newspaper ad
   B. encyclopedia
   C. telephone directory
   D. thesaurus

4. Diane is writing a paper and needs another word to use for the word "trip." Which reference should she use?

   A. appendix
   B. bibliography
   C. thesaurus
   D. encyclopedia

5. Shawn is buying his first car. Where would he look for the best price?

   A. **Reader's Guide**
   B. newspaper ad
   C. table of contents
   D. bibliography

6. Where would Maria look to find books of African-American folktales?

   A. encyclopedia
   B. **Reader's Guide**
   C. ad
   D. card catalog

7. Aaron wants to find out which page in his history book tells about the causes of World War I. What part of the book should he look in?

   A. bibliography
   B. appendix
   C. index
   D. title page

8. Zack needs to know the page number for the beginning of Chapter 6. Where should he look?

   A. index
   B. table of contents
   C. bibliography
   D. appendix

9. Brittany needs to know the definition of the word "lugubrious." Where should she look?

A. dictionary
B. thesaurus
C. **Reader's Guide**
D. encyclopedia

10. Charles needs to do a report on sea creatures that dwell on the bottom of the ocean. Which of the following resources would he most likely **not** turn to?

A. encyclopedia
B. **Reader's Guide**
C. newspaper index
D. card catalog

11.

Marketing and Sales Division Building

	Office No.
Mr. Arnold Bass	218
Ms. Susan Chapel	128
Mr. Dale Fletcher	222
Mr. Ken Greene	207
Mrs. Cheryl Love	105
Ms. Gail Spears	109
Mr. Ben Tinley	215
Mrs. Jessie Ulrich	112
Mr. Sam Walton	111

Ms. Stone, a new accounts manager in the Marketing and Sales Division Building, will have her name added to the above alphabetized building directory between

A. Mrs. Cheryl Love and Ms. Gail Spears.
B. Mr. Ben Tinley and Mrs. Jessie Ulrich.
C. Ms. Gail Spears and Mr. Ben Tinley.
D. Ms. Susan Chapel and Mr. Dale Fletcher.

12. If the guide words lance - late were at the top of a page in the dictionary, which word could be included on that page?

A. laundry
B. laser
C. lamp
D. lake

13. Where would you find alphabetized definitions of terms describing the body in a biology book?

A. table of contents
B. index
C. bibliography
D. glossary

14. Where would you look for a book on speed reading?

A. a card catalog
B. telephone directory
C. an index
D. a table of contents

Statistical Index	
Space Research and Technology,	
Federal Outlays	509, 983
Spain. See Foreign Countries	
Spanish-American War, cost	548
Spices, imports	1105,1107,1109
Sporting and athletic goods	
Sports	407,408,1130
Consumer Price Indexes	748
Sporting goods and bicycle shops,	
retail	1278
Sports	309,404,412
Expenditures	393,407
Sports Associations	92
Sports Industry Receipts	395
Spot Market Price Index	760
Squid	1152,1158

15. On what page(s) would you find information about pepper and cloves?

A. 1109
B. 760
C. 983
D. 393

Use the following information on the Dewey Decimal System to answer questions 16-20.

Section Numbers	Category	Examples
000 - 099	General Works	Encyclopedias
100 - 199	Philosophy	psychology, ethics
200 - 299	Religion	mythology, world religions
300 - 399	Social Sciences	law, government, economics, education
400 - 499	Languages	dictionaries, grammars
500 - 599	Science	astronomy, biology, chemistry, physics, math
600 - 699	Technology	medicine, business, engineering, farming, homemaking
700 - 799	Arts & Recreation	dance, painting, music, hobbies
800 - 899	Literature	poetry, plays, short stories, novels
900 - 999	History	biography, geography, travel

16. What section would have a book entitled The Cry in the Night? _______________

17. In which category would you find a book on the catfish farming? _______________

18. Which category would have a book on battles during the Civil War? _______________

19. In which section would you find a book of poems by Emily Dickenson? _______________

20. In which section would you find a book titled Plants that Eat Insects? _______________

Chapter 7

ANALYSIS OF LITERATURE

Analyzing literature improves your understanding of what you are reading. Then you can learn to think critically about reading selections taken from speeches, short stories, poems, plays, articles, essays, ads, and editorials. You will be taught how to analyze the following elements of literature:

1) **Argument and Fallacy**
2) **Propaganda**
3) **Author's Purpose**
4) **Structural Devices**
5) **Rhetorical Devices**
6) **Types of Literature**

In this chapter, you will be learning about these elements. You will also complete practice exercises about analyzing literature.

ARGUMENT AND FALLACY

An **argument** often presents opinions that have a positive or negative slant. A writer will use reasons to support a claim or assertion about a topic or issue. You may be asked to analyze an ad, article, or editorial taken from a newspaper or magazine. An **advertisement** tries to persuade you to purchase a product such as a car or a service such as trash collection. An **editorial** presents a viewpoint on a controversial issue such as violence on television or raising the speed limits.

When you read a selection from a book, magazine, or newspaper, you will usually need to identify the statement that best describes the argument. Follow these tips for analyzing an argument:

Tips for Analyzing an Argument

1. **Identify the opinion or viewpoint on the issue.** It will generally appear near the beginning of the selection, but it may also appear at the end as a conclusion.
2. **Read the supporting reasons for the opinion.**
3. **Decide whether the reasons or examples support the argument.**

Hint 1: A **valid argument** contains good logic, solid evidence, or clear reasons and examples from the reading selection.

Hint 2: A **fallacy** or **false argument** contains poor logic, weak evidence, or faulty reasons and examples from the reading selection.

To identify the statement that best describes the argument, you should also learn the main kinds of fallacies used in arguments. **Fallacies** are pieces of information that try to falsely persuade you to accept an opinion or viewpoint about an issue.

Main Types of Fallacies

Name	Example
1. **Jumping to Conclusions** - a claim with little proof to support it.	Vote for the people's choice! Sun Soap is the best!
2. **Ad Hominem** - attacking the person rather than his or her ideas.	Tom dresses like a nerd! How could he run for president of the Student Council!
3. **Circular Argument** - part of an argument is used as evidence to support it.	Looks are more important than talent because looks mean everything.
4. **Testimonial** - famous persons endorse a product, even though they aren't experts.	Bill Cosby loves Jell-O. Robin Williams drives a Lexus.
5. **Either-Or Fallacy** - there are only two sides to an issue.	Either we eliminate all weapons from this earth, or we'll blow each other up!

Now let's read some selections, and answer questions about the arguments.

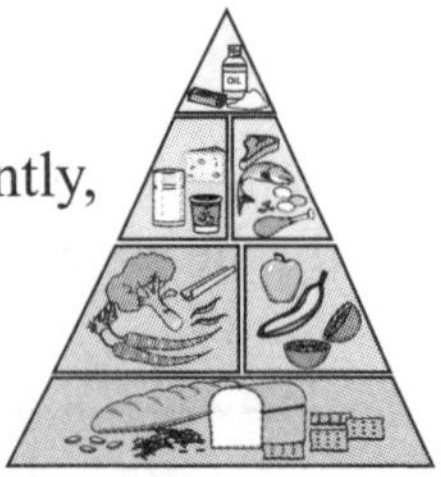

Metabolism refers to how the body burns energy. People with high metabolisms burn more calories than people with low metabolisms. Consequently, they have an easier time losing weight. One-half of the women and one-fourth of the men in the United States are trying to lose weight and become fit. The sad truth is that most of us will regain our original weight in a year or less.

What's the real secret for losing weight and keeping it off? The answer is developing and maintaining a healthy metabolism. Here are some tips for improving your metabolism and melting away that extra fat:

1) **Drink plenty of cold water.** Filling up on water decreases the appetite. Three quarts of water each day are ideal.
2) **Don't skip meals, especially breakfast.** Eat small meals every two to three hours. In this way, carbohydrates and protein will not be converted into fat.
3) **Eat fat-burning foods.** Raw vegetables, whole grains, fruits, and legumes are your best choices. Consume fruits between meals for extra energy, so they won't be converted to fat.
4) **Exercise regularly.** Aerobic exercises like running and walking are best. Also try lifting weights–a good muscle builder and fat burner. Exercise before you eat. It will decrease your appetite and increase your metabolism.

1. Which one of the following statements best describes the writer's argument?

   A. The writer states that people with high metabolisms lose weight easier, which is an invalid argument.
   B. The writer develops a valid argument.
   C. The writer jumps to conclusions based on limited information.
   D. The writer does not support the argument with valid reasons.

Rapidly Burn Off Pounds And Inches

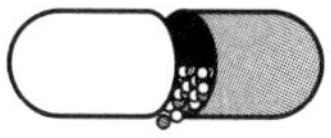

This is it! The diet pill researchers around the world have hailed for its powerful, quick-working ingredients that help people shed stubborn fat– fast! People can lose up to 5 pounds the first 48 hours without complicated calorie counting or suffering from biting hunger pains.

People Can Lose 10, 20, 50, Even 100 pounds!

Super Diet Pill Satisfies Need For Fast Action Without Strenuous Dieting

So fast-working, people can see a dramatic difference in just two days. Users, even those with long-time weight problems, find they can burn off up to a pound of fat and fluid every five hours over a weekend alone.

50% Fat Loss In 14 To 21 days

Incredibly, testing showed people lost 15, 20, 30, or more pounds without making major sacrifices or drastic changes! What's more, it works so fast that people shed as much as 50% of their fat in just two to three weeks.

2. Which one of the following statements best describes the argument of the writer in the above selection?

   A. The writer constructs a valid argument.
   B. The writer explores only two sides of an issue.
   C. The writer uses the personal testimony of famous people.
   D. The writer jumps to a conclusion.

Responding to the Metabolism Passage

To find the right answer for question 1, you must locate the statement that best describes the argument of the writer in the above selection. As you read the passage, you must decide whether the argument is valid, which is always one of the choices, or whether there are fallacies in the argument. **The best way to select your answer is to read each answer choice and see which one accurately describes the argument in this passage.**

The best answer for question 1 is B. The writer constructs a valid argument by presenting substantial evidence about the proven methods of increasing metabolism. Choice A is wrong because it is a known fact that individuals with higher metabolisms by definition burn their body's energy supply faster. Choice C is wrong because the passage provides a great deal of information to support the argument. Choice D is incorrect because the writer does offer valid reasons for the argument. These reasons are based on the widely accepted evidence about how the body metabolizes food.

Responding to the Diet Pill Passage

Choosing an answer for the second passage requires you to read the ad carefully.

First, you must identify the writer's opinion or viewpoint about losing weight.

Basically, the ad promotes a powerful diet pill that helps you shed pounds fast.

Secondly, you must review the supporting reasons to see whether the argument is valid or whether it is a fallacy.

Thirdly, you must find the statement that best describes the argument.

When you analyze the supporting reasons for this fast-working diet pill, you realize that the writer offers very limited information about the diet pill. Little proof is presented to support the claims. The writer never mentions the names of the diet pill researchers, the people who lost weight, or where and when the testing was done. Therefore, D is the best answer because the ad jumps to conclusions.

Choice A would be wrong because the supporting evidence about the diet pill is not well documented. Choice B is incorrect because the ad focuses on only the favorable aspects of the product. Choice C is wrong because the users of the diet pill are ordinary people, not famous celebrities.

PRACTICE 1: ARGUMENTS AND FALLACIES

Directions: Read each of the following selections. Check **"Valid"** if the all the sentences in the argument are valid and explain why the arguments are valid. Check **"Fallacies"** if one or more of the sentences in the argument are fallacies. Then list any fallacies, and explain why they are fallacies.

1. When you bite into a Dreambar, you'll sail into a galaxy of gooey goodness. Chewing that rich chocolate center sends waves of delight zooming through you. And who can resist the peanut and oatmeal layer wrapped around the outside. "That's why kids like Dreambars for snacks," says football linebacker Denzel Conner. "They provide that extra energy kids need to do their homework." Make your dreams come true. Have a Dreambar today!

Valid ________

Fallacies ________

Explanation ____

____

2.  There can be no question that Congress is more efficient than it was in its early days. Legislative business in both houses can now be conducted effectively; many weapons of obstruction that the rules once permitted have been eliminated. It is in the nature of a partisan body that some members will object to the manner in which the rules and procedures are applied. Congress would not be Congress – indeed, democracy would be in danger–if there were not complaints about how the institution was being run. But the long view yields the conclusion that, although Congress might conduct its business better in the future, it is operating more effectively now than it did in the past.

–from *To Make Laws* by James H. Hutson

Valid ________

Fallacies ________

Explanation ____

____

____

3. We either follow Trey Weiner, or we support Curtis Dornsky for district representative. Trey is a true leader who walks his talk. It doesn't matter that he wears old clothes and drives around in a beat-up pickup truck. He speaks for the people of this city. On the other hand, Curtis Dornsky wants the voters to focus on his good looks and his flashy Fifth Avenue suits. He talks about reducing taxes, but look how he dresses. He also drives a shiny new Lexus and a fancy Cadillac. Either you vote for the defender of the common people or the champion of the rich and famous. The other candidates just don't have a chance against these two competitors. When I vote next Tuesday, there's only one candidate I'll choose. His name is Trey Weiner.

– editorial in *The Wilson Gazette*

Valid ________

Fallacies ________

Explanation ____

____

____

4. In the Catskills I found something I'd missed after four decades of living in cities: simple courtesy. Like a friendly wave, for example. It is unthinkable not to return one…Walt Meade, a naturalist who lives in Roxbury, on the Catskill's northern slope, says, "I was going to Grand Gorge when Jane Hubble drove by and waved. But I didn't see her till it was too late. The next time I saw her, she berated me, "I wasted a perfectly good wave on you, Walt Meade. And I don't know if I'm going to wave at you again." Time after time, stories of compassion come out of the Catskills. "When my dad's barn burned down, the neighbors put a new one up in three days." "When our daughter was killed, the neighbors just came in and took over." The genuineness of the Catskills calls out like a distant memory…

– Paraphrase from *National Geographic*

Valid ________

Fallacies ________

Explanation ____

____

____

5. Doctors are a regular set of humbugs, and most of them are quacks. They go off to school and learn some recipes for curing diseases. Then they manage in one way or another to get the teachers in their school to give them a certificate, and then they'll go out into some town or village or city and rent some space over a drugstore and get some bones and an old skull and a lot of books and spread them around the room and call it an office. They put up a sign and call themselves doctors. Then they guess what your illness is and collect their money.

–from *Shams* by John S. Draper

Valid ________

Fallacies ________

Explanation ____

____

____

PRACTICE 2: ARGUMENT AND FALLACY

A. Other Fallacies. Two other fallacies that are important are **False Cause** and **Ignoring the Question.** Find definitions and examples of these fallacies in an English or Language Arts book.

B. Reasons for Arguments. Mark either **Agree** or **Disagree** next to each statement. Then write reasons for your opinion. Exchange your opinion and the reasons for it with a partner or in a group. Then determine whether the argument is valid or whether it contains fallacies.

		Agree	Disagree
1.	A black cat crossing your path brings bad luck.	______	______
2.	Looks are more important than intelligence.	______	______
3.	Jeans and pants must be worn with belts.	______	______
4.	Students who cheat in school should be expelled.	______	______
5.	The speed limit should be increased.	______	______
6.	A school dress code is necessary.	______	______
7.	Money solves your problems.	______	______
8.	A high school diploma is important.	______	______
9.	Children are just like their parents.	______	______
10.	Television has too much violence.	______	______

C. Fallacies in Ads. Find examples of valid arguments and fallacies from this chapter in newspaper and magazine ads, articles, editorials, or television commercials. Then share your examples with the class and your teacher. See if they agree with your findings.

D. Perform Skits. In a small group, create a television advertisement for a product or service. Use scenes, props, posterboard, etc. to create a realistic presentation. Perform two versions of the advertisement, one with a valid argument and one with fallacies. The class then analyzes each version to determine which is a valid argument and which has fallacies. Discuss your findings.

PROPAGANDA

A writing that purposely tries to influence others is called **propaganda**. It is found in editorials, magazines, television commercials, political statements, and everyday conversation.

TYPES OF PROPAGANDA

Testimonials - a frequently used technique in which famous persons endorse a product even though they are <u>not</u> qualified as experts.

Example: Chuck Norris endorses anti-perspirant. Michael Jordan endorses cereal.

Transfer - a technique in which the public's feelings on one thing are somehow connected to another unrelated thing.

Example: "If federal employees are hired based on their political membership, then this nation is not truly a democracy." Democracy, rule by popular consent of the governed, is not related to one employer's hiring policy.

In-Crowd Appeal - a kind of flattery which encourages viewers to identify with an admired, envied group.

Example: A super model stands in front of a new sports car. The viewers are supposed to connect the desirability of the woman to the desirability of the new car.

Bandwagon - a technique in which the reader is made to feel that a great movement is beginning. The reader would be an idiot or an enemy if he/she does not join the movement.

Example: "Millions of people sign on to the Internet everyday and receive the latest information. If you don't get on-line, you will be left behind." Do you have to jump on this bandwagon? No qualifications are required to put information on the Internet.

PRACTICE 3: RECOGNIZING PROPAGANDA

Directions: Read the following passages. Write **"balanced"** if the statement seems to be truthful or fair. Write **"propaganda"** if the statement seems to distort or slant information. Then explain your choices.

1. Buy Youth-filled Vitamin E supplements today. They're going to make you look younger and feel happier! Over one hundred thousand people are already taking advantage of this supplement to look years younger. Why shouldn't you?

____

____

2. Do you want the state government to tax even more of your income? Don't let greedy Uncle Sam pocket more of your money. Write to your congressman today, and send a "no more taxes" message to the leaders of our state.

____

____

3. Bring your friends to see the latest Laser Light Show at the Gigantic Gold Dome. Penny Starway, the best new voice in country music, was thrilled: "This show has the prettiest lights and images I have ever seen! If you want to see the best in laser technology, come on down to the dome."

____

____

4. There is still a great deal of controversy about the future of the space program. While some people believe it is a waste of much needed funds, others point to the great scientific and technological advances that have resulted from the exploration of space. Supporters of the program most frequently cite the wide uses of microprocessors as one of the major contributions to space-related research.

____

____

5. The County Government meeting broke up after a long debate. The man's supporters claim he is the duly elected representative of the people and should be allowed to take his seat on the council. His opponents disputed this, saying that his previous protests of council activities disqualified him from holding public office.

____

____

6. When looking for the best travel agency, try Globe World Travel. Thousands of satisfied customers have been on the tours we offer. Imagine a moonlight walk in Paris, a lion safari in East Africa, or a shopping spree in Singapore! Many of the nation's top business leaders choose Globe World Travel for their vacations. Why don't you?

____

____

7. Grace Chisolm, the well-known newscaster, has this to say about the Cheetah XR71A: "It drives like a sea breeze. I can definitely tell this car is going to redefine the future of the automotive industry." Like Ms. Chisolm, we at Sunrise Motors believe this sports car looks better, rides better, and feels better than anything else in its class.

____

____

8. I stand as firm as the rock of Gibraltar on the right that women have to shape the thoughts, socially and politically, of the world. They can make our country better and purer, just as they appreciate their own rights. I am in favor of women's rights–in their rights to rise up in the majesty of the nature their Creator gave them and emancipate themselves from the foolish fashions and sentiments of the age. When they do rise, they will be more respected by all mankind than all the rulers of the earth from Adam down to the present day.

– Clarissa's speech in *Shams* by John S. Draper

____

____

AUTHOR'S PURPOSE

Author's purpose refers to the reason why an author writes a selection. Knowing the author's purpose helps us to better understand a reading passage. For example, if the author is telling a story with characters, plot, and setting, then the author's purpose is **to relate an adventure**. Technically, this purpose is **to narrate**. A **narrative** means to tell a story through a series of related events.

You should become familiar with the various reasons an author communicates information in a reading selection. These purposes are listed below with definitions and examples.

Purpose	Definition	Reading Selection
To inform	To present facts and details	"Ocean Fishes"
To entertain	To amuse or offer enjoyment	"Time I Slipped in the Mud"
To persuade	To urge action on an issue	"Raise Penalties for Polluters"
To instruct	To teach concepts and facts	"Tips For Healthy Living"
To describe feelings	To communicate emotions through words	"When My Dog Died"
To create suspense	To convey uncertainty	"Will Tom Win the Race?"
To motivate	To incite	"You Can Lose Weight!"
To cause doubt	To be skeptical	"Are Adults Responsible?"
To describe an event	To narrate	"My Trip to Mobile"
To teach a lesson	To furnish knowledge	"Mastering Exponents"
To introduce a character	To describe a person's traits	"First Look at Captain Nemo"
To create a mood	To establish atmosphere	"Gloom in the House of Usher"
To relate an adventure	To tell an exciting story	"Lost in a Cave"
To share a personal experience	To tell about an event in your life	"The Time I Learned to Share"

PRACTICE 4: AUTHOR'S PURPOSE

Directions: Based on the previous list of author's purposes, identify the author's purpose for the following reading passages. Then discuss your choices with your class or the instructor.

1. The fire crackled musically. From it swelled light smoke. Overhead the foliage moved softly. The leaves, with their faces turned toward the blaze, were colored shifting hues of silver, often edged with red. Far off to the right, through a window in the forest, could be seen a handful of stars lying, like glittering pebbles, on the black level of the night.

– Stephen Crane, *Red Badge of Courage*

A. To describe an event
B. To create a mood
C. To persuade
D. To teach a lesson

2. The blood carries oxygen from the lungs to each cell in the body. In addition, the blood carries carbon dioxide from the cells to the lungs where it is expelled as a waste product. Nutrients like protein and glucose depend on the blood for their dispersal throughout the body.

A. To motivate
B. To entertain
C. To relate an adventure
D. To inform

3. **Letter to His Son**

The South, in my opinion, has been aggrieved by the acts of the North, as you say. I feel the aggression and am willing to take every proper step for redress. It is the principle I fight for, not individual or private benefit. As an American citizen, I take great pride in my country, her prosperity and institutions, and would defend any state if her rights were invaded. But I can anticipate no greater calamity for the country than a dissolution of the Union. It would be an accumulation of all the evils we complain of, and I am willing to sacrifice everything but honor for its preservation. I hope, therefore, that all constitutional means will be exhausted before there is a resort to force.

– Gen. Robert E. Lee, Jan. 23, 1861

A. To introduce a character
B. To cause doubt
C. To persuade
D. To entertain

4. 

Columbus' own successful voyage in 1492 prompted a papal bull dividing the globe between rivals Spain and Portugal. But the Portuguese protested that the pope's line left them too little Atlantic sea room for their voyages to India. The line was shifted 270 leagues westward in 1494 by the Treaty of Tordesillas. Thus, wittingly or not, the Portuguese gained Brazil and gave their language to more than half the people of South America.

A. To teach a lesson
B. To describe feelings
C. To relate an adventure
D. To inform

5. At the start of every school year, each student is given a handbook that lists all the school rules. The conduct code in our high school requires that students be respectful and responsible toward each other and their teachers. When disruptive behavior threatens the safety of the students or teachers, the school administrator will determine a penalty which will be communicated to the parents.

Yesterday, between classes at our high school, David spray painted the back of Sam's new leather jacket. Ignoring the pleas of students and teachers, Sam chased David down the hall, wrestled him to the floor, and punched him in the stomach twice. Students nearby quickly grabbed Sam and David and pulled them apart just as Mr. Freel, the principal, arrived on the scene. Based on what students and teachers observed, Mr. Freel suspended Sam and David for ten days.

A. To share a personal experience
B. To create a mood
C. To teach a lesson
D. To describe feelings

6. Twelve-year-old Nadia told us a story that seemed unbelievable but was true about her family's journey to the United States. In Romania, her father was involved in the politics of Romania, opposing the communist regime of Ceausescu. Because of death threats made against her family, Nadia and her family had to leave the country in the middle of the night. They had arranged for a boat to meet them, so they could sail the Black Sea to freedom in Bulgaria. Because they left in a hurry, they took nothing with them except their clothes. The boat never came, so they swam into the sea until a boat from Bulgaria discovered her family swimming. All of them survived the swim except for Nadia's little brother, Dimitry. From that country, they obtained refugee status and traveled to the United States. This experience made Nadia and ourselves very thankful for the lives we have here.

A. To instruct
B. To describe an event
C. To relate an adventure
D. To persuade

7. During Napoleon's war with England, both England and France seized neutral ships and goods. In addition, they were conscripting United States merchant sailors into their navies, enraging the people of the United States. In August 1810, Napoleon publicly repealed his previous decrees and declared that neutral ships could freely trade in France without risk of confiscation or conscription. President Madison believed Napoleon's words. When Britain refused to promise the same thing, Congress declared war on England and began invading Canada, starting the War of 1812.

A. To inform
B. To describe an event
C. To relate an adventure
D. To persuade

8. Hand grippers can help give your arms those bulging biceps you're after, but only if they offer enough resistance. If you can squeeze them repeatedly for one to two minutes, and your hands don't get tired, they're too weak for you. You can keep buying stronger ones or make something at home that can do the same job.

A. To instruct
B. To persuade
C. To describe an event
D. To entertain

9. There was no escape from the severe regimen Ida was compelled to follow. The work she had to do, the rules she had to observe. Breakfast at seven-thirty sharp because the store had to be opened by her father at eight, which meant rising at seven; luncheon at twelve-thirty, so as to satisfy her father and her own noon recess hour which was completely filled in by this; dinner invariably at six-thirty because there were many things, commercial and social, which fell upon the shoulders of William Zobel at night. And between whiles, from four to six on weekdays and later from seven to eight at night, as well as all day Saturdays, store duty in her father's store.

– Theodore Dreiser, *Typhoon*

A. To relate an adventure
B. To introduce a character
C. To persuade
D. To teach a lesson

10. My family came to America in 1985. No one spoke a word of English. In school, I was in an English as a Second language class with other foreign-born children. My class was so overcrowded that it was impossible for the teacher to teach English properly. I dreaded going to school each morning because of the fear of not understanding what people were saying and the fear of being laughed at.

– Yu-Lan (Mary) Ying, an eyewitness account about learning English

A. To cause doubt
B. To entertain
C. To share a personal experience
D. To create suspense

PRACTICE 5: AUTHOR'S PURPOSE

Directions: In a group or on your own, review 6 passages from a newspaper or magazine. Using the list of purposes from this section, identify the author's purpose in each selection. Exchange your passages with a classmate to see if he/she identifies the same purpose. Then discuss your findings with the class or with your teacher.

STRUCTURAL DEVICES

Structural Devices refer to elements that help you understand a story, poem, or play. In this part of the chapter, you will be learning about these structural devices. These devices are **plot, character, setting, point of view, mood,** and **theme** or **interpretation.**

Now let's review these structural devices and some of their features. Study them and then apply what you learn to some sample passages of literature.

Setting and Its Features

setting - includes the place and time in a story. The setting of Poe's *Cask of Amontillado* is a murky wine cellar in the evening.
place - location where a story takes place. The Uncle Remus tales of Joel Chandler Harris take place in rural Georgia.
time - when the story occurs. Crane's *Red Badge of Courage* takes place during the Civil War.

Plot and Its Features

plot - pattern of events in a story leading to a conclusion. The plot of *Moby-Dick* centers around Captain Ahab's pursuit of a great white whale.

climax - the turning point in a story. In Poe's "Fall of the House of Usher," the climax occurs when the reader discovers that Usher's dead sister is alive.

conflict - the struggle between different forces in a story. These struggles can be with nature, with one's self, with others, or with society. In Jack London's *Call of the Wild*, the dog Buck struggles with nature and society until he joins a wolfpack.

foreshadowing - clues or hints of events to come. In *The Wizard of Oz*, a harsh wind blows through the trees before the wicked witch appears.

suspense - anticipation about what will happen in a story. In "Little Red Riding Hood," we worry about what the wolf will do to the little girl.

Character and Its Features

character - an imaginary person that appears in a literary work. Celie and Nettie are the main characters in Alice Walker's *The Color Purple.*

antagonist - an opponent or rival of the hero. The antagonists in Hemingway's *Old Man and the Sea* are the sharks.

dialogue - conversation between two people in a story. Huck and Jim engage in many dialogues as they travel along the Mississippi River in Mark Twain's *Huckleberry Finn.*

narrator - the person telling a story. In Angelou's *I Know Why the Caged Bird Sings*, the narrator is a young girl who is also the main character.

protagonist - the hero or main character. The protagonists are Romeo and Juliet in Shakespeare's famous play of the same name.

Point of View and Its Features

point of view - the perspective from which a writer tells a story. Harper Lee writes *To Kill A Mockingbird* from the point of view of Scout, a young girl living in a small town in Alabama.

first person point of view - narrator tells the story from the "I" point of view. In *House On Mango Street*, Esperanza tells her story as the main character.

third person point of view - writer tells story describing characters as "he," "she," or "they." Irving's *Rip Van Winkle* is an example of this point of view.

Mood and Tone

mood - the atmosphere of a literary work. The writer often creates a mood through details in the setting and plot. The **tone** is a feeling or attitude conveyed to the reader in a work of literature. In "The Cask of Amontillado," Poe creates a mood of mystery and gloom. A tone of humor and mischief pervades *Tom Sawyer* by Mark Twain.

Types of Moods and Tones (Learn what these words mean.)

angry	dramatic	mocking	sad
anxious	fearful	optimistic	satirical
boring	happy	pessimistic	suspenseful
calm	humorous	poetic	sympathetic
cynical	lighthearted	relaxed	tragic
depressed	lofty	threatening	remorseful
lackadaisical	gloomy	tense	nervous
hysterical	lethargic	pensive	tearful
expectant	disgusting	macabre	beguiling

Theme or Interpretation

theme or interpretation - the message or meaning in a story, poem, or play. The reader is then able to gain insights into literature and life. The theme of Paul Laurence Dunbar's "We Wear the Mask" is that we all must wear masks that hide our true selves. One interpretation of Kate Chopin's "Story of an Hour" is that life is full of surprises that can kill you.

Tips for Understanding Structural Devices

1. **Study the definitions and examples of plot, character, setting, point of view, mood, and theme from this section.**

2. **Complete the following practice passages.**

3. **Apply them to the exercises at the end of this chapter.**

PRACTICE 6: STRUCTURAL DEVICES

Directions: Read each of the following passages. Then answer the questions about structural devices.

20,000 Leagues Under The Sea

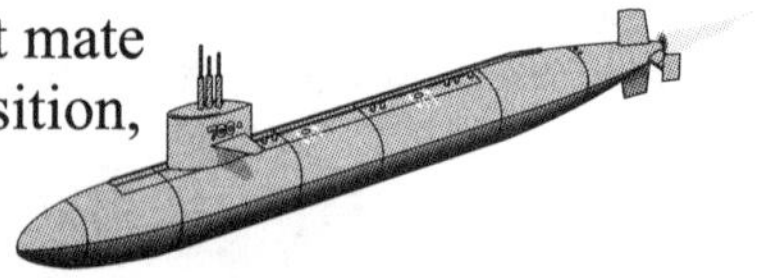

When I got up, I saw that Captain Nemo and his first mate were on the platform. They were examining the ship's position, exchanging several words in their incomprehensible language.

Here was our situation. Two miles to starboard rose Gueboroar Island, whose coast extended from north to west like an immense arm. Toward the south and east, we could already make out the tops of several coral formations which the ebb tide was beginning to uncover. We had gone aground at high tide, which would make it difficult to refloat the *Nautilus.* Nevertheless the ship had suffered no damage, for her hull was solidly joined. But even though it could never sink or spring a leak, there was a serious danger of its remaining grounded forever on these reefs, and that would be the end of Captain Nemo's submarine.

I was thinking of all this when the captain came over looking as cool and calm as ever. He seemed neither disturbed or unhappy.

"An accident?" I asked.

"No, an incident," he replied.

"But an incident," I retorted, "that will force you once again to live on that land you have been fleeing!"

– Jules Verne

1. The story is told from the point of view of

A. the first mate.
B. Captain Nemo.
C. first person narrator.
D. the third person.

2. At the end of the selection, the mood is

A. tense.
B. happy.
C. relaxed.
D. boring.

3. The main conflict in this passage is a struggle with

A. society.
B. one's self.
C. Captain Nemo.
D. nature.

4. The setting of this passage is

A. near the sea.
B. on a reef.
C. under the sea.
D. on an island.

5. The best statement of the plot in this passage is that:

A. the Nautilus ran aground near shore, so Captain Nemo and the narrator argue.
B. Captain Nemo and the narrator disagree about where the Nautilus will land.
C. Captain Nemo found a submarine near Gueboroar Island and wants to own it.
D. the Nautilus will be sailing out to sea after a few days of rest.

The Hermit's Hut

Thomas, bearing the unconscious monk in his arms, and somewhat faint from his own wounds, staggered in the direction of the chiming bell. He had but a short distance to go from the scene of combat to the tiny chapel, where a hermit was saying his prayers.

At the sound of Thomas' clattering footsteps, the hermit turned with a start and hastened toward him disclosing a kindly face lit by large brown eyes.

"Brother," said Thomas, "here is a holy man badly wounded for my sake. I beg you to use your skill with herbs to heal him."

The hermit responded quickly and led them into his chambers. Thomas carried the monk with tenderness and laid him down tenderly on the hermit's couch.

"I best be alone with him," said the hermit. "Go outside and wait 'till I come to you. I think the brother is not wounded unto death."

Thomast went out obediently as the good monk faintly called his name. "Be not troubled," said the hermit. "He does not know that he calls you. He is delirious."

Alone with the monk, the hermit began to look at the wound. The hermit looked at the soft white flesh of the shoulder with surprise. Then on impulse, he removed the hood and confirmed his thought. Long hair cascaded over the monk's delicate face. He paused in dismay.

6. What is the setting?

   A. a tiny chapel
   B. a cabin
   C. a doctor's quarters
   D. a house

7. The mood of this story is

   A. humorous.
   B. dramatic.
   C. relaxed.
   D. suspenseful.

8. Who is **not** involved in the dialogue of this story?

   A. the hermit
   B. the enemy
   C. Sir Lancelot
   D. the monk

9. What is the theme of this story?

   A. the joy of life
   B. death is coming
   C. unexpected surprise
   D. falling in love

A Fishing Trip

The traffic began moving again. Josh was glad to be finished building houses in Spartanburg. Now he was ready to relax for a couple of weeks in the Blue Ridge Mountains. The drive home would take about two hours on Interstate 26.

When Josh got home, he'd pack the tent, sleeping bags, food, and cooking gear in the truck. Then he'd pick up his son, David. They'd be together for the whole weekend in a secluded mountain woodland with no one around for miles. They'd fish the streams and rivers with fly rods. The cool air and water would refresh his mind and spirit. Josh could already smell the freshly caught trout sizzling over an open fire.

10. From which point of view is the story told?

A. first person	C. David
B. second person	D. third person

11. Who is the protagonist in the story?

A. David	C. narrator
B. Josh	D. the mountains

12. The mood in this story is

A. humorous.	C. suspenseful.
B. sad.	D. relaxed.

13. Which statement best expresses the theme of the story?

A. The best fishing is trout fishing.
B. Josh builds houses for a living.
C. Josh and David are going for a fishing trip this weekend.
D. Everyone needs time to relax away from home.

PRACTICE 7: STRUCTURAL DEVICES

A. Passage Practice. Read this passage from *The Red Badge of Courage*. Identify the **plot, character (s), setting, point of view, mood, and theme** in the passage. Then compare your answers with your classmates.

Upon his fellows he beamed tenderness and good will. "Gee! ain't it hot, hey?" he said affably to a man who was polishing his streaming face with his coat sleeves.

"You bet!" said the other, grinning sociably. "I never seen such dumb hotness." He sprawled out luxuriously on the ground. "Gee, yes! An' I hope we don't have more fightin' till a week from Monday."

There were some handshakings and deep speeches with men whose features were familiar, but with whom the youth now felt the bonds of tired hearts. He helped a cursing comrade to bind up a wound of the shin.

But, of a sudden, cries of amazement broke out along the ranks of the new regiment. "Here they come ag'in! Here they come ag'in!" The man who had sprawled upon the ground started up and said, "Gosh!"

The youth turned quick eyes upon the field. He discerned forms begin to swell in masses out of a distant wood. He again saw the tilted flag speeding forward.

The shells, which had ceased to trouble the regiment for a time, came swirling again, and exploded in the grass or among the leaves of the trees. They looked to be strange war flowers bursting into fierce bloom.

B. Team Activity. Review 1 or 2 stories or plays you have read in class. Each team writes a **structural device** on the front of 5 × 8 cards and an **example** of the device from the literature selection on the back of the cards. The leader flashes either side of the card to the opposing team, and team members must identify the other side. For instance, if the leader flashed an example, the team members would have to identify the structural device.

C. Mood. Review the types of moods learned in this chapter. Which ones would accurately describe the mood in the short stories and poems in your literature book. Which types of moods would apply to these selections?

D. Theme. Divide your class into teams. Then focus on 3 or 4 stories or poems that all your classmates have read. On 5 × 8 cards, write both valid and invalid themes. Then shuffle the cards. A quizmaster flashes a card before each team. The team decides whether it will support or reject the theme, giving reasons for the answer. The team with the most points is the winner.

E. Literature Practice. Read or listen to several of your favorite short stories or poems or some from the list below. Then answer the accompanying questions about structural devices.

Short Stories

Poe's "Masque of the Red Death"
London's "To Build a Fire"
Thurber's "Secret Life of Walter Mitty"
Henry's "The Gift of the Magi"

Poems

Poe's "The Raven"
Brooks' "The Bean Eaters"
Ortez's "My Father's Song"
Shakespeare's "All the World is a Stage"

Questions

1. What is the plot? What are the conflicts? What is the climax? Do any events foreshadow the outcome or build suspense?
2. Who are the characters? Who is the protagonist? Who is the antagonist? Is there a narrator? Is there dialogue? Why is it important?
3. How do the setting and mood affect the plot and characters?
4. What is the theme of the story or poem? Would you change the ending? Why? Why not?

RHETORICAL DEVICES

Rhetorical devices are ways of expressing ideas that are unusual. Writers use rhetorical devices to achieve special effects in a passage. Authors achieve these effects by the way they arrange their words.

In this part of the chapter, you'll be learning about rhetorical devices. These devices can be found in **poetry, stories, essays, speeches, editorials, and advertisements**. Here are some important rhetorical devices used in literature.

alliteration	**onomatopoeia**
analogy	**personification**
euphemisms	**rhyme**
hyperbole	**simile**
metaphor	

Take some time now to learn about these rhetorical devices. Study these devices. Then you'll apply what you've learned to some sample passages.

Rhetorical Devices

alliteration - the repetition of the same consonants in lines of poetry or prose. Examples: 1) "Droning a drowsy syncopated tune,"– Langston Hughes (repetition of "d" and "o" sounds). 2) "I like to see it lap the miles. / And lick the valleys up," – Emily Dickinson (repetition of l sounds)

analogy - a comparison between two things or ideas. Examples: comparing life to a journey, comparing students in a school to the members of a family.

euphemisms - using mild words to describe something instead of using offensive or sexist words. Examples: 1) **passed away** for died 2) **perspire** for sweat
3) **restroom** for bathroom 4) **sanitation engineer** for trash man.

hyperbole - exaggeration to create an effect. Examples: 1) "I would rather die than eat Brussels sprouts!" 2) I was so surprised you could knock me over with a feather!

metaphor - direct comparison between two unlike things without using the words "like" or "as." Examples: 1) The sun was a ball of fire.
2) "Life is but an empty dream!" Longfellow

onomatopoeia - words whose sound suggests their meaning. Examples: 1) **splash, buzz, hiss, boom** 2) "The moan of doves in immemorial elms; / And murmuring of innumerable bees," Tennyson

personification - giving human qualities to something not human. Examples: 1) "As she sang softly at the evil face of the full moon." Jean Toomer 2) "The oak trees whispered softly in the night breeze." John Steinbeck

rhyme - occurs when the last words have the same sounds. Examples: 1) "The old horse thrust his long head out, / And grave with wonder gazed about:" Whittier **(out** and **about** rhyme.)
2) "Happy the man who, safe on shore, / Now trims, at home, his evening fire; / Unmov'd, he hears the tempests roar, / That on the tufted groves expire:" "The Hurricane" by Philip Freneau (rhymes are on **shore/roar** and **fire/expire)**

simile - comparison between two things using "like" or "as." Examples:
1) "Sometimes I feel **like** a motherless child" - African-American Spiritual
2) "My love is **like** a red, red rose" Robert Burns.
3) Free **as** a bird.

Tips for Understanding Rhetorical Devices

1. **Study the definitions and examples of:**

   alliteration, analogy, euphemisms, hyperbole, metaphor, onomatopoeia, personification, rhyme, and simile.

2. **Complete the following practice passages.**
3. **Apply them to the exercises at the end of this chapter.**

PRACTICE 8: RHETORICAL DEVICES

Directions: For practice, read each of the following passages. Then, answer the questions about rhetorical devices.

You ought to see my Cindy
She lives way down south;
She's so sweet the honey bees
Swarm around her mouth.
Oh, Cindy is a pretty girl.
Cindy is a peach;
She threw her arms around my neck.
And hung on like a leech.

And if I were a sugar tree
Standing in the town
Every time my Cindy passed
I'd shake some sugar down.

– Traditional Folk Song

1. Write down the words that **rhyme** in this song. ______________________________

____

2. Which of the following lines from the song contain a **hyperbole?**

A. lines 1-2
B. lines 3-4
C. lines 5-6
D. lines 9-10

3. Which of the following lines are an example of a **metaphor?**

A. line 5
B. line 6
C. line 7
D. line 8

4. Which of the following lines are an example of a **simile?**

A. line 5
B. line 6
C. line 7
D. line 8

5. Cite some examples of **alliteration** in the song. ______________________________

____

Common Sense

(In 1776, Thomas Paine wrote a pamphlet urging Americans to fight for independence from England. This paragraph is taken from it.)

"The heart that feels not now is dead; the blood of his children will curse his cowardice who shrinks back at a time when a little might have saved the whole, and made them happy. I love the man that can smile in trouble, that can gather strength from distress, and grow brave by reflection. 'Tis the business of little minds to shrink; but he whose heart is firm, and whose conscience approves his conduct, will pursue his principles unto death. My own line of reasoning is to myself as straight and clear as a ray of light. Not all the treasures of the world, so far as I believe, could have induced me to support an offensive war, for I think it murder; but if a thief breaks into my house, burns and destroys my property, and kills or threatens to kill me, or those that are in it, and to "bind me in all cases whatsoever" to his absolute will, am I to suffer it?"

– Thomas Paine *Common Sense*

6. List examples of alliteration in the passage. ______________________________

____

____

7. Which lines in the passage contain an **analogy?**

A. 1-2
B. 3-4
C. 5-7
D. 8-10

8. In your own words, describe the analogy. ______________________________

____

9. Which line in the passage is an example of **personification?**

A. 1
B. 2
C. 3
D. 6

10. Explain why your choice is a personification. ______________________________

____

11. Which line in the passage is an example of a **simile?**

A. 5
B. 6
C. 7
D. 8

We Wear the Mask

We wear the mask that grins and lies,
        It hides our cheeks and shades our eyes, –
This debt we pay to human guile;
With torn and bleeding hearts we smile,
And mouth with myriad subtleties.

Why should the world be over-wise,
In counting all our tears and sighs?
Nay, let them only see us, while
        We wear the mask.

We smile, but O great Christ, our cries
To thee from tortured souls arise.
We sing, but oh the clay is vile
Beneath our feet, and long the mile;
But let the world dream otherwise,
        We wear the mask!

– Paul Laurence Dunbar

12. Line 4 of this poem is an example of ______________________.

13. What does the author personify in line 14? ______________________________

14. Cite two examples of alliteration in the first stanza. ______________________________

____

15. Why are "sighs" (line 7) and "cries" (line 10) examples of onomatopoeia? ____________

____

____

Tips for Answering Questions About Structural and Rhetorical Devices

1. **Read the literary selection at least twice.**
2. **Try to summarize the selection in your own words.**
3. **Decide which answer best describes the structural or rhetorical device you are asked to find.**
4. **Choose your answer, and then confirm it by going back to the selection.**

PRACTICE 9: RHETORICAL DEVICES

A. **Passage Practice.** Locate rhetorical devices in poems or stories from your literature book. Identify **alliteration, analogy, euphemism, hyperbole, metaphor, onomatopoeia, personification, rhyme,** and **simile** in any passage. Then compare your answers with your classmates.

B. **Media Search.** Find examples of rhetorical devices in magazines, newspapers, ads, poetry, stories, speeches, or editorials. Clip them out, and attach them to a paper summarizing the use of each device in 1-2 sentences. Exchange your examples with a partner or in a group. Then see if they can find the rhetorical device without looking at your answers.

C. **Creative Writing.** Write a poem based on your reflections of photos or paintings. Then create metaphors, similes, onomatopoeia, hyperbole, etc. from your reflections. For example, if you write a poem about life, you might begin "Life is a roller coaster." Or you could describe a photo of a donut as "Donuts are delightfully delicious."

D. **Team Activity.** Do an activity like Practice 7B with rhetorical devices from poetry.

E. **Collage.** Create a collage based on the statement: ____ is like ____. (Examples: Life is like _____; Friday is like _____; etc.) Cut out pictures that reflect your feelings on the subject. Then paste them on a posterboard and describe your poem collage to the class.

TYPES OF LITERATURE

Writers use many different forms of literature to communicate their messages. Some of these forms have been used for centuries while others are more recent inventions.

Fiction - narrative writing drawn from the imagination rather than from history or fact. The term is most frequently associated with novels and short stories. There are many examples. They vary from "The Lady or the Tiger?" to *Gulliver's Travels.*

Nonfiction - factual writing which is meant to inform the reader. Examples include newspaper or magazine articles and speeches.

Biography - a written account of a person's life; a life history. Examples include William Roper's *Life of Sir Thomas Moore* and Kroeber's *Ishi, Last of His Tribe.*

Autobiography - the story of a person's life as written by that person. One famous example is Helen Keller's *The Story of My Life.*

Fantasy - a written work that takes place in an exaggerated world with bizarre characters in it. Example: J.R.R. Tolkien's *Lord of the Rings* trilogy.

Science Fiction - a written work in which scientific facts, assumptions, or hypotheses form the basis of adventures in the future, on other planets, or in different dimensions of time and space. Example: Ray Bradbury's *Fareinheit 451.*

Mystery - a term used to designate a work in which mystery or terror plays a controlling part. Example: Sherlock Holmes's *Hound of the Baskervilles.*

Romance - written works describing extravagant places, remote locations, heroic events, and passionate love. Examples: Hawthorne's *The Scarlet Letter* and Fitzgerald's *The Great Gatsby.*

Allegory - a device used to convey a deeper meaning based on the actions of the characters. It is considered an extended metaphor comparing a story with another meaning outside of the story. Examples include the parables of Jesus, John Bunyan's *Pilgrim's Progress*, and Orwell's *Animal Farm.*

Novel - any extended fictional narrative almost always written in prose. Examples: James F. Cooper's *The Last of the Mohicans* and Stephen King's *It.*

Short Story - a story varying in length from 500 to 15,000 words. Generally, these stories contain a plot and reveal the characters in the story through actions and thoughts. Examples of these include Chaucer's *Canterbury Tales*, Mark Twain's "The Celebrated Jumping Frog of Calaveras County," and Richard Connell's "The Most Dangerous Game."

Epic - a long narrative poem in elevated style presenting characters of high position in adventures, always including a central heroic figure. Examples include Homer's *The Odyssey* and the Old English *Beowulf.*

Fable - a brief tale told to point a moral. The characters are frequently animals, but people and inanimate objects can also be central. Examples include George Orwell's *Animal Farm* and Joel C. Harris's *Uncle Remus* stories.

Tall Tale - a humorous tale common on the North American frontier. Tall tales use realistic detail and a literal manner to explain seemingly impossible deeds and events. Usually, these events are accomplished by a superhuman character. Examples include the legends of Paul Bunyan and Pecos Bill.

Poem - concentrated words expressing strong feeling. A *poem* can also be spoken. It contains significant meaning, sense impressions, and figurative language. Poets write poems for emotional pleasure in stanzas and for the beauty of the word combinations. Examples include "Psalm 51," Robert Frost's "The Road Less Traveled," and Hughes's "A Dream Deferred."

Folk Tale - a simple story set in the past. These stories contain animal, human, or superhuman characters. Supernatural events are included which resolve conflicts. Often, events in folk tales happen in threes. A good selection of folk tales can be found in *Grimm's Fairy Tales*.

Myth - a story with supernatural characters and events used to explain religious beliefs or rituals. Myths are also written to explain certain natural phenomena. The journey of the Greek goddess, Persephone, to the underworld, for example, is used to explain the changing of the seasons.

Legend - a story associated with some period in the history of a people or nation. The story is written to glorify a human hero or an object that has significance to a people. Examples include *The Iliad* and *The Odyssey*.

PRACTICE 10: TYPES OF LITERATURE

Directions: Read the following passages. Circle the type of literature you are reading, and then explain why you selected your answer.

The Fox and the Grapes

A hungry fox came into a vineyard where there hung delicious clusters of ripe grapes. His mouth watered to be at them; but they were nailed up to a trellis so high, that with all his springing and leaping he could not reach a single bunch. At last, growing tired and disappointed, the fox said, "Let someone else take them! They are but green and sour; so I'll leave them alone."

– Aesop (ca. 6th century B.C.)

1. myth   fable   fantasy

2. Why did you select this answer?____

____

The First Woman

Once there was a beautiful woman who lived in a pleasant valley on the earth. The rest of the world was filled with rocks and mountains. In this valley, summer was the ruling season, and honey and fruit were always available. Her only companions were the beaver and the doe. She was the reigning spirit of this world, and nothing ever grew old or died.

One morning the woman followed a scarlet butterfly to a remote waterfall where the butterfly disappeared. Realizing she was lost, the woman fell asleep from exhaustion. When she woke, a being like herself stooped down and lifted her off the ground. Clothed in a robe of clouds, the man being told her he saw her as he traveled across the sky.

Because he rescued her, the man being had broken the command of the Great Spirit. He would remain on earth and share her companionship. For many moons, they lived happily in the valley. The woman bore a child. Sad because he broke the law, the man sought the guidance and forgiveness of the Great Spirit. The Great Spirit took pity on the man and the woman. He opened up many more valleys and plains for the future inhabitants, but because of the broken command, the Great Spirit caused the man and woman to labor for their food. They would also suffer from cold, grow old, and die when their heads became white as the feathers of swans.

3. myth nonfiction autobiography

4. Why did you select this answer? ______________________________

____

Ancient Forest Rises from Italian Clay

Workers were digging for clay to supply a tile factory in Italy's Umbria region when they struck wood-old tree trunks, in fact. Upright but listing like Pisa's tower, they looked, felt, and even smelled like living trees.

But these relatives of modern sequoias and bald cypresses are about two million years old. Buried by an ancient earthquake, they were preserved by the moist clay. Sixty trees, some of them five feet in diameter and 26 feet high, have been exposed on a 25-acre site near Perugia; the tops of three dozen more break the surface. No sequoias, nor anything resembling them in the family called Taxodiaceae, live in Italy today, suggesting that the climate used to be far damper.

Exposure to air has led to some decay of the trees. "The primary object is to find some way to preserve them," says the site director, Sergio Vergoni of Umbria's archeological superintendency. His team has erected roofs over the trunks to provide protection from the elements and is monitoring their status.

Analysis of the trees revealed that some lived for a thousand years. "They are not petrified," Vergoni says, "They are wood; they still could be burned."

5. allegory biography nonfiction

6. Why did you select this answer? ______________________________

____

My Bondage and My Freedom

"Make a noise," "make a noise," and "bear a hand," are the words usually addressed to the slaves when there is silence amongst them. This may account for the almost constant singing heard in the Southern states. There was, generally, more or less singing among the teamsters, as it was one means of letting the overseer know where they were, and that they were moving on with the work. But, on allowance day, those who visited the great house farm were peculiarly excited and noisy. While on their way, they would make the dense old woods, for miles around, reverberate with their wild notes. These were not always merry because they were wild. On the contrary, they were mostly of a plaintive cast, and told a tale of grief and sorrow. In the most boisterous outbursts of rapturous sentiment, there was ever a tinge of deep melancholy. I have never heard any songs like those anywhere since I left slavery, except when in Ireland.

– Frederick Douglass

7. fable autobiography tall tale

8. Why did you select this answer?____

____

Dr. North

So Dr. North left his secret mark upon the neighborhood– as all of us do, for good or for ill, upon our neighborhoods, in accordance with the strength of that character which abides within us. For a long time I did not know that it was he, though it was not difficult to see that some strong good man had often passed this way. I saw the mystic sign of him deep-lettered in the hearthstone of a home; I heard it speaking bravely from the weak lips of a friend; it is carved in the plastic heart of many a boy. No, I do not doubt the immortalities of the soul; in this community, which I have come to love so much, dwells more than one of John North's immortalities– and will continue to dwell. I, too, live more deeply because John North was here.

He was in no outward way an extraordinary man, nor was his life eventful. He was born in this neighborhood: I saw him lying quite still this morning in the same sunny room of the same house where he first saw the light of day. Here among these common hills he grew up, and save for the few years he spent at school or in the army, he lived here all his life long.

In old neighborhoods and especially farm neighborhoods, people come to know one another– not clothes knowledge, or money knowledge– but that sort of knowledge which reaches down into the human springs of human character.

9. science fiction romance biography

10. Why did you select this answer?____

____

The Comeback of Rabies

Rabies, a deadly disease to both animals and humans, is on the increase in many areas of Florida. In fact, the number of reported human exposures to rabies has not been as high since the 1940s. This particular strain of rabies was brought to Florida by Texas coyotes. Truckloads of these coyotes are imported into the state by hunting clubs and are used in fox hunts. The disease has always been found among wild animals, but the real problem is that fewer than half of all dogs, cats, and farm animals have been vaccinated against it. In 1994, twenty cats, ten dogs, and three horses contracted rabies, an increase of 500% in the last five years. Domestic animals must be vaccinated, for they are the ones most likely to have contact with humans.

11. nonfiction   epic   novel

12. Why did you select this answer?______________________________________

____

Mark Twain

Mark Twain was the pen name of Samuel Clemens. Clemens was born in 1835 in Florida, Missouri. When he was four, his parents moved to the town of Hannibal, Missouri, where he experienced some of the adventures he wrote about in his novels *Tom Sawyer* (1876) and the *Adventures Of Huckleberry Finn* (1884). These two novels are some of his best known works and are still enjoyed over 100 years later by children and adults around the world.

In his 20s, Clemens was an apprentice pilot on a Mississippi River steamer. Life didn't just stop there. With the West opening up, he followed and went to California. This is where he won literary success with his reading and journalism. In San Francisco, he began his career as a lecturer, delighting audiences with his manner and wit. By the late 1860s, he traveled Europe and the Middle East and wrote about these trips in *Innocents Abroad.*

After some financial ups and downs, Clemens built a mansion in the 1890s, now a museum at Redding Connecticut, where he passed away in 1910, at the height of his fame. Clemens' legacy to the world is his literary style which produced several wonderful books, many more than are mentioned here. Readers of all ages should choose books by Mark Twain. They are some of the best stories written.

13. fiction   biography   mystery

14. Why did you select this answer?______________________________________

____

You ought to see my Cindy
She lives way down south;
She's so sweet the honey bees
Swarm around her mouth.

Oh, Cindy is a pretty girl.
Cindy is a peach;
She threw her arms around my neck.
And hung on like a leech.

And if I were a sugar tree
Standing in the town
Every time my Cindy passed
I'd shake some sugar down.

15. nonfiction   folk tale   poem

16. Why did you select this answer? ____

____

The Hunter

A hunter had been all day looking for deer in the mountains without success until he was completely tired out and sat down on a log to rest and wonder what he should do. A buzzard, a bird which always has magic powers, came flying overhead and spoke to him, asking him what was his trouble. When the hunter had told his story, the buzzard said there were plenty of deer on the ridges beyond if only the hunter were high up in the air where he could see them. The buzzard proposed that they exchange forms for a while. The buzzard would go to the hunter's wife while the hunter would go to look for deer. The hunter agreed, and the buzzard became a man and went home to the hunter's wife, who received him as her husband, while the hunter became a buzzard and flew off over the mountain to locate the deer.

After staying some time with the woman, who thought always it was her real husband, the buzzard excused himself, saying he must go again to look for game, or they would have nothing to eat. He came to the place where he had first met the hunter and found him already there, still in buzzard form, awaiting him. He asked the hunter what success he had had, and the hunter replied that he had found several deer over the ridge, as the buzzard had said. Then the buzzard restored the hunter to human shape and became himself a buzzard again and flew away. The hunter went where he had seen the deer and killed several, and from that time on, he never returned empty-handed from the woods.

17. nonfiction   legend   folk tale

18. Why did you select this answer? ____

As the old man walked the beach at dawn, he noticed a young man ahead of him picking up starfish and flinging them into the sea. Finally, catching up with the youth, he asked why he was doing this. The young man explained that the stranded starfish would die if left until the morning sun.

"But the beach goes on for miles, and there are millions of starfish," commented the old man. "How can your effort make any difference?"

The young man looked at the starfish in his hand and then threw it safely in the waves. "It makes a difference to this one," he said.

– Anonymous

19. allegory fantasy autobiography

20. Why did you select this answer? ______________________________

____

CHAPTER 7 REVIEW

Read the following poem, and answer each question.

Sympathy

I know what the caged bird feels, alas!
When the sun is bright on the upland slopes;
When the wind stirs soft through the springing grass
And the river flows like a stream of glass;
When the first bird sings and the first bird opes,
And the faint perfume from its chalice steals-
I know what the caged bird feels!

–Paul Laurence Dunbar

1. Which point of view is used in this stanza? ______________________________

2. In your own words, state the theme or message of this poem. ____________________

____

3. Write the line in this poem that is a simile. Then explain why it is a simile. __________

____

____

4. List two examples of alliteration in this poem. ___________________________

____

Directions: Read the following story carefully, and then answer the questions.

The Cave

Traveling into northern Alabama, four high school seniors began their journey. Chad, a football player; Doug, an apprentice auto mechanic; Steve, a deer hunter; and Mike, a computer whiz all had one thing in common: they ate together at lunch. For weeks, they had planned this trip. Winter break had just begun, so they were ready for high adventure. They purchased exit markers, rope, helmets, and cave lights attached to their helmets so they could see. Steve's father owned about 600 acres of land near the Alabama-Tennessee border. About a month ago, Steve saw an old cave he'd heard stories about and was just waiting for the best time to explore it.

It was one of the coldest days of the winter when they left in Chad's Jeep Cherokee. They parked the vehicle and had to walk about 2 miles in the forest before they reached the entrance. Mike screamed, "There's smoke coming out of that hole!" "Will you hush, you little book worm. Don't you know that caves are always warmer than the land in the wintertime? That's just mist!" Steve said. The cave entrance was slippery and muddy. Spiders crawled through the opening, and bats regularly flew in and out. Once they were past the entrance, however, there were no more bugs. "It sure is a lot warmer in here than it is outside," Doug muttered.

They crawled, jumped, and sloshed their way through the cave. Everyone was taken away by the beauty of the cave. Crystal stalactites and stalagmites dotted the cave floor and ceiling. Chad reached his hand out to grab one of the pretty crystal formations. "Don't you touch that," Steve yelled. "I've heard talk from long ago that there's some sort of cave guardian here. The story is that the Guardian is supposed to be real mean and nasty, and it strikes whenever someone tries to steal part of the cave's formations." Chad dropped his hand, and the group continued crawling forward.

A few minutes later, the passage opened up into a huge cavern. The ceiling was about 100 feet high. Beautiful crystal formations resembling amethyst and topaz were everywhere. Mike screamed when he tripped on a bone on the cave floor. "Don't worry, Mike, it was probably some animal that crawled down here and died a long time ago," Steve said. While the rest were occupied comforting Mike, Chad was carefully examining a two foot long crystal shard. He couldn't resist any longer. Chad reached up and started breaking the shard with his hands. Suddenly, a low growl filled the cavern. "What was that?" everyone asked. Two yellow eyes appeared out from a ledge near the ceiling. A voice was heard, saying "Get! Out!"

The group broke into a run. Steve was leading everyone else out of the cave. "Don't look back. Whatever you do, don't look back," he yelled. They could feel a presence behind them all the way to the cave's entrance. They stumbled through the forest,.and they were near exhaustion when they reached the jeep. Steve spoke, "Chad, get us out of here." Chad fumbled for his keys and jumped in. Steve heard something behind him. Then he saw the Guardian coming. Steve told everyone, "Mike and I are going to run in front of the jeep. When you see the Guardian, you'd better run it over."

Mike and Steve waited for the Guardian to catch up with them, scared out of their minds. Then, they dashed in front of the jeep. Chad waited until the spider creature was in front of him, pushed the gas pedal, and ran over the Guardian. A flash of blue light flared from beneath the jeep, and the guardian was nothing but a pile of big crab legs. "Let's get out of here for good," Steve said.

5. Who is the main character? ______________________________

6. Is the author's purpose to persuade, to cause doubt, or to relate an adventure? Explain your answer.

____

____

Cite examples of the following in this story.

7. foreshadowing ______________________________

____

8. conflict ______________________________

____

9. climax ______________________________

____

10. suspense ____

____

11. What lesson do the characters learn from their experience? ______________________

____

Directions: Read the following examples of propaganda. Then answer the questions.

Some people care about their smiles. Other people care about their teeth. Sparkle toothpaste cares about everyone's smiles and everyone's teeth. Its patented "Clean Smile" formula whitens teeth and brightens smiles. Bring some Sparkle into your life today!

12. What is the purpose of this advertisement?______________________________

____

13. What makes this ad propaganda? ______________________________

____

Directions: Read the poem "Work," and answer the questions below.

WORK

Work, work, my boy, be not afraid;
    Look labor boldly in the face;
Take up the hammer or the spade,
    And blush not for your humble place.

There's glory in the shuttle's song;
    There's triumph in the anvil's stroke;
There's merit in the brave and strong,
    Who dig the mine or fell the oak.

– Eliza Cook, 1879

14. What types of propaganda does the author use in this poem? ____________________

____

15. What makes this poem propaganda?______________________________

____

____

Directions: Read the poem below, and answer the questions.

No willing grave received the corpse
    of this poor lonely one; –
His bones, alas, were left to bleach
    and moulder 'neath the sun!

The night-wolf howl'd his requiem,–
    the rude winds danced his dirge;
And e'er anon, in mournful chime
    sigh's forth the mellow surge!

The spring shall teach the rising grass
    to twine from him a tomb;
And, o'er the spot where he doth lie,
    shall bid the wild flowers bloom.

But, far from friends, and far from home,
    ah, dismal thought, to die!
Ah, let me 'mid my friends expire,
    and with my fathers lie.

–Rufus B. Sage

16. What is the setting for this poem? ______________________________

17. Why was the poem written? ______________________________

____

18. Based on the first three stanzas, the point of view is ______________________.

19. The point of view changes in the last stanza. This point of view is ____________.

20. Personification is the main rhetorical device used in this poem. List two examples of personification in the poem.

____

____

Directions: Read this passage. Then answer the questions that follow.

Christera

Christera walked carefully between the yawning craters of Lovos. Moments before, her bubble rocket had crash-landed on a ridge of soft volcanic sand. Little was left of the vast meteor shower that carried her off course, hurling the rocket into this strange place. All that remained of her misfortune were flaming bits of meteors that still fell occasionally from the sky.

She stared into the black void of space. Somewhere out there was a burning cinder or perhaps a swirl of smoky debris. That was all one would find of the planet Earth. Because of the great A-War, she and thousands like her had sought a way out of annihilation. The famous bubble rockets were the answer, but only a few people had been able to secure them. She was sure the rest had perished.

Where were the others, she wondered? Did they reach the earth-like planet Geos, or did they too lose their way?

Ahead of her, Christera saw rocks of many colors, and they glowed. She heard an odd sound like water rushing over rocks. She listened more closely for other sounds. Suddenly, there was a noise like a squeal, perhaps human but possibly an animal. She was not sure. She pulled out her laser gun, stopped, and listened again. Was she safe or was she about to confront an alien? Christera did not know, but she was not going to take any chances.

21. What type of literature is this passage? List two reasons for your choice.

____

____

22. What is the author's main purpose in the passage? ____________________

____

23. Describe any conflicts in this story. ____________________________

____

____

24. Where does the story take place? ______________________________

25. What do you think will happen next in the story? In two to three paragraphs, write the rest of this story. Use your own paper.

READING PRACTICE EXAM 1

Read the passage, and answer the questions below.

1) Because he saw a boy with greater obstacles learning to swim, Tommy overcame his fears and swam. 2) After he mastered that movement, Daisy taught him how to kick his legs forward in the water. 3) Tommy began by holding his breath and plunging his body into the water. 4) Daisy, his swimming partner, taught him how to cup his hands and move them from over his head to his side in the water. 5) Twelve-year-old Tommy had never learned to swim, but when he saw a boy with cerebral palsy his same age learning to swim, he knew he had to try. 6) Finally, Tommy was swimming on his own.

1. Which of the following is the correct order of these sentences?

   A. 5-2-4-3-6-1
   B. 5-3-4-2-6-1
   C. 1-6-3-4-2-5
   D. 1-6-2-4-3-5

2. According to the passage, what does Tommy do after he learns how to move his arms in the water?

   A. Tommy saw a boy who had cerebral palsy learn how to swim.
   B. Daisy becomes his swimming instructor.
   C. Tommy learns how to kick his legs in the water.
   D. Tommy learns how to hold his breath while in the water.

Read the passage and answer the questions below.

1) Facing the east, Sherry saw the orange light of the sun rising. 2) Sherry wanted to watch the dawn today on a rocky hillside in the state park. 3) Shooting stars were visible from a meteor shower on the western horizon. 4) Sherry was taken away by the beauty of this moment. 5) Turning her gaze upwards, Sherry noticed the stars of the night sky were still visible. 6) Facing the west, Sherry saw that the night sky was still black in color. 7) The sun's rays were just beginning to illuminate the trees here. 8) The full moon shone brightly near the center of the sky.

3. If Sherry began looking east and then moved her eyes to the west, what is the correct order for this passage?

   A. 2-6-3-5-8-1-7-4
   B. 4-7-1-8-6-3-5-2
   C. 2-5-3-6-8-1-7-4
   D. 2-1-7-5-8-6-3-4

4. If Sherry began looking west and then moved her eyes towards the east, what is the correct order of the passage?

   A. 2-6-3-5-8-1-7-4
   B. 2-5-3-6-8-1-7-4
   C. 4-7-1-8-6-3-5-2
   D. 2-1-7-5-8-3-6-4

For questions 5-6, select the word that means the <u>same</u> as the underlined word.

5. The minister resolved the <u>conflict</u> between my two brothers.

   A. enjoyment
   B. agreement
   C. disagreement
   D. discussion

6. What new laws did the <u>legislature</u> pass this year?

   A. organization
   B. governing body
   C. democrats
   D. pioneers

For questions 7-8, select the word that means the <u>opposite</u> of the underlined word.

7. Brett's injury resulted in a <u>temporary</u> leave from the basketball team.

   A. long
   B. permanent
   C. limited
   D. brief

8. To <u>recruit</u> high school graduates, the United States Army offers good pay and benefits.

   A. enlist
   B. discourage
   C. contact
   D. discharge

For questions 9-11, select the word or phrase that matches the meaning of the underlined word.

9. Be <u>punctual</u> for your job interview tomorrow.

   A. on time
   B. well-dressed
   C. clean
   D. polite

10. Just a few years ago, computers were <u>massive</u> machines.

    A. complex
    B. rare
    C. large
    D. small

11. I felt so <u>inadequate</u> I almost wanted to leave.

    A. strong
    B. cool
    C. helpless
    D. ridiculous

12. Which of the following would most likely contain the gross national product of the United States?

    A. encyclopedia
    B. dictionary
    C. thesaurus
    D. atlas

13. George would like to find out the current asking price of a 1995 Jeep Cherokee. Where should he look to find this information?

A. dictionary
B. encyclopedia
C. newspaper
D. glossary

Read the passage. Select the best answer.

Try the new fragrance, Swan Song, just once, and you won't believe the results! With exclusively patented pheromones, this fragrance will attract handsome men to you wherever you are. Try it today and receive a complimentary Swan Song umbrella.

14. The propaganda in this advertisement convinces the reader to

A. go out on a date.
B. change her life.
C. buy an umbrella.
D. buy Swan Song perfume.

15. Which passage contains propaganda?

A. The labor union and Gramwell Corporation sat down at the bargaining table last week. The labor union is striking because it wants the company to hire a higher proportion of full-time employees. Gramwell Corporation, however, believes the company would not remain competitive or in business for long if it places more people on full-time status.

B. Vote for Courtney Hart in the next election. She's all heart when it comes to protecting the people from big business and big government. Her political record is perfect. She has worked the hardest to reduce corruption and the power of special interest groups at the state level. If you're trying to choose, it's not hard. Vote Hart!

C. Your vote is crucial on election day. Elect someone with a record of perfect attendance in all sessions of City Government. Elect the person with the most experience in this office. Compare the facts, and make the best choice.

D. Compare this candidate's experience with the opponent's. Compare the voting records on the crucial issues. Compare the amount of campaign contributions received by special interest groups. Be knowledgeable when you make your decision.

Read the poem. Select the best answers.

A Beautiful Girl Combs Her Hair

Awake at dawn
she's dreaming
by cool silk curtains

fragrance of spilling hair
half sandalwood, half aloes
windlass creaking at the well
singing jade

the lotus blossom awakes, refreshed
her mirror
two phoenixes
a pool of autumn light

– Stanzas I-III by Li Ho (about 810 A.D.)

16. What is the woman being compared to in this poem?

A. a mirror
B. a lotus blossom
C. a windlass
D. a phoenix

17. In the poem, "the lotus blossom awakes" means that

A. the flower is waking up.
B. the flower is opening its petals.
C. the girl is going to sleep.
D. the girl is waking up.

18. Which passage contains propaganda?

A. Grace Chisolm, a well-known psychic, had this to say about Batwing XR 71A. "It drives like a dream. I can definitely tell this car is going to redefine the future of the automotive industry." Like Ms. Chisolm, we at American Motors believe this sports car looks better, rides better, and feels better than anything else in its class.

B. Try all the other fine jewelry stores in the area. Then visit us. At Simpson & Hyde, we offer a selection of over 6,000 pieces of jewelry in every price range. Our staff undergoes two months of training before they are allowed to help customers like you. Compare and see the difference.

C. For overnight and 2-day deliveries of goods at the lowest price available, try Value Express. We promise to go 5% below the lowest quote for shipment in the Birmingham area. All packages are tracked with scanners to ensure accuracy in shipments.

D. When looking for the most knowledgeable travel agents, try Globe World travel. Each of our travel agents has personally been on the tours we offer. They can tell you what to see and what to avoid on your trips overseas. For experienced travel agents, try Globe World.

Gunther's Furlough

Gunther hurried home, his first furlough since they forced him to join. He couldn't wait to be in the arms of his wife for one night.

The bombs were rumbling off in the distance. The blackout made the once familiar streets seem like something from a horror movie. Bombed out buildings cast unfamiliar shadows in the streets where he once played ball. He must hurry. The rumbling was getting louder.

The police officer stopped him. "Let me see your identity card." Gunther opened his wallet. "Why are you away from your unit?"

"I have a one day pass to see my wife. I live four blocks from here."

"Let me see your pass."

Gunther reached in his coat pocket and produced the paper. "You'll find it's all in order, Sir. The bombs–is it like this every night?"

"Except when it's raining. It's only safe when it's raining. Have a good night," he said as he handed back Gunther's papers.

"Thank you, sir," Gunther yelled back as he started running down the street. The rumbling was getting louder now. He thought he could hear the whistle of the bombs as they dropped though the air. And then, they were dropping all around him. Fires started to light up the sky. He must get home to his Marlene. He must get home. Only two more blocks now.

He began to get a sick feeling as he turned the corner. The closer he got to home, the more he was overcome with dread. One more corner–there were people rushing to his house! It had taken a direct hit. He rushed into the crowd shouting "My wife! Has anyone seen my wife?"

We haven't seen anyone come out," an old man answered. Neighbors were hooking up hoses trying to put out the fire. The seventy year old frame house was going quickly. Suddenly Mrs. Heinrich shouted, "I heard a moan! Over here! Come quick!"

Gunther rushed to where an outside wall had fallen on a woman. He could see Marlene's face. Her eyes were closed. Gunther started to lift the wall by himself. Rescuers pitched in to help. He quickly grabbed his wife by the arms and pulled her out as the wall collapsed with a loud thud. The noise made Gunther's heart skip a beat as he realized how heavy was the timber that had fallen on Marlene.

19. What is the main idea of this story?

    A. Good will always triumph over evil.
    B. Love must face many challenges in the midst of a war.
    C. Gunther is happy that he will see his wife while on leave.
    D. Gunther's house caught on fire from a bombing.

20. Which of the following is the story's point of view?

    A. Gunther
    B. first person
    C. second person
    D. Marlene

21. Which of the following sentences is an example of foreshadowing in this story?

    A. "Let me see your pass."
    B. Gunther rushed to where an outside wall had fallen on a woman.
    C. The police officer stopped him.
    D. "I live four blocks from here."

Who Robbed The Zoo?

Only a rat would think of stealing from a zoo, but that's exactly what happened Tuesday. A thief with a gun robbed the cashier at the Daytonville Zoo just after closing. Over $5,000 in cash was taken.

According to the cashier and two witnesses, a woman in her 40's entered the main ticket booth and demanded all the cash from the zoo's safe. The robber also released two large rats from a bag to scare the cashier. The robber then fled on foot.

"I was never so scared in my life," said the cashier after the incident. Zoo officials were able to capture the rats later and feed them to the pythons.

Police were unable to catch the thief, but they believe that the woman planned the place and time of the robbery. Anyone having any information about the robber is asked to contact police.

22. Which of the following statements is a fact?

    A. "I was never so scared in my life," said the cashier.
    B. Only a rat would think of stealing from a zoo.
    C. They believe that the woman planned the robbery.
    D. A thief with a gun robbed the cashier at the Daytonville Zoo just after closing, police said.

23. Where did the story above take place?

    A. at a grocery store
    B. near the pythons
    C. at a ticket counter
    D. in a police station

State Playoffs Start Today

Five months ago, 220 high school football teams started their journey to the state championship. As of Friday, only three of the teams remain in the playoffs, and only one will become the state champion.

North Metro (15-1) plays Long Hill (13-1) for the class AAA title at 7 PM in Dodge Memorial Stadium. North Metro's star quarterback, Rob Sanders, leads the league in pass completions. He will be a challenge for the Long Hill Raiders, but Long Hill's offense will keep Sanders on his toes while he looks for openings in the line.

The winner of tonight's playoff will meet the undefeated Washington Warriors (14-0). Stunning victories in their last two games of the season make them the team to beat in the state. The final playoff will be next Saturday at Roger's Stadium in Jones County. A crowd of 8,000 spectators is expected, and WHIA will televise the game from the stadium.

24. Which of the following statements is an opinion?

    A. The final playoff will be next Saturday at Roger's Stadium in Jones County.
    B. Stunning victories in their last two games of the season make them the team to beat in the state.
    C. Rob Saunders leads the league in pass completions.
    D. As of Friday, only three of the teams remain in the playoffs.

Directions for a Science Experiment

1. Place a small amount of water in a glass dish.
2. Make a two inch diameter circle of sewing thread.
3. Float the thread on the water.
4. Sprinkle pepper on the water inside the circle.
5. Put one drop of a dish washing detergent in the circle.

25. According to the science experiment above, when should you sprinkle the pepper?

A. after adding dish washing detergent
B. before putting the water in the glass
C. after floating the thread on the water
D. at the beginning of the experiment

Directions for Cutting a Circular Cake

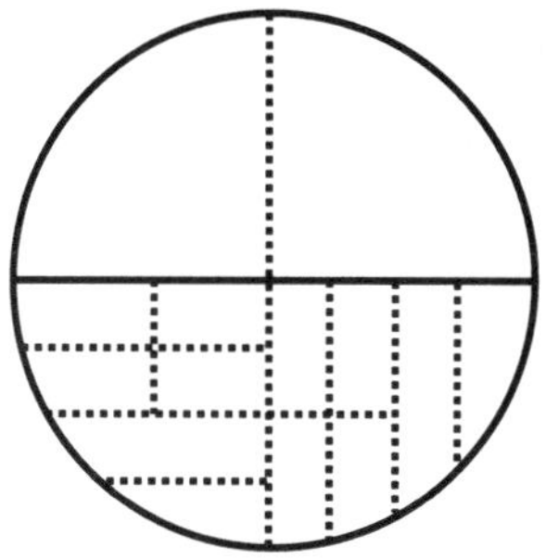

1. Allow the cake to cool, and then frost.
2. Cut cake into quarters.
3. Cut quarters into slices.
4. Pieces near the center can be cut in half.

26. According to the directions above, when should you cut the cake into quarters?

A. after the cake is cool and frosted
B. immediately after the cake comes out of the oven
C. after you cut the slices
D. last

Population Trends

The age structure will shift toward relatively fewer children and youth and a growing proportion of middle-aged and older people well into the 21st century. The decline in the proportion of children and youth reflects the lower birth rates that prevailed during the 1970s and 1980s; the impending large increase in the middle-aged population reflects the aging of the "baby boom" generation born after World War II; and the very rapid growth in the number of old people is attributable to high birth rates prior to the Great Depression of the 1930s, together with improvements in medical technology that have made it possible for most Americans to survive into old age.

Minorities and immigrants will constitute a larger share of the population of the United States in 2005 than they do today. Substantial increases in the number of Hispanics, Asians, and blacks are anticipated, reflecting net immigration and higher birth rates among blacks and Hispanics. Substantial inflows of immigrants, both documented and undocumented, are expected to continue. The arrival of immigrants from every corner of the world has significant implications for the labor force because immigrants tend to be of working age but of different educational and occupational backgrounds than the U.S. population as a whole.

27. Which age group will increase the fastest in the 21st century?

A. Hispanics
B. older people
C. children and youth
D. blacks

28. What is the author's purpose in writing this article?

A. to alarm the reader into action
B. to explain the population trends and shifts in the foreseeable future
C. to explain the problems associated with the aging of the population
D. to amuse the reader with interesting facts

Manned Space Flight

For thousands of years, we have dreamed of the day when we would explore the vast universe that surrounds our planet. This aspiration stemmed not only from our curiosity, but also from our fundamental thirst for knowledge and our readiness to accept a challenge.

When Orville Wright made the first powered airplane flight in 1903 at speeds of 50 kilometers (31 miles) per hour, the significance of his achievement was barely recognized. Yet in little more than half a century following that historic event at Kitty Hawk, we succeeded in orbiting the Earth at speeds measured in thousands of miles per hour and set foot on the Moon.

Viewed in terms of time and distance, the challenge of space exploration seems insurmountable. Yet, a review of the technological accomplishments of the 20th century indicated that what appears as "impossible" is merely "difficult." The exploration of space is following the pattern by which flight within the atmosphere was mastered. Each new development provides a platform from which to take the next step, and each step adds an increment of scientific knowledge, technological skill, and previously undreamed of benefits to mankind.

– **NASA**

29. The best statement of the main idea is that:

A. the space age began with the first powered airplane flight in 1903 at Kitty Hawk.
B. In the 20th century, advances in technology have provided many benefits to mankind.
C. past achievements in technology have made exploration of the universe now possible.
D. the launching of satellites into the universe is one of many accomplishments of the Space Age.

The Hunter

A hunter had been all day looking for deer in the mountains without success until he was completely tired out and sat down on a log to rest and wonder what he should do. A buzzard, a bird which always has magic powers, came flying overhead and spoke to him, asking him what was his trouble. When the hunter had told his story, the buzzard said there were plenty of deer on the ridges beyond if only the hunter were high up in the air where he could see them. The buzzard proposed that they exchange forms for a while. The buzzard would go to the hunter's wife while the hunter would go to look for deer. The hunter agreed, and the buzzard became a man and went home to the hunter's wife, who received him as her husband, while the hunter became a buzzard and flew off over the mountain to locate the deer.

After staying some time with the woman, who thought always it was her real husband, the buzzard excused himself, saying he must go again to look for game, or they would have nothing to eat. He came to the place where he had first met the hunter and found him already there, still in buzzard form, awaiting him. He asked the hunter what success he had had, and the hunter replied that he had found several deer over the ridge, as the buzzard had said. Then the buzzard restored the hunter to human shape and became himself a buzzard again and flew away. The hunter went where he had seen the deer and killed several, and from that time on, he never returned empty-handed from the woods.

30. In which order did the events in this selection occur?

A. The hunter flew over the mountains.
The buzzard became the hunter.
The hunter killed several deer.

B. The buzzard took on a human shape.
The hunter killed several deer.
The buzzard married the hunter's wife.

C. The buzzard became the hunter.
The hunter became the buzzard.
They returned to their original shapes.

D. The hunter and the buzzard exchanged shapes.
The hunter saw deer on the ridges.
The hunter returned empty-handed from the woods.

31. The hunter was tired because he

A. saw the buzzard in the sky.
B. could not find any deer.
C. killed several deer.
D. flew around the sky as a buzzard.

32. What is the main idea of this passage?

A. Buzzards live a better life than hunters.
B. The woman always thought the buzzard was her husband.
C. The buzzard and the hunter hunted deer together.
D. The buzzard helped the hunter find some deer.

33. The author's main purpose in writing this story is

A. to persuade
B. to share a personal experience.
C. to entertain
D. to describe feelings.

Wilma Rudolph

Nothing has been easy for Wilma Rudolph. Born in Clarksville, Tennessee, she was the twentieth of 22 children. Her mother worked as a domestic, and her father was a railroad handyman. As a child she suffered pneumonia, scarlet fever, and polio and wore a brace on her leg when she was six years old. It was not an auspicious beginning for an Olympic medal winner, but her mother's determined effort to take her to Meharry Medical College in Nashville for weekly treatment continued until she would walk.

Encouragement of track coach Ed Temple inspired her to run. Wilma ran in America, in Australia, and in the 1960 Rome Olympic games where she won three gold medals, broke two world records, and brought the crowd to its feet in waves of applause. When she joined the Women's Sports Hall of Fame in 1980, she became the first black woman to receive that honor and the first to so honor the Hall of Fame.

34. Which of the following statements is most likely true?

A. Wilma Rudolph preferred running to walking.
B. Wilma Rudolph grew up in a middle class family.
C. Wilma Rudolph always wore a brace.
D. Wilma Rudolph became a successful athlete.

35. Which of the following statements is an opinion?

A. Wilma Rudolph won three gold medals in the Rome Olympics.
B. Nothing has been easy for Wilma Rudolph.
C. Wilma brought the crowd to its feet in waves of applause.
D. Wilma wore a brace on her leg when she was six years old.

36. Wilma Rudolph came to Meharry Medical College for

A. rehabilitation.
B. track training.
C. a gold medal.
D. applause.

37. The author's purpose in this passage is

A. to amuse the reader about Wilma Rudolph.
B. to encourage women to become athletes.
C. to describe Wilma Rudolph's rise to fame.
D. to criticize people who make fun of handicaps.

Read the following map. Then answer questions 38 and 39.

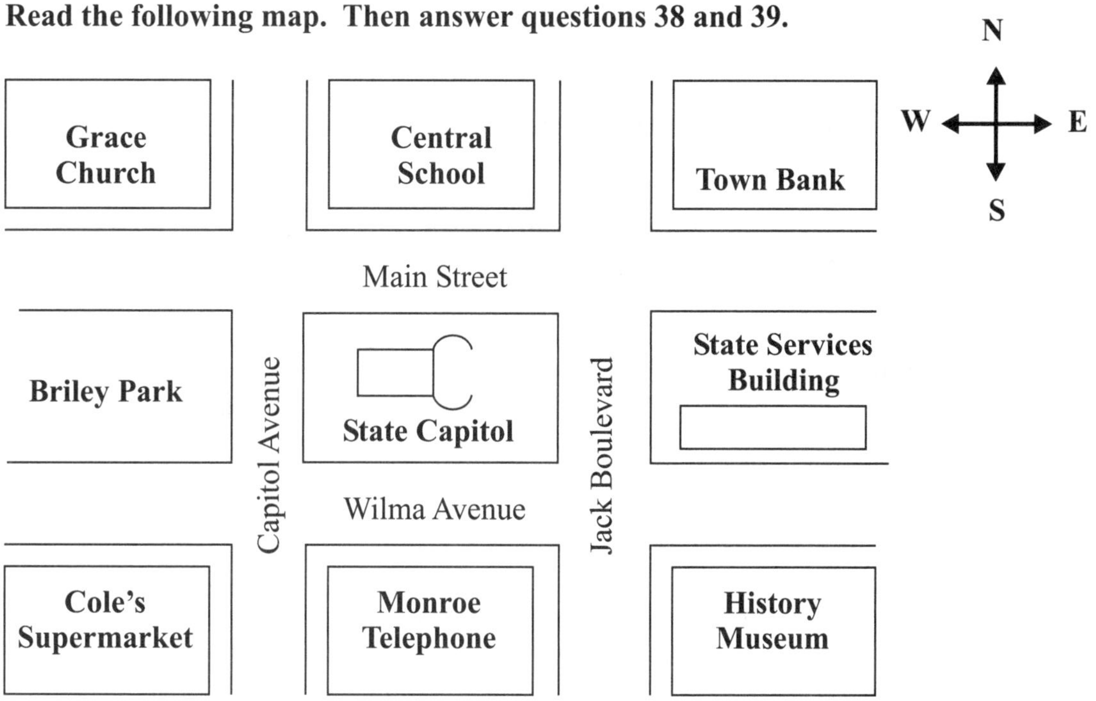

38. In what direction is the Museum from the Church?

    A. north
    B. southwest
    C. south
    D. southeast

39. If you walked from the Supermarket to the Bank, in which directions would you go?

    A. north, east
    B. east, west
    C. east, south
    D. west, north

Excerpt from the Declaration of Independence

…That whenever any Form of Government becomes destructive of these ends (Life, Liberty, and the pursuit of Happiness), it is the right of the People to alter or abolish it, and to institute new Government, laying its foundation of such principles and organizing its powers in such form, as to them shall seem most likely to effect their Safety and Happiness…

40. Based on this passage, which of the following conclusions is correct?

    A. Government, once established, can never be abolished.
    B. Three branches of government shall rule the nation.
    C. The government can be abolished or altered if it interferes with rights such as Life or Liberty.
    D. The rights of Life and Liberty are naturally acknowledged by all governments.

The Quest

Traveling at an easy canter through the forest of Esterwild, the human Kitiara was sitting astride her horse, Thunder. Her Dwarf friend, Regis, was riding beside her on a pony called Dancer. "Regis, when are we going to find that glowing herb, Canaris? Every day, the people of our village grow sicker from the Creeping Death," Kitiara remarked. "I know it's here. Drat it anyway. The stuff grew all over the place last year when I was here," muttered Regis. Dusk approached quickly, and the two lit torches to light their path through the all too quiet forest.

"Aha!" cackled Parsnip, "I am very poor troll, but soon I very rich!" He quickly closed his leather pouch, and the area around him grew dark. The troll glanced up and saw the two travelers approaching his way. "Mm...dwarf make tasty dinner and woman nice dessert."

The two didn't know what hit them. A large spear quickly dispatched Dancer, throwing Regis to the ground. The large troll pounced on him, clawing away at his armor to expose his back. Weaponless, Kitiara took Parsnip's large leather pouch from his belt. "Yoo Hoo!" she screamed. "I got your money." As she bolted, Parsnip turned around to give chase. Taking the opportunity, Regis threw his warhammer and neatly severed Parsnip's right arm. The troll screamed in agony, and Regis and Kitiara watched in horror as the one troll suddenly became two. Remembering an old nursery rhyme, Kitiara shouted, "Fire!" Both torches were hurled at the newly made trolls, and the forest was lit up with the sight of two trolls, their flesh crackling and popping into the night sky.

Opening Parsnip's pouch, Kitiara smiled with glee. The glow from the pouch bathed the two travelers in a warm light.

41. What happened after Kitiara opened the pouch?

    A. She saw Canaris in the pouch.
    B. She was warmed by the fire that killed the trolls.
    C. She found money to save the village.
    D. She was glad to have the troll's magic potion.

42. What caused Kitiara to search for the glowing herb, Canaris?

    A. This herb grows plentifully in the forest of Esterwild.
    B. Parsnip stole the Canaris, and Kitiara wants it back.
    C. Kitiara needs the herb, Canaris, to heal the villagers suffering from the Creeping Death.
    D. The dwarf, Regis, uses the herb to improve his strength.

43. When does the attack on Kitiara and Regis take place?

    A. at dawn
    B. at midnight
    C. in the early afternoon
    D. in the early evening

44. Which of the following is an example of foreshadowing in this story?

A. Her dwarf friend, Regis, was riding beside her on a Pony called Dancer.
B. "I know it's here."
C. Dusk approached quickly, and the two lit torches to light their path through the all too quiet forest.
D. Opening Parsnip's pouch, Kitiara smiled with glee.

45. Who is the protagonist in this story?

A. Parsnip
B. Kitiara
C. Regis
D. Dancer

46. What is the mood of this story?

A. lighthearted
B. lackadaisical
C. satirical
D. suspenseful

The TVA (Tennessee Valley Authority)

As the TVA (Tennessee Valley Authority), started in 1933, rushed its physical works to completion and developed its numerous coordinated applications of physical and social science, it became evident that in the Tennessee Valley, of all places, was emerging one of the marvels of the modern world. The event was as unimaginable and surprising as the rise of a Marxist socialist state in backward Czarist Russia had been earlier. It was something nobody would have predicted for the Tennessee Valley. Nevertheless, this unprophesied technological eruption made happy not only the immediate recipients of TVA blessings but also many anxious Americans who had begun to wonder whether the United States could adapt its political mechanisms to modern needs. Abroad, the totalitarian regimes were boasting about their efficiency. Theirs seemed to Americans a cruel efficiency, gained at the cost of liberty. The TVA, it was now said with pride, answered the totalitarian challenge. It proved that a democratic government could be even more efficient than a totalitarian regime. Yet this government could also be kind and good and not in any way oppressive.

47. According to the passage, why was the Tennessee Valley Project considered a marvel of the modern world?

A. The project was impressive.
B. The project was politically popular.
C. The project required millions of dollars.
D. The project combined technology and politics.

48. Which of the following statements is a valid conclusion for this passage?

A. The Tennessee Valley Project replaced the oppressive Marxist Socialist State.
B. The Tennessee Valley Project impressed many Americans.
C. The Tennessee Valley Project built many roads and bridges over a large area.
D. The Tennessee Valley Project improved the living standards of the United States and and Russia.

49. According to the passage, who benefitted from the Tennessee Valley project?

A. immediate recipients
B. the American people
C. the modern world
D. totalitarian regimes

50. Which of the following statements is a fact?

A. Totalitarian regimes thought that Americans were cruel in their efficiency.
B. The Tennessee Valley Authority was one of the marvels of the modern world.
C. Application of physical and social science created the Tennessee Valley Authority.
D. Democratic government is more efficient than a totalitarian regime.

Firewalking Made Easy

For centuries, people around the world have stood in awe of the ability of Eastern mystics to walk across burning coals with bare feet. "It's only physics," says John Campbell, a visiting professor from New Zealand.

At the University of Georgia, Dr. Campbell delivered a lecture entitled "The Physics of Firewalking." There are some things you can touch when they're red-hot, and charcoal is one of them," Campbell stated. The skin on the bottom of the foot is tough and comes into contact with the hot coals for only a second as you walk across them. Charcoal transports heat slowly so the heat in the middle of the coals isn't carried outward fast enough to burn your skin.

Campbell then prepared a 10 foot hot bed of coals in front of one of UGA's dormitories and demonstrated before a cheering audience. Many students and teachers took off their shoes and socks and followed him.

"The trick isn't mind over matter," Campbell said. "It's only common sense."

51. What was the author's purpose in writing the passage?

A. to teach a lesson
B. to motivate
C. to describe feelings
D. to share a personal experience

52. What is the main idea of this passage?

A. Dr. Campbell delivered a lecture on firewalking at the University of Georgia.
B. Hot charcoal transports heat slowly.
C. The nature of red-hot charcoal permits people to walk barefoot on burning coals without injury.
D. Many people respect the wisdom of Eastern mystics because they understand how charcoal burns.

53. From this passage, one can infer that John Campbell

A. lives in one of UGA's dormitories.
B. walks on hot coals frequently.
C. is a practicing physician from New Zealand.
D. is an authority on firewalking.

54. When did the students and teachers walk on the hot coals?

A. before the lecture
B. during the lecture
C. after the lecture
D. late at night

55. Where would you find alphabetized definitions of terms describing the body in a biology book?

A. table of contents
B. index
C. bibliography
D. glossary

56. Where would you look for a book on speed reading?

A. a card catalog
B. telephone directory
C. an atlas
D. Reader's Guide to Periodical Literature

Hand Grips

Hand grips can help give your arms those bulging forearms you're after, but only if they offer enough resistance. If you can squeeze them repeatedly for one to two minutes, and your hands don't get tired, they're too weak for you. You can keep buying stronger ones or make something at home that can do the same job.

Try tying a 3 pound barbell plate to a rope. Then drill a hole through the middle of an old rake handle. Standing straight with your feet one shoulder-width apart, roll the rake handle horizontally until the weight is lifted up. Then slowly unroll letting the weight back down. When this gets too easy, just add more weight. Doing this exercise three or four times each day will work your forearm muscles and help you in any sport where you throw or hit a ball. It will also give you an impressive handshake.

57. What is the author's purpose in writing the passage?

A. to entertain
B. to persuade
C. to describe an event
D. to instruct

58. What is the main idea of this section?

A. Keep buying stronger hand grips to improve your hand strength.
B. You can strengthen your grip with store-bought grips or a home-made variation.
C. Squeezing a rake handle 3-4 times a day is the best way to build your grip.
D. Lifting weights builds forearms the fastest.

59. What should you do before you roll the rake handle horizontally?

A. Insert the other end of the rope into the rake handle and tie it.
B. Drill a hole through the middle of the rake handle.
C. Stand straight with your feet one shoulder width apart.
D. Unroll the rope to let the weight down.

The Case of the Missing Video Game

Brian, Jeremy, Katie, and Allison were taking turns playing Brian's video game, *Sewer Monsters*. Allison told Katie, "You know, Katie, what's so great about us is that we share everything in common."

"Will you girls please play instead of talk?" Brian asked. The girls kept talking, so Brian and Jeremy went outside to shoot hoops. When they returned from the basketball game, Katie was doing her nails in her bedroom, and Allison was playing the video game. Allison went into the kitchen to grab a snack. Brian and Jeremy took this as an opportunity to go in the living room and play *Sewer Monsters*. However, the cartridge was missing from the game system.

"Girls!" they shouted. "The game is missing."

"Don't look at me," Allison said. "I just went into the kitchen." Allison's small purse, however, had a suspicious bulge in it.

"You know I couldn't have taken it," Katie said. "My nails are still wet, and I wasn't in this room when you two started shouting."

"I just don't like being accused," Allison said. "Come on, Katie, let's go outside." Slinging their purses on their shoulders, the two girls went outside together.

When the girls came back in, Jeremy and Brian both looked upset. Brian said, "OK, Allison, empty your purse."

Looking very mad, Allison said, "Fine then!" She turned her purse upside down, and there was no cartridge in the mess on the table.

Jeremy and Brian looked at each other and said, "Then who has the game cartridge?"

60. What is the best statement of the main idea in this passage?

A. Four siblings decide to play video games, basketball, and do their nails.
B. The four siblings try to decide who took the video game *Sewer Monsters*.
C. Brian and Jeremy play *Sewer Monsters* and basketball well.
D. Allison and Katie agree to share everything in common, including video games.

61. Based on the facts above, who now has the game cartridge?

A. Allison
B. Brian
C. Katie
D. Jeremy

62. What is the climax of the story above?

A. Allison dumps her purse out on the table.
B. Brian and Jeremy go outside to play basketball.
C. Allison plays *Sewer Monsters* in the living room.
D. Katie walks into her bedroom and paints her nails.

63. If the guide words Bland - Blevins were at the top of a page in the telephone book, which listing could be included on that page?

A.	Blair	C.	Blanton
B.	Blalock	D.	Bligen

64. If you were looking for the name Terrell in the telephone book, which words could you find at the top of the page?

A.	Tennison - Tharp	C.	Terza - Thackston
B.	Terryberry - Thisse	D.	Tener - Terranova

Participating Dentists

Stephen Campbell, DDS
John Glasser, DDS
Peggy King, DDS
Paul McLendon, DDS
D. Janet Taylor, DDS
Gary Terkiewicz, DDS
Leigh Thomaston, DDS
Marysia Triggs, DDS
Brenda Warner, DDS

65. Harry K. Telzig will be added to the alphabetized list of participating dentists in the dental plan. His name will be added between

A. Leigh Thomaston, DDS and Marysia Triggs, DDS.
B. Janet Taylor, DDS and Gary Terkiewicz, DDS.
C. Gary Terkiewicz, DDS and Leigh Thomaston, DDS.
D. Marysia Triggs, DDS and Brenda Warner, DDS.

66. The appendix is the part of the book that gives information on

A. supplementary material not essential to the text itself.
B. the author, title, and publication.
C. page references for names, places, and subjects in a book.
D. chapter titles and page numbers.

67. Cheetah is to mammal as iguana is to _______.

A.	amphibian	C.	reptile
B.	fish	D.	eagle

68. Justice is to unbiased as injustice is to _______.

A. falsehood
B. bravery
C. bribery
D. prejudiced

69. Salt is to pepper as sugar is to _______.

A. cinnamon
B. chocolate
C. milk
D. jelly

70. A clock is to time as a liter is to _______.

A. volume
B. coke
C. length
D. quart

71. During the 1880s and 1890s, Andrew Carnegie was a prominent leader in the steel industry and one of the richest men in the world. With his money, he established 1,681 libraries in urban centers across the United States. In 1956, the Library Services Act gave libraries strong federal support.

What would have likely happened if Andrew Carnegie had not promoted libraries in urban areas?

A. Libraries would have been more promoted in colleges and universities.
B. City libraries would have had to wait many decades before they were built.
C. Libraries would have flourished regardless of his help because everyone could read.
D. Libraries would have been built in the suburban United States.

Television Viewing Patterns

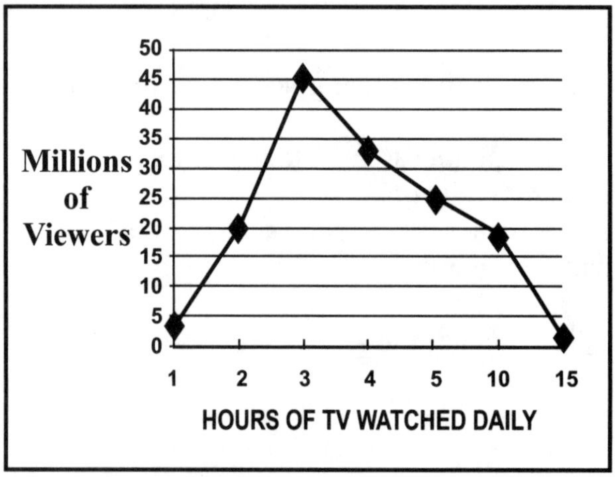

72. About how many viewers watch TV 5 hours per day?

A. 10 million
B. 15 million
C. 20 million
D. 25 million

The Cave

Traveling into northern Alabama, four high school seniors began their journey. Chad, a football player; Doug, an apprentice auto mechanic; Steve, a deer hunter; and Mike, a computer whiz all had one thing in common: they ate together at lunch. For weeks, they had planned this trip. Winter break had just begun, so they were ready for high adventure. They purchased exit markers, rope, helmets, and cave lights attached to their helmets so they could see. Steve's father owned about 600 acres of land near the Alabama-Tennessee border. About a month ago, Steve saw an old cave he'd heard stories about and was just waiting for the best time to explore it.

It was one of the coldest days of the winter when they left in Chad's Jeep Cherokee. They parked the vehicle and had to walk about 2 miles in the forest before they reached the entrance. Mike screamed, "There's smoke coming out of that hole!"

"Will you hush, you little book worm, don't you know that caves are always warmer than the land in the wintertime. That's just mist!" Steve said.

The cave entrance was slippery and muddy. Spiders crawled through the opening, and bats regularly flew in and out. Once they were past the entrance, however, there were no more bugs.

"It sure is a lot warmer in here than it is outside," Doug muttered.

They crawled, jumped, and sloshed their way through the cave. Everyone was taken away by the beauty of the cave. Crystal stalactites and stalagmites dotted the cave floor and ceiling. Chad reached his hand out to grab one of the pretty crystal formations.

"Don't you touch that," Steve yelled. "I've heard talk from long ago that there's some sort of cave guardian here. The story is that the Guardian is supposed to be real mean and nasty, and it strikes whenever someone tries to steal part of the cave's formations."

Chad dropped his hand, and the group continued crawling forward. A few minutes later, the passage opened up into a huge cavern. The ceiling was about 100 feet high. Beautiful crystal formations resembling amethyst and topaz were everywhere. Mike screamed when he tripped on a bone on the cave floor.

"Don't worry, Mike, it was probably some animal that crawled down here and died a long time ago," Steve said.

While the rest were occupied comforting Mike, Chad was carefully examining a two foot long crystal shard. He couldn't resist any longer. Chad reached up and started breaking the shard with his hands. Suddenly, a low growl filled the cavern.

"What was that?" everyone asked.

Two yellow eyes appeared out from a ledge near the ceiling. A voice was heard, saying "Get! Out!"

The group broke into a run. Steve was leading everyone else out of the cave. "Don't look back. Whatever you do, don't look back," he yelled. They could feel a presence behind them all the way to the cave's entrance. They stumbled through the forest and were near exhaustion when they reached the jeep.

Steve spoke, "Chad, get us out of here."

Chad fumbled for his keys and jumped in. Steve heard something behind him. Then he saw the Guardian coming.

Steve told everyone, "Mike and I are going to run in front of the jeep. When you see the Guardian, you'd better run it over."

Mike and Steve waited for the Guardian to catch up with them, scared out of their minds. Then, they dashed in front of the jeep. Chad waited until the spider creature was in front of him, pushed the gas pedal, and ran over the Guardian. A flash of blue light flared from beneath the jeep, and the guardian was nothing but a pile of big crab legs.

"Let's get out of here for good," Steve said.

73. Who incites the anger of the Guardian?

A. Derek
B. Mike
C. Steve
D. Chad

74. Where was the cave located?

A. Mike's father's property
B. on the edge of the forest
C. a state park in northern Alabama
D. two miles into the forest

75. What is the main idea for this passage?

A. Strong bonds of friendship can overcome any obstacle.
B. Exploring new environments is very satisfying.
C. Some people live in a world of fantasy.
D. Life is full of ordinary events.

76. Which describes the greatest conflict in this story?

A. Chad versus Steve
B. unity versus individuality
C. responsibility versus irresponsibility
D. Steve versus the Cave Guardian

77. In what section of the newspaper would you find reviews of the latest movies?

A. Entertainment section
B. Obituaries
C. Advertisements
D. Front Page

78. In the classified section of the newspaper you would find information about

A. the latest football draft picks.
B. election results.
C. powerboats for sale.
D. horoscopes.

79. In what section of the newspaper would you find funeral notices?

A. Sports section
B. Classified section
C. Front page
D. Obituaries

80. In the sports section of a newspaper, you would find information about

A. theater performances.
B. hockey scores.
C. refrigerators for sale.
D. the latest events around the world.

81. The <u>table of contents</u> is the part of the book that gives a list of

A. key words used in the book with their definitions.
B. page references of the names, places, and subjects in a book.
C. chapter titles and page numbers at the front of the book.
D. additional material not essential to the text itself.

82. Which part of the book would you use to learn the definition of "alchemy" ?

A. glossary
B. preface
C. appendix
D. bibliography

83. Which part of the book would you use to find a list of page references of the names, places, and subjects in a book?

A. glossary
B. index
C. preface
D. title page

Read the following passage. Then answer questions 84-86.

During the 1830s, fur trading reached its golden age in the unsettled West. However, it was a time of great danger. Competing fur companies, potentially hostile Native Americans, and the dangers of nature awaited "mountain men" at every turn. One of the legends from that time tells of Scott, a fur trapper, who got sick on a company expedition. He had to be carried. While traveling, he and two of his comrades became separated from the main group. The main group had established a meeting point in case of separation. When the three arrived there, the company had already left. Since Scott could not walk, his friends left him. They were out of supplies and had no weapons for food or protection. They overtook the main group after several days of fast traveling on foot. Scott was found dead when the company returned the following year.

84. What caused the two men to leave their wounded friend?

A. They were tired of carrying him.
B. They were afraid they would all die if they didn't catch up with the rest of the group since they had no food or weapons.
C. Their friend was sick, and they might catch a disease.
D. They wanted to walk fast.

85. Where did the story take place?

A. the mountains of Oregon
B. the California gold rush
C. the woods of the Midwest
D. the mountains of the West in the 1830s

86. Which is the best summary of the story?

A. Patience and perseverance are their own reward.
B. Survival in the Old West could mean making cruel life and death decisions.
C. Competition divides people from each other.
D. Some people want to die alone.

The Marquis de Lafayette: Hero of Two Revolutions

The French nobleman and soldier whose name is about three feet long, but who is commonly known as the Marquis de Lafayette, is a model of revolutionary spirit. A wealthy orphan, he was only 16 years old when he heard that the United States had declared independence from Great Britain. From the moment he heard the news, he determined to be part of the American fight for independence. Though very young, he disobeyed orders and sailed to America to be part of the Continental Army. He fought with General George Washington, who also became his friend.

Lafayette returned to France to convince the French to support the Americans in their fight. Because of his efforts, several French officers and troops sailed to America and fought with the Americans against England. One of these officers was Admiral Rochambeau, who, along with Lafayette and another French officer, brought about the defeat of the British in Yorktown. That was one of the most decisive victories of the American Revolution. For this reason alone, Lafayette has become an important figure in American history.

Lafayette had a noble and honest character, which won him the respect of his troops and of his countrymen. When he returned to France after the American Revolution, the French gave him a hero's welcome, calling him a "hero of two worlds." Lafayette hated the oppressive rule of kings and fought for the rights of people. While in France, he fought successfully for a more democratic form of government called the National Assembly. Later, he wrote and introduced to the Assembly the "Declaration of the Rights of Man and of the Citizen." That document was equivalent to the American Declaration of Independence. In fact, Thomas Jefferson helped Lafayette in writing it. The French Revolution against royalty soon followed, and France, after a few tumultuous years, followed in the American footsteps towards freedom.

Before he died, Lafayette became an honorary citizen of the United States. Both the Americans and the French deeply mourned his death in 1834. He was one of the greatest champions of liberty that ever lived.

87. Why did the Marquis de Lafayette sail to America at age 16?

A. He wanted to fight in the American Revolution.
B. He was only 16 years old and was seeking adventure.
C. He was an orphan and lived a lonely life in France.
D. America offered more freedom than France did.

88. From this passage, one could infer that

A. Lafayette's countrymen resented him for fighting for another country.
B. the French understood the American need for independence.
C. the French took pride in fighting the wars of other nations.
D. the French would adopt some of American culture as their own

89. Which statement best summarizes the main idea of the passage?

A. It takes help from foreign countries to win a revolution.
B. The Marquis de Lafayette lived a very exciting life and won a lot of admiration.
C. The Marquis de Lafayette was a man who lived and died for the cause of freedom.
D. The Marquis de Lafayette was a soldier who was not afraid of danger or defeat.

90. If you wanted to find out the approximate distance that Lafayette sailed from France to America, where would you look?

A. Thesaurus
B. encyclopedia
C. Bibliography
D. atlas

READING PRACTICE EXAM 2

Read the passage, and answer the questions below.

1) If you are buying a used car, also know the blue book value for the vehicle. 2) Most importantly, you should know what your budget is so that you shop for what you can afford. 3) Many people find it helpful to bring someone skillful in negotiations with them the first time they buy. 4) There are many points to consider when deciding to purchase a vehicle. 5) Also, make sure you drive the vehicle and have it inspected by a mechanic before you buy. 6) Finally, keep in mind that prices are negotiable, so try to drive the price down as low as possible. 7) Remember, find out all the facts because a car purchase is a very important decision. 8) Next, when you find a vehicle you like, check with Consumer Reports to find out its strong points and its weak points.

1. What is the correct order for the passage from most important to least important?

   A. 7-3-6-5-1-8-2-4
   B. 4-7-3-5-1-8-2-6
   C. 4-2-8-1-5-6-3-7
   D. 6-2-8-1-5-3-7-4

2. According to the passage, what is the last important thing to remember when purchasing a vehicle?

   A. Remember that the price of the vehicle is negotiable.
   B. Remember to write down the blue book value for the vehicle.
   C. Remember what your budget for a car is before you shop.
   D. Remember to check with Consumer Reports to find out the qualities of the vehicle.

Read the following passage, and answer the questions that follow.

1) Further out from the epicenter, people and buildings remained intact but suffered from radiation poisoning and burns. 2) When the United States dropped the atomic bomb on Hiroshima on August 6, 1945, the destruction was terrible. 3) The ground was heated to such an extent at ground zero that it melted and hardened like cement. 4) 129,000 people were killed in a four square mile area from ground zero. 5) Further out, the shock wave flattened all buildings in a ½ mile radius. 6) Up to one mile away, the blast cracked brick walls twelve inches thick. 7) Those that looked at the blast were permanently blinded by the intensity of the light. 8) The legacy of this bombing continues to be with us to this very day.

3. What is the correct order for this passage starting from the center of the blast and working outward?

   A. 2-1-7-4-6-5-3-8
   B. 4-6-2-7-1-3-8-5
   C. 8-3-5-6-4-1-7-2
   D. 2-3-5-6-4-7-1-8

4. According to the passage, how did the blast affect life beyond the four square mile mark from ground zero?

   A. It flattened all buildings.
   B. It caused the earth to melt and harden.
   C. People suffered from radioactive poisoning and burns.
   D. Massive fatalities were reported past this point.

The Madman

At last, when his wits were gone beyond repair, he came to conceive the strangest idea that ever occurred to any madman in the world. It now appeared to him fitting and necessary, in order to win a greater amount of honor for himself and serve his country at the same time, to become a knight adventurer and roam the world on horseback, in a suit of armor. He would go in quest of adventures, by way of putting into practice all that he had read in his books; he would right every manner of wrong, placing himself in situations of the greatest peril such as would make him famous to the eternal glory of his name. As a reward for his valor and the might of his arm, the poor fellow could already see himself crowned Emperor…and so, carried away by the strange pleasure that he found in such thoughts as these, he at once set about putting his plan into effect.

– Miguel de Cervantes, adaptation from *Don Quixote*

5. After reading the passage, one could conclude that

   A. someone can be focused on a mission, yet be mentally insane.
   B. the man in this passage will not likely become a great knight and conqueror.
   C. literally putting what you read into practice is always a good idea.
   D. the best way to serve your country is to ride the world on horseback.

6. In this passage, the writer suggests that following one's dreams

   A. means reaching for the highest goal.
   B. can also be a great way to escape reality.
   C. is the best way to achieve a healthy, happy life.
   D. requires quick action with little preparation.

Tons of Toads

The best laid plans of toads and men . . . In June 1935, Australia's sugar industry imported 101 cane toads from Hawaii in the hope that they would eat the cane beetles threatening the sugar crop. The toad, described by one as "ugly even by toad standards" did not have any interest in eating cane beetles. But it made itself at home. It now exists over half of Queensland and is spreading into New South Wales and the Northern Territory. A single female has been known to lay 54,000 eggs in a clutch, and females may lay eggs twice a year. Australia's toad population is now in the millions–and growing.

And the cane toad, which can grow to more than eight inches long, is dangerous. It eats baby snakes and frogs, and when other animals try to eat it, it secretes a poison that can kill a dog in 15 minutes. Even humans can die from ingesting the poison. Biologists have suggested introducing a parasite or disease to control the pests.

7. If the cane toad population is not controlled, what is most likely to occur?

   A. The number of cane beetles will increase.
   B. Biologists will find a parasite to kill the toads.
   C. Snakes and dogs will disappear in Australia.
   D. The cane toads will spread to other parts of Australia.

8. What is the best summary of the meaning of this passage?

   A. Australia's cane toad population is very large.
   B. Cane toads can lay 54,000 eggs at a time.
   C. Cane toads are poisonous and can kill humans.
   D. Cane toads were imported to Australia for one purpose, but they have become pests.

The World of Cyberspace

Is it a person, place, or a thing? Actually, cyberspace is the place where you communicate information using a personal computer and a telephone line. Persons, places, things, and ideas are the information generated in cyberspace. Other names for this world are the information superhighway or the electronic highway.

Why bother with cyberspace? Information 24 hours a day is one reason. Imagine an incredibly rich library of computer software available at any time of the day or night. Add to that newspapers, encyclopedias, magazines, games, discussion groups, and contests with prizes. Most importantly, you can connect with millions of people around the world.

You'd never have the chance to meet these people in the real world, but in cyberspace you can. Friendships and businesses can now operate in cyberspace whether you live in the United States or Korea.

What do I need to enter cyberspace? All you need is a personal computer, a modem which connects the computer to the telephone line, and an on-line service provider such as CompuServe, America On-Line, or Prodigy. Then you'll be ready to travel, join discussion groups, go shopping around the world, and make new friends too.

9. The best generalization of this passage is that

A. with a computer and a modem, you cannot access the world of cyberspace.
B. another name for cyberspace is the information superhighway.
C. encyclopedias and discussion groups are now available on CompuServe, America On-Line, or Prodigy.
D. cyberspace is the place where you can find people, places, things, and ideas.

Offer Education

In reference to the article on ending prison education plans, I find these "get tough" measures shortsighted and lamentable. Rather than denying educational opportunity, the prison system should incorporate educational incentives with work requirements. Illiteracy imprisons the mind and shackles human potential. While withdrawing funding for college classes, policy-makers should pledge to upgrade the GED program, even to make it obligatory for high school dropouts and to offer scholarship incentives.

Unfortunately, we are too ready to expend vast sums on incarceration but very little money on effective prevention and rehabilitation. The politics of vengeance is alive and well and self-destructive.

– Barbara Allen Kenney

10. Which of the following statements best describes the argument of the writer in the selection above?

A. The writer constructs a valid argument.
B. The writer explores only two sides of an issue.
C. The writer attacks the person rather than the problem.
D. The writer does not directly address the issue.

Lawyers

It is a plain fact that lawyers, instead of being the preservers of the rights of the people, are the great disturbers of their rights. They make it their special business to counsel men to all kinds of quarrels and fusses, so they can charge an exorbitant fee for defending persons from a difficulty they have gotten them into by their advice.

It isn't safe nowadays for a man of property to make a will and die, or die without one, for as sure as he does, a lot of lawyers will buzz around some of his heirs and get them to bust up the will. They will gather around that estate like so many hungry buzzards around a carcass, and they'll linger around it until every dollar is consumed, and then the poverty-stricken heirs can go to the Devil, for all they care. They are grand preservers of the people's rights, aren't they? Show me a single right that some of them have not trampled upon. I will admit there are a good many things a lawyer can do that will benefit some, once in a while, and also there are some very honorable lawyers, but not many. The great run of them are figuring all the time how they can thrive upon the misfortunes and errors of others.

– excerpt from *Shams* by John S. Draper

11. Which of the following statements best describes the argument of the writer in the above selection?

A. The writer believes most lawyers work for the people.
B. The writer wants to portray lawyers as impartial searchers of the truth.
C. The writer wants people to know that lawyers fight for your legal rights.
D. The writer feels that lawyers are greedy and work for selfish reasons.

12. Which of the following fallacies does this argument contain?

A. The writer attacks the personal life of lawyers.
B. The writer attacks the person rather than a group.
C. The writer jumps to conclusions.
D. The argument does not contain any fallacies.

Select the word that means the same as the underlined word.

13. Darnell's speech contained many concrete examples.

A. hard
B. colorful
C. specific
D. abstract

14. My uncle's fish stories are often exaggerated.

A. true
B. sad
C. hilarious
D. overstated

Select the word that means the opposite of the underlined word.

15. A majority of people in this state like baseball.

A. population
B. minority
C. large number
D. variety

16. The musicians gave an impressive performance.

A. amazing
B. interesting
C. lively
D. inferior

When a Friendship is Over

When you are a teenager, if there is one thing that you can count on in life, it is that people change. The person you are today is not the person you will be four years from now. And while you are busy changing, so are your friends. These changes can be painful. Any time you choose to care about another person, you risk a painful, but rarely fatal, broken heart.

Relationships grow and die. Friends grow in different directions. Boyfriends and girlfriends leave. Children grow up and move away. Parents die. We may even surpass the people we used to look up to. All these events can lead to pain.

Pain comes into everyone's life sooner or later. Painful experiences help us learn. When an important relationship ends, and you feel badly, allow yourself to experience that feeling.

It is appropriate to be miserable when you are. It's normal to cry and express your feelings. It's also possible to go to class, study, work, eat, sleep, get your laundry done, and feel miserable at the same time.

If the pain of a broken relationship is getting you down, do something nice for someone who isn't expecting it. When you make someone else smile-well, it can be contagious. If depression is a problem, exercise, study outside in the sunlight, call a friend and talk about it. Whatever you do, don't soak in the pain too long. Get up and do something.

If you feel severely depressed and stay that way, talk to a professional before it starts affecting your health. When friends and family can't help, most schools have counselors available. Take action. There is no need to let the end of a relationship keep you down.

17. According to the passage, how should you react if your relationship ends badly?

    A. Forget about it and go on in life.
    B. Seek professional help.
    C. Express your emotions to others.
    D. Find a way to get revenge.

18. After reading the passage, one would conclude that everyday activities can

    A. continue in spite of pain.
    B. help to regain happiness.
    C. become boring.
    D. indicate one's lifestyle.

19. Which of the following statements is a fact?

    A. Depression can affect your health.
    B. Severely depressed people should talk to someone.
    C. The problem causing depression will pass away.
    D. Parents die.

20. According to the passage, in every relationship you should prepare yourself for

    A. exciting, fun-filled experiences.
    B. the risk of painful changes.
    C. less time devoted to career.
    D. an increased, combined income.

21. According to the passage, what causes changes in relationships?

A. People get tired of each other.
B. Natural disasters, wars, and plagues
C. People move, die, or surpass the people they looked up to.
D. Getting a job

22. According to the passage, what is likely to happen if someone stays depressed?

A. His or her health will be affected.
B. Friends will avoid him/her.
C. He or she will sleep more.
D. He or she will attempt suicide.

For questions 23-26, select the word or phrase that matches the meaning of the underlined word.

23. <u>Fatigue</u> is more common in adults than children.

A. disease
B. energy
C. joy
D. weariness

24. Headache, nausea, and fever are <u>symptoms</u> of the flu.

A. signs
B. causes
C. purposes
D. principles

25. Studies of volcanoes provide unique opportunities to <u>decipher</u> how the earth was formed.

A. feel sorry for
B. disapprove
C. figure out
D. exaggerate

26. Her whispers were <u>inaudible</u> in the crowded mall.

A. heard
B. spoken
C. unheard
D. loud

Pumpkin Pie

1	**pie crust**
2	**eggs**
H	**cup sugar**
21	**teaspoon cinnamon**
1	**teaspoon nutmeg**
1	**teaspoon salt**
1	**(16-oz.) can pumpkin**
1	**(12-oz.) can evaporated milk**

Heat oven to 425°. Prepare pie crust according to package directions for filled one-crust pie using 9-inch pie crust. In large bowl, beat eggs slightly. Add remaining ingredients; blend well. Pour into crust-lined pie pan. Bake at 425° for 15 minutes. Reduce oven temperature to 350°, and continue baking for 45 minutes or until knife inserted near center comes out clean. Cool. Store in refrigerator.

27. What must be done immediately before the ingredients are placed in the pie pan?

    A. The ingredients must be blended well.
    B. The crust must be baked at 425° for 15 minutes.
    C. The eggs must be added to the ingredients.
    D. The remaining ingredients must be added.

28. Which passage contains propaganda?

    A. When trying to decide something as important as who you want to govern your state, consider this: Which candidate has more experience in political leadership? Who has lived in our state longer? Who financed his campaign without using a single penny of special interest groups' funds? Consider the facts and cast your vote for the best candidate.

    B. It's that time of year again. It's time to take a look at the facts. Over the past four years, the state income tax has risen 23%. The crime rate is up 17%. Standardized test scores at both the junior high and high school level dropped 8%. Isn't it time to face the facts? Please vote in the November election.

    C. This year, vote for the candidate who is the right choice for our country. Someone who has experience serving this country in overseas diplomacy as well as domestic. Someone who really has a grasp on how to best benefit our country on the international playing field. Make your decision and vote in this election.

    D. Yes, this year, only one candidate stands for truth, integrity, and reason. Our candidate does not resort to mud slinging to get into office. He would rather spend his time showing the voters what he would do for them in office. He is committed to the voter and to the principles that have made this country great. Please cast your ballot the right way in this election. Vote for Bill Johnson.

Read the passage below. Then answer the questions that follow.

During Napoleon's war with England, both England and France seized neutral ships and goods. In addition, they were conscripting United States merchant sailors into their navies, enraging the people of the United States. In August 1810, Napoleon publicly repealed his previous decrees and declared that neutral ships could freely trade in France without risk of confiscation or conscription. President Madison believed Napoleon's words. When Britain refused to promise the same thing, Congress declared war on England and began invading Canada, starting the War of 1812.

29. Based on this passage, which sentence below shows events in the correct time sequence?

    A. Napoleon decided that the United States could trade freely in France after the War of 1812.
    B. England refused to honor the trading status of neutral nations, so the United States went to war with England.
    C. Napoleon allowed the United States to trade freely with France after the United States declared war on England.
    D. The United States declared war on England. Then England began conscripting soldiers from United States merchant ships.

30. Which of the following causes of the War of 1812 is best supported by the passage?

    A. England was preparing to retake their lost colonies in North America.
    B. President Madison wished to conquer English territory in Canada.
    C. Napoleon promised not to harm United States trading ships or crews.
    D. United States' citizens were angry that England ignored the United States' neutral trading status.

31. What is the best title for this passage?

    A. President Madison and Napoleon
    B. Napoleon's Free Trade with the United States
    C. The Origins of the War of 1812
    D. The War of 1812 in Canada

The Swing

Cindy, Jennifer, Tara, and Amy were all friends and classmates at the local middle school. One day at around 5:00 p.m., they decided they would sit in the playground and tell ghost stories. Cindy told a graveyard ghost story, Jennifer told a haunted house ghost story, and Amy told an abandoned prison ghost story. Now, it was Tara's turn.

All the other girls couldn't wait for Tara to tell her story. She was the best storyteller of all of them. "All right," Tara said, "I'll tell you my story." The girls leaned forward to listen. "Did you know this playground is haunted?"

"Oh, come on," Cindy said. "Who's ever heard of a haunted playground?"

"No, really, it's true," Tara said with a devious grin. The girls waited as Tara began her story. "About twenty years ago, there was a woman who came here every day to let her daughter play on the playground. Her daughter was strong and very healthy, so her mom didn't watch her all that closely. One day, at about this same time, her daughter, Julie, pumped the swings really hard, fell out, and died. The mother, heartbroken by what happened, died about a week later. To this day, it is said that this mother still walks the playground with Julie, watching her play on the swings, and sometimes watches over the other children that play here."

Abruptly, Tara said, "Look, I think there's something in that building over there!" All the girls turned and looked. While they weren't looking in Tara's direction, Tara ran, pushed the swing on the swing set, and ran back to the girls, telling them, "Look at the swing set!" The girls turned around and started screaming. Tara laughed and said, "Tricked you! I pushed the left swing just a few seconds ago."

"Then why are both swings swinging on the swing set?" Amy asked. Tara turned around, saw both swings swinging and screamed for everyone to run away.

As they ran out, they could hear a woman whispering, "Come on Julie, you can do it. This time I am here to catch you."

32. Where does the story above take place?

A. the park
B. a haunted house
C. a playground
D. a graveyard

33. What is the main idea of this story?

A. Tara tells a ghost story that turns out to be true.
B. Four girls exchange ghost stories on a playground.
C. Four girls run out of a park after hearing the voice of a ghost.
D. Tara tricks her friends into believing her ghost story.

34. Who told the last story?

A. Cindy
B. Julie
C. Tara
D. the mother

After the Blast

At first glance, the beach at Bikini Atoll, a small island in the Pacific Ocean, looks like a tropical paradise. In truth, the land and water share a poisoned past, from the era when 23 atomic tests were conducted at Bikini Atoll.

In 1946, all 167 Bikini residents were relocated. Then 42,000 people and 90 vessels used the island for target practice. This was to be the first peace time testing of nuclear weapons.

Testing continued until November 1958. The most damaging explosion came on March 1, 1954, when a 15 megaton hydrogen bomb, code-named Bravo, was exploded on the island. This bomb was the most powerful ever exploded by the United States. It was a thousand times more powerful than the bomb dropped on Hiroshima. Not only did it open a mile-wide crater on Bikini Atoll, but it also vaporized one small island and part of another.

To this day, the soil on Bikini contains too much radioactive cesium to permit the Bikinians, now numbering 2,025, to return from their exile.

35. Why was an atomic bomb exploded on Bikini Island in 1954?

    A. Few people lived on the island, so they moved to a new location.
    B. Nuclear bombs were being tested for use as weapons.
    C. The soil was already radioactive from earlier blasts.
    D. The United States was preparing to drop a bomb on Hiroshima.

36. Which of the following statements is an <u>opinion</u>?

    A. In 1946, all 167 Bikini residents were relocated.
    B. This bomb was the most powerful ever exploded by the United States.
    C. Bikini Atoll should not be used for nuclear testing.
    D. 42,000 people and 90 vessels used the island for target practice.

37. The author's purpose for writing this passage is

    A. to create suspense.
    B. to introduce a character.
    C. to inform.
    D. to persuade.

38. Based on the passage, the damage to Bikini Atoll suggests that

    A. no more nuclear bombs will be dropped on the island.
    B. more powerful bombs will be dropped on the island in the future.
    C. the island will remain uninhabited for some time to come.
    D. people will be able to return to the island.

39. Which statement best express the main idea of this passage?

    A. Nuclear testing on Bikini Atoll damaged the island and displaced its residents.
    B. Bikini Atoll looked like a tropical paradise, but no one lives there.
    C. The soil on Bikini Atoll is contaminated with radioactive cesium.
    D. On March 1, 1954, the United States dropped a powerful atomic bomb on Bikini Atoll.

Sea Adventure

Four men in an open life boat caught glimpses of the steamer sinking into the sea…

A seat in this boat was not unlike a seat on a bucking bronco, and, by the same token, a bronco is not much smaller. The craft pranced and reared and plunged like an animal. As each wave came, and she rose for it, she seemed like a horse leaping a fence outrageously high. A great disadvantage of the sea lies in the fact that after successfully going across one wave, you discover there is another behind it just as important and just as nervously anxious to do something effective in the way of swamping boats.

"Good thing it's an on-shore wind," said the cook. "If not where would we be?"

"That's right," said the correspondent.

The busy engine master nodded his assent.

Then the captain in the bow chuckled in a way that expressed humor, contempt, tragedy, all in one. "Do you think we've got a show, now, boys?" said he.

Whereupon the three went silent, save for a little hemming and hawing. To express any particular optimism at this time they felt to be childish and stupid, but they all doubtless possessed this sense of the situation in their mind. A young man thinks doggedly at such times. On the other hand, the ethics of their condition was decidedly against an open suggestion of hopelessness. So they were silent.

"Oh well," said the captain, soothing his children, "we'll get ashore all right."

But there was that in his tone which made them think, so the engine master said, "Yes, if this wind holds!"

The cook was bailing water, "Yes! If we don't break apart in the surf."

– Stephen Crane's "Open Boat"

40. What is the author's point of view in this story?

A. first person
B. third person
C. the captain
D. the correspondent

41. What caused the four men to be together?

A. They were old friends.
B. They worked together.
C. They were fishermen.
D. They were in a lifeboat trying to make it to shore.

42. The author's main purpose in writing this passage is to

A. motivate.
B. persuade.
C. create suspense.
D. describe feelings.

43. What caused the crew to be optimistic in this situation?

A. The ship was gaining water.
B. The ship was receiving an on-shore wind.
C. The waves were crashing high.
D. The surf was breaking the life boat apart.

44. Which of the following is the main idea of this passage?

    A. Everyone shares a similar perspective about the world.
    B. Many lives are lost at sea each year.
    C. Every crisis produces both hope and despair.
    D. Trust in God can save you from any danger.

45. Some people care about their smiles. Other people care about their teeth. Sparkle toothpaste cares about your smile and your teeth. Its patented "Clean Smile" formula whitens your teeth and brightens your smile. Bring some Sparkle into your life today!

    The propaganda in this advertisement tries to convince you to

    A. smile more often.
    B. purchase Sparkle toothpaste.
    C. whiten your teeth.
    D. care about your teeth.

46. Which passage contains the most propaganda?

    A. Try the new Sleep-Inducing Mattress by Snyder & Company. This mattress has a patented system of stretchable fibers. These fibers provide an additional level of comfort on top of our regular mattress. Stop by, and try it today!

    B. The new Liberty Child Care Service gives you the liberty that you should enjoy by right. All parents should be able to go out on special occasions. Remember, parents have rights, too! So, enjoy them with Liberty Child Care!

    C. The Roloflex twisting machine works all the major muscle groups of the upper and lower body. This isometric exercise machine uses twisting and rolling motions from your own body to increase your muscle size and definition. Stop by, and roll your way to fitness!

    D. Just in time for Christmas, the Whirro peeler has made its appearance. This one-of-a-kind peeler actually cleans the dirt off of food as you place it in! No more peeling! No more washing! The Whirro peeler is also 50% faster and 70% easier to use than any other peeler. Think of the convenience, and buy a Whirro peeler today!

Injuries to Teenagers

Many injuries occur in teenagers due to an active lifestyle.

Motor vehicle related deaths are responsible for nearly 80% of all injury deaths in teenagers. One out of every fifty teens requires hospitalization for motor vehicle (occupant) related injuries each year. Auto safety classes and the use of seatbelts are very important as protective measures for the safety of our teens.

The second leading injury threat to the lives of teenagers is drowning, while burns are third and poisoning fourth. The most common poison ingestions in teens involve alcohol and drugs.

The most common type of nonfatal injury in teenagers is sports injuries. Approximately one out of fourteen teenagers has required hospitalization for a sports injury. Football caused nearly 20% of these injuries, with basketball, roller-skating and baseball causing most of the other injuries.

47. What is the main idea in this passage?

    A. Car accidents, drownings, and sports injuries occur frequently among teenagers.
    B. Teenagers are responsible for their own deaths because they are poor drivers.
    C. A good number of teens die in the hospital after a motor vehicle accident.
    D. Teens put themselves at risk every time they get into a car.

48. According to the passage, what conclusion can be made about sports?

    A. Football is one of the main causes of sports injuries among teenagers.
    B. Baseball is one of the safest sports to play.
    C. Sports are fun and keep teenagers fit and healthy.
    D. Sports injuries are the least common injuries among teenagers.

49. Which of the following statements from the passage is an opinion?

    A. Motor vehicle-related deaths are responsible for nearly 80% of all injury deaths in teenagers.
    B. One out of every fifty teens requires hospitalization for motor vehicle (occupant) related injuries each year.
    C. The second leading injury threat to the lives of teenagers is drowning, while burns are third, and poisoning fourth.
    D. Auto safety classes and the use of seatbelts are very important as protective measures for the safety of our teens.

50. According to the passage, what is the second leading cause of injury-related deaths in teens?

    A. poisoning
    B. drowning
    C. burns
    D. alcohol and drugs

T. G. Sheppard

Suddenly, in the shadow of the Smoky Mountains, as a brilliant light show fills the stage, T.G. Sheppard emerges to the applause of the packed house and smoothly glides into the opening bars of the song. But just as quickly as he appears, he descends from the stage and begins mingling with the hand-clapping audience.

As the melody goes on, he quickly shakes hands, smiles at the ladies in the audience, pauses for camera shots, hugs young children, breaks the song momentarily to welcome the crowd, and then ascends back to the stage in the closing bars of the song.

Less than five minutes have passed since curtain time, but in these brief moments T.G. Sheppard has won the heart of his audience, and it's a bond that is drawn tighter over the next two hours as he weaves his own hit songs, popular melodies and big-band sounds, personal glimpses into his life, and comedic routines into a theatrical presentation that ends in somewhat of an emotional parting that seems to end all too soon.

51. According to the passage, why is T.G. Sheppard a popular entertainer?

    A. He plays several musical instruments.
    B. He sings about the Smoky Mountains.
    C. He entertains for several hours.
    D. He mingles with his audience.

52. "In the shadow of the Smoky Mountains" means that

    A. Sheppard's performance is close to the Smoky Mountains.
    B. Sheppard's performance is far from the Smoky Mountains.
    C. Sheppard's performance is on top of the Smoky Mountains.
    D. Sheppard's performance is beyond the Smoky Mountains.

53. What is the author's purpose for writing this passage?

    A. to teach a lesson
    B. to create suspense
    C. to relate an adventure
    D. to describe

54. Which of the following statements is a <u>fact</u>?

    A. T. G. Sheppard glides smoothly into the opening bars of the song.
    B. T. G. Sheppard pauses for camera shots and hugs young children.
    C. T. G. Sheppard has won the heart of his audience.
    D. T. G. Sheppard's show ends in an emotional parting that seems to end all too soon.

Pilgrim Life

When the Pilgrims landed in November of 1620 in what is now Massachusetts, they needed to provide food and shelter if they were to survive. There were no stores and markets for buying things, and no houses for the Pilgrims to move into. All their needs had to be met by themselves, and even the smallest hands contributed to that effort. The Pilgrims overcame many hardships to establish a colony. The winter was long and cold, and much work had to be done for spring planting. Their hard work that first year was rewarded with a bountiful harvest in the autumn of 1621, and the Pilgrims celebrated the first Thanksgiving as a time of gratitude.

Over the next several years, Plymouth grew into a successful community of 180 colonists. By 1627, more than one-third of them were age 16 or younger. There were no schools, but the children were always learning by working. The work centered on providing food. The children's chores varied depending on their age and abilities, but by the time they were six, most were working a full day alongside their parents. Tending to the animals, working in the fields, and preparing meals took up most of the daylight hours.

55. Which of the following statements is the main idea of the above passage?

A. School is not always available for families with children.
B. Surviving winter is a great challenge.
C. Thanksgiving is a time to be grateful.
D. Overcoming hardship is essential for survival in a new environment.

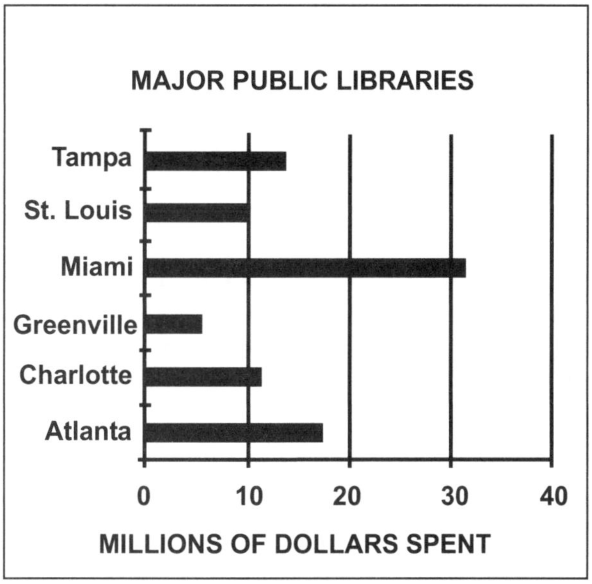

56. According to the graph above, which two cities spent the most on their public libraries?

A. Charlotte and St. Louis
B. Atlanta and Miami
C. Tampa and Miami
D. Greenville and Atlanta

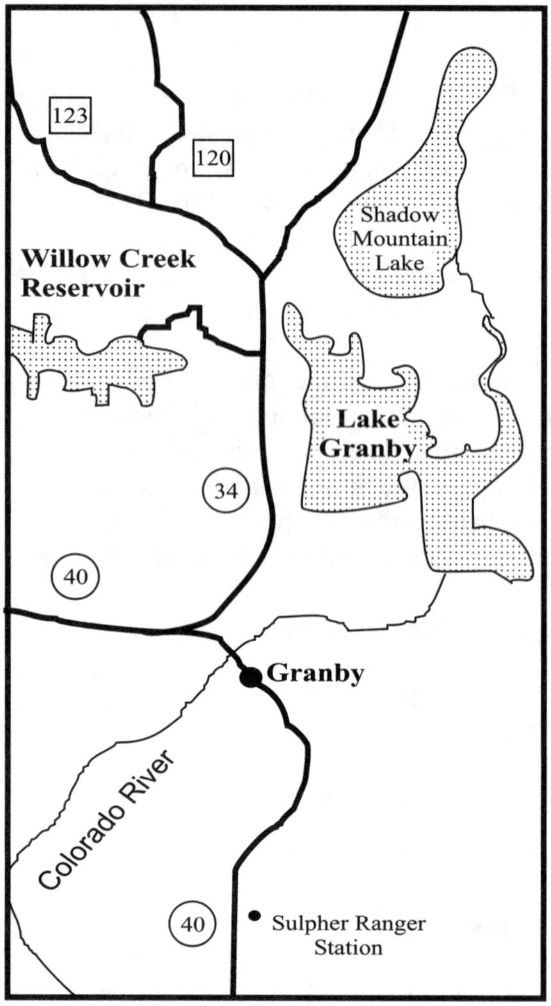

57. According to the map on the left, which highway runs parallel to Lake Granby?

A. 40
B. 120
C. 34
D. 123

Nonstop Bus Service to Airport

Downtown to Airport					
Leave Downtown					**Arrive Airport**
Ramada	**Hilton**	**Marriott**	**Sheraton**	**Holiday Inn**	
7:30 AM	**7:36**	**7:42**	**7:50**	**7:57**	**8:20 AM**
8:45	**8:51**	**8:57**	**9:05**	**9:12**	**9:35**
10:00	**10:06**	**10:12**	**10:20**	**10:27**	**10:50**
11:30	**11:36**	**11:42**	**11:50**	**11:57**	**11:20**

58. According to the schedule above, how many stops does the bus make downtown before it arrives at the airport?

A. 2
B. 3
C. 4
D. 5

Office Mart had a sale on computers in all 21 of its stores. Below is a chart showing how many of each brand were sold.

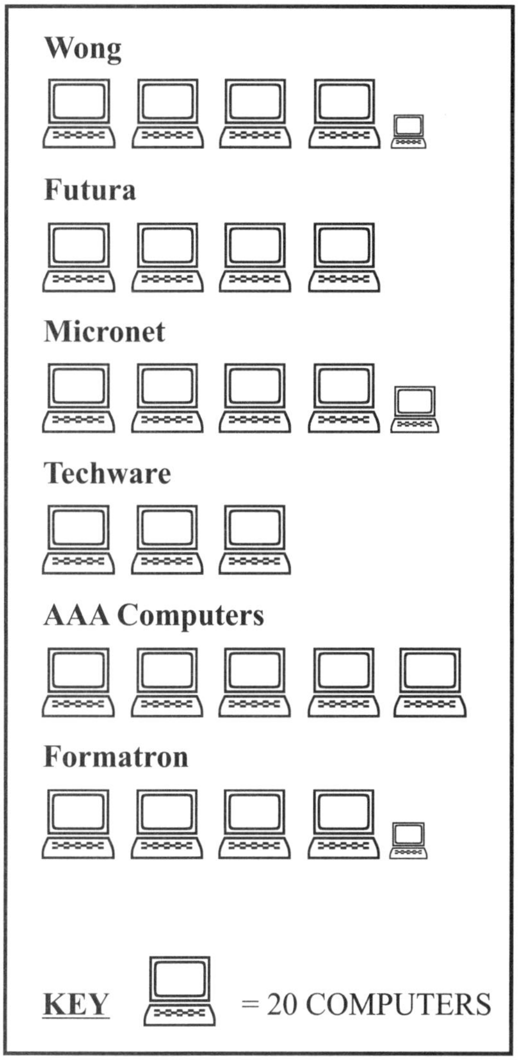

59. How many brands sold more than 80 computers?

    A. 3
    B. 4
    C. 5
    D. 6

60. Computer is to monitor as VCR is to _______.

    A. television
    B. CD player
    C. movie theater
    D. remote control

61. Actor is to entertainment as engineer is to _______.

    A. college
    B. calculator
    C. biology
    D. structure

62. Underground mine is to skyscraper as cave is to _______.

    A. river
    B. mountain
    C. boulder
    D. gold

63. Anger is to calmness as mental illness is to _______.

A. sickness
B. sanity
C. exercise
D. intelligence

FACULTY OFFICES BUILDING

Office	Number
Dr. George Amerson	227
Dr. Samuel Buchanan	106
Dr. Linda Faraway	304
Dr. Jennifer Heinrich	118
Dr. Jim McPherson	208
Dr. Gloria Nunez	116
Dr. Peter Phillips	326
Dr. Andrew Thompson	107
Dr. Victoria Wesselman	213
Dr. Sarah Whitman	302

64. Dr. Lamont, a new faculty member in the Faculty Offices Building, will have his name added to the above alphabetized building directory between

A. Dr. Jim McPherson and Dr. Gloria Nunez.
B. Dr. Linda Faraway and Dr. Jennifer Heinrich.
C. Dr. Jennifer Heinrich and Dr. Jim McPherson.
D. Dr. Peter Phillips and Dr. Andrew Thompson.

65. If the guide words Sound - Sporting were at the top of a page in the yellow pages, which listing could be included on that page?

A. Steam Cleaning
B. Speech Pathologists
C. Shoe Repair
D. Security Consultants

Common Sense

. . . 'Tis the business of little minds to shrink; but he whose heart is firm, and whose conscience approves his conduct, will pursue his principles unto death. My own line of reasoning is to myself as straight and clear as a ray of light. Not all the treasures of the world, so far as I believe, could have induced me to support an offensive war, for I think it murder; but if a thief breaks into my house, burns and destroys my property, and kills or threatens to kill me, or those that are in it, and to "bind me in all cases whatsoever" to his absolute will, am I to suffer it?

– Thomas Paine's *Common Sense*

66. What is the author's purpose in writing this passage?

A. to persuade
B. to inform
C. to relate an adventure
D. to share a personal experience

67. When the author says his reasoning is "as straight and clear as a ray of light," he means that

A. he is confused.
B. he is excited about the future.
C. he is certain about what he will do.
D. he will use a flashlight to find his way.

68. In what section of the newspaper would you find opposing views on a current event?

A. Front page
B. Classified section
C. Advertisements
D. Editorial section

69. In the obituaries of a newspaper, you would find

A. restaurant reviews.
B. biographies on the recently deceased.
C. news on medical advancements.
D. information about basketball championships.

70. In what section of the newspaper would you find the latest department store sale?

A. Classified section
B. Advertisements
C. Obituaries
D. Front Page

71. Which part of a book would you use to locate additional charts and graphs not found in the book's chapters?

A. Appendix
B. Glossary
C. Table of contents
D. Bibliography

72. The title page is the part of the book that gives information on

A. page references for the names, places, and subjects in a book.
B. the author, title, and publication of the book.
C. books, articles, etc., used or referred to by an author.
D. supplementary material not essential to the text itself.

73. Which part of a book would you use to locate the page numbers that discuss the Cuban Missile Crisis?

A. Title page
B. Index
C. Glossary
D. Appendix

74. Which part of a book would you use to find other writings on a specific subject referred to by the author?

A. Preface
B. Appendix
C. Glossary
D. Bibliography

75. If the guide words Towing - Trailer were at the top of a page in the yellow pages, which listing could be included on that page?

A. Toys
B. Tire Dealers
C. Transmissions
D. Travel Agencies

76. If you have the encyclopedia volume labeled So-Sz, which subject could you find in that volume?

A. Race Relations
B. Temperature
C. Snow
D. Spelling

What I Lived For

An honest man has hardly need to count more than his ten fingers, or in extreme cases he may add his ten toes, and lump the rest. Simplicity, Simplicity, Simplicity! I say, let your affairs be as two or three, and not a hundred or a thousand; instead of a million count half a dozen, and keep your accounts on your thumbnail. In the midst of this chopping sea of civilized life, such are the clouds and storms and quicksands and thousand-and-one items to be allowed for, that a man has to live, if he would not founder and go to the bottom and not make his port at all, by dead reckoning, and he must be a great calculator indeed who succeeds. Simplify, Simplify. Instead of three meals a day, if it be necessary eat but one; instead of a hundred dishes, five; and reduce other things in proportion.

–Thoreau's *Walden*

77. When the author refers to "this chopping sea of civilized life," he means that

A. life is peaceful.
B. life is like salty water.
C. life is stressful.
D. life is sad.

Blitzkrieg

It was called blitzkrieg–lightning war, and the Germans unveiled it in Poland during September of 1939. It consisted of stuka dive bomber attacks, fast tank movements, and mobile infantry deployments, all of which were backed up by heavy bomber attacks. The keys to this whole new tactic were mobility and coordination of a multi-force attack. It was a strategy the Germans developed to avoid the slow, turgid warfare of World War I. It can be reasonably said that this new air-ground, multi-force concept revolutionized modern warfare.

In 1939, the German blitzkrieg overwhelmed Poland. By the end of the first day of the Polish campaign, the Polish air force had been largely destroyed; most of it was caught on the ground before it could take off, and thus the Germans had almost immediate air supremacy. Also, German high level bombers attacked Warsaw, reducing most of the Polish rear to shambles. On the ground, the German military machine streamed across the Polish border - tanks, the armored cars, and the armored infantry and artillery of the mechanized panzer divisions. All of these were supported by waves of Junkers-87 dive bombers, the deadly stukas.

78. Which statement from the passage is a conclusion drawn by the author?

A. It can be reasonably said that this new air-ground, multi-force concept revolutionized modern warfare.
B. Also, German high-level bombers attacked Warsaw, reducing most of the Polish rear to shambles.
C. It was called blitzkrieg - lightning war, and the Germans unveiled it in Poland that September of 1939.
D. All of these were supported by waves of Junkers-87 dive bombers, the deadly stukas.

A Life Saved or a Life Lost?

Once in India there was a high priest by the name of Devasha who lived in a certain village. His wife, Yajna, was also of high birth. In time, she became pregnant, and the couple had a son whom they named Kanji. This son was a great gift, a precious diamond to be cherished and treasured.

Shortly after the child's birth, Yajna went to the river to bathe. Devasha stayed with the child and cared for him in his mother's absence. Soon, a messenger notified the high priest that presents for performing sacred ceremonies were arriving. In a hurry, Devasha left a pet mongoose to guard the child.

A few minutes later, a poisonous snake slithered toward the child. At the moment that the serpent was about to strike the child, the mongoose saw the snake and quickly killed it out of love for his master.

When the mongoose saw his master return from his duty, he happily ran toward Devasha with the blood of the snake on his fur. Thinking that the mongoose had killed his son, the high priest strangled the mongoose with his bare hands.

When he arrived home, Devasha discovered his son alive and well. Next to his son, he saw the snake that the mongoose killed. He was stricken with grief and wailed loudly. Returning from the river, his wife, Yajna, learned of the incident and denounced her husband for his foolish action.

79. Based on this passage, we can infer that:

A. Yajna was very upset at the mongoose's actions.
B. Devasha loved his son very much.
C. The mongoose was trying to befriend the snake.
D. Devasha does not jump to conclusions.

80. What is Devasha likely to do in the future?

A. Devasha will learn to trust no one.
B. Devasha will ask questions before making assumptions.
C. Devasha will buy a pet serpent.
D. Devasha will always stay near Kanji.

81. Shoes are made for walking. Bentley boots are made for bigger challenges like hiking across mountains, forging new trails, or climbing rocks. These boots will make you feel like a warrior. Do yourself a favor. Hike over to your nearest Bentley Outlet soon.

The propaganda in this advertisement persuades you to

A. become a warrior.
B. strive for bigger challenges.
C. walk in some new boots.
D. try on Bentley boots.

The New Colossus
(A Poem about the Statue of Liberty)

Not like the brazen giant of Greek fame,
With conquering limbs astride from land to land;
Here at our sea-washed, sunset gates shall stand
A mighty woman with a torch whose flame
is the imprisoned lightning, and her name
Mother of Exiles. From her beacon-hand
Glows world-wide welcome; her mild eyes command
The air-bridged harbor that twin cities frame
"Keep, ancient lands, your storied pomp!" cries she
With silent lips. "Give me your tired, your poor
Your huddled masses yearning to breathe free,
The wretched refuse of your teeming shore
Send these, the homeless, tempest-tost to me,
I lift my lamp beside the golden door!"

– Emma Lazarus

82. Lines 9-11 suggest that

A. the ancient world should keep their traditions favoring the rich.
B. the ancient world is rich with ceremony and art.
C. the statue welcomes the less fortunate people.
D. the ancient world is more courteous and ceremonial than the United States.

83. The phrase "the wretched refuse of your teeming shore" means

A. the garbage from your beaches.
B. people who desperately search for a better life.
C. the excess seafood that is spoiled and left on the beach.
D. the toxic waste that flows from the rivers into the sea.

Directions for Performing a Magic Trick

1. Show the audience the rabbit and the inside of the hat.
2. Place the rabbit inside the hat.
3. Wave your magic wand around the hat and say, "Presto!"
4. Turn the hat upside down to demonstrate that the rabbit disappeared.

84. According to the magic trick above, when should you wave your magic wand?

A. after you say, "Presto!"
B. before you place the rabbit in the hat
C. after you turn the hat upside down
D. after you place the rabbit in the hat

How to Make an Omelet

Step 1 Cut up one cup green peppers, one cup onions, and one cup mozzarella cheese.

Step 2 Place the vegetables in the frying pan with two tablespoons oil over medium heat; fry for 6 minutes.

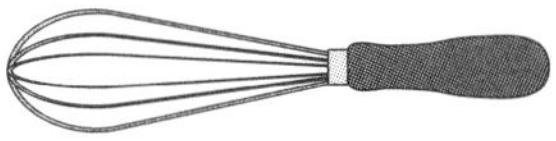

Step 3 Whisk 10 eggs together in a bowl.

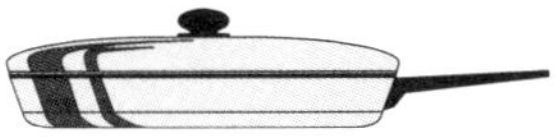

Step 4 Pour eggs into the frying pan, add the cheese to the top, cover for 5 minutes, and serve.

85. In making an omelet, a person must first

A. place the vegetables in the frying pan.
B. whisk ten eggs together in a bowl.
C. cut up the vegetables and the cheese.
D. add the cheese to the top of the eggs.

Directions for Changing Car Oil

Step 1	Start the engine, and allow it to reach its normal operating temperature. Turn off the engine when it is warm.
Step 2	Raise the vehicle and support it on jack stands.
Step 3	Place the drain pan under the oil plug, and loosen the plug. Wait for all the oil to drain into the pan.
Step 4	Plug the oil pan, and remove the drain pan from under the vehicle.
Step 5	Replace the oil filter, refill the engine oil, remove the jack stands, and start the car.

86. Before the oil pan is plugged, a person must

A. make sure all the oil is drained from the car.
B. remove the jack stands.
C. replace the oil filter.
D. refill the engine with oil.

Decorating a Christmas Tree

Step 1 Place the evergreen tree in a pot of water.

Step 2 Decorate the tree with lights and streamers.

Step 3 Hang ornaments on the tree limbs.

Step 4 Place a star or other large ornament on the top of the tree.

87. According to these directions, when should you hang up the tree ornaments?

A. before the tree is placed in water
B. after the tree is decorated with lights
C. after a large ornament is placed on top of the tree
D. before the tree is decorated with lights

A Warrior's Quest

"After so many years, what's another day," Vlad muttered to himself as he waited for the return of his long-lost daughter, Kyla. They had been separated by a tragic mishap five years ago. Vlad sat down and started pounding the dirt with his boot in exasperation. His thoughts kept returning to the way his daughter smiled and skipped around the woods at their home. She was so courteous and fragile-his eyes grew mistier by the minute.

Hearing the thunder of many horses, Vlad quit his thoughts, drew his broadsword, and stepped into the woods. Pale, ghost-like forms traveling on horses with red eyes slowly rode along the path close to his hiding place. "These evil, ugly freaks have been following me for too long," he muttered softly to himself. In a piece of bad luck, one of the horses looked directly in Vlad's direction and began stomping hysterically. Realizing he would be discovered, Vlad leapt up and attacked the first horseman, neatly impaling him through the chest. Meanwhile, the three remaining ghost riders encircled him. Throwing a net that neatly entangled him in a crushing heap, the ghost riders circled around Vlad clockwise and prepared themselves for a feast.

At this moment, a robed figure and a panther, Manx, jumped down on the horses from a ledge and attacked the ghost riders from behind. Strong, soft hands quickly cut one of the riders to pieces with a dagger while Manx finished off a ghost rider dinner on another horse. The remaining ghost rider galloped away faster than light.

By this time, Vlad had cut himself free of the net and stood up, saying, "Thank you, sir. You saved me just in the nick of time." "Actually, I thought I was a few years late," the figure said as the hood fell down. Recognizing the figure, Vlad fainted and fell to the ground with a thud.

88. According to this passage, what is the turning point in this story?

    A. Vlad jumps into the woods to hide.
    B. Vlad attacks the first horseman and impales him through the chest.
    C. The ghost riders entangle Vlad in a net.
    D. A robed figure and a panther come to Vlad's rescue.

89. What is the author's purpose in writing this story?

    A. to relate an adventure
    B. to create a mood
    C. to motivate
    D. to cause doubt

90. What is the main lesson of this story?

    A. Help can come at the most unexpected times.
    B. We can never have enough friends.
    C. Always go into forests alone.
    D. Wild pets offer the best protection on the open road.